CENTRE FOR EDUCATIONAL RESEAR

What Schools for the Future?

OECD

ORGANISATION FOR ECONOMIC CO-OPERATION AND DEVELOPMENT

Foreword

The origins of this volume lie in a meeting of OECD Ministers of Education convened in 1996 in Paris (OECD, 1996a). Their theme was "lifelong learning for all". The analysis, discussion and conclusions all pointed forcefully to the key role of schooling in the overall panoply of lifelong learning opportunities, which had previously suffered relative neglect compared with the part played by the different sectors of continuing education and training. Specifically, the Ministers invited the OECD to "assess alternative visions of the 'school of tomorrow'", an invitation which has led directly to the analysis of trends and scenarios in this report.

However, the ways in which schools can make their most effective contribution to the "lifelong learning for all" objective are still ill-understood. Moreover, forward-looking methodologies have been developed in only rudimentary fashion in education compared with many other sectors. This work had thus to begin with fundamental questions rather than a well-established body of analysis. What will schools look like in the future? What big trends are most influential in shaping education and how might these unfold in coming years? What policy questions need to be tackled today for desirable pathways into the future to become more likely?

These are the questions addressed in Part I. Chapter 1 examines the "driving forces" in the wider environment of schooling, reviewing key economic, social, cultural and policy trends and discussing some of their educational implications. Chapter 2 focuses more closely on developments in education systems and schools themselves. Chapter 3 presents the scenarios constructed through this project for school systems over the next 10-20 years – six are presented, grouped into "status quo", "re-schooling" and "de-schooling" futures. Chapter 4 concludes the Secretariat Report. It reviews the main arguments, identifies implications for lifelong learning, and identifies questions for, and tensions among, the policies for the long-term development of schooling. Part II complements the Secretariat Report with eight chapters contributed by experts from Europe, North America and the Pacific area at different stages of the "Schooling for Tomorrow" project.

The work has been implemented through a series of seminars and events since the original Hiroshima conference that launched the "Schooling for Tomorrow" project in November 1997 (which resulted in the 1999 *Innovating Schools* publication).[1] The international OECD/Netherlands seminar held in Scheveningen in April 1998 provided a valuable forum of discussion as well as a couple of the expert papers included in Part II. In October 1999, OECD/CERI was a partner in the L'École Horizon 2020 ("The School in 2020") conference held in Poitiers, France. A small expert seminar on forward-looking methodologies was convened in Futuribles headquarters in February 2000. There were two meetings of invited experts in OECD headquarters in 1999 and 2000 that both brainstormed ideas and reviewed progress. At regular intervals throughout, the work has profited from the valuable advice of the CERI Governing Board.

One of the most important events during this phase of the project has been the major international OECD/Netherlands conference on "Schooling for Tomorrow" that took place in Rotterdam in November 2000, chaired by former Swedish Minister of Education, Ms. Ylva Johansson. This event allowed *inter alia* for a day's discussion of trends and scenarios by two working groups. The views of the participants were surveyed as to the desirability and likelihood of the different scenarios (see Chapter 12).

Within the OECD, there has been close co-operation with the International Futures Advisory Group to the Secretary-General (its four recent publications on the economy, technology, society and governance in the 21th century are referred to in Riel Miller's chapter).

Since the Rotterdam event, the OECD Ministers of Education have convened again in Paris (April 2001), this time on the broad theme "Investing in Competencies for All". The results of the "Schooling for Tomorrow" project were reported back to the Ministers as a response to their initial request for this analysis at their previous 1996 meeting.[2] These results also informed the ministerial discussion paper.

Drawing on the inputs of many colleagues, the discussions held at the different conferences and meetings, and the expert papers reproduced in Part II and other technical reports, the main author within the OECD Secretariat was David Istance. The volume is published on the responsibility of the Secretary-General of the OECD.

---

1. Parallel work on innovation has been carried out under the "Schooling for Tomorrow" project, including a seminar on networks in Lisbon, September 2000 and the main Rotterdam conference held six weeks later. The project has also generated a major activity on ICT and the Quality of Learning [publications to date are Learning to Bridge the Digital Divide (2000) and E-Learning: The Partnership Challenge (2001)].
2. Chapter 5, "What Future for our Schools?", in Education Policy Analysis, 2001 Edition (OECD, 2001a).

Acknowledgements

Many people have taken part in the events, meetings and informal discussions referred to in the foreword. We are unable to acknowledge them individually but extend a general thanks to all, in recognition that this volume could not have been produced without their valuable contributions.

Particular thanks are due to the authors of the expert papers reproduced in Part II, some of whom have been active in other ways in the "Schooling for Tomorrow" project: Martin Carnoy (Stanford University, USA), Gosta Esping-Andersen (University Pompeu Fabra, Spain), Walo Hutmacher (University of Geneva, Switzerland), Kerry J. Kennedy (University of Canberra, Australia), Alain Michel (Inspecteur général de l'Éducation nationale, France), Riel Miller (International Futures Programme, OECD), Sten Söderberg (National Agency for Education – Skolverket, Sweden), and Hans F. van Aalst (Consultant, Netherlands).

Thanks are also due to those who organised or hosted the seminars/conferences. In France, *Futuribles International* hosted an expert seminar (Paris, February 2000), and they were co-organisers, with EPICE (*Institut Européen pour la Promotion de l'Innovation et de la Culture dans l'Éducation*), of a conference held in Poitiers (October 1999). Two "Schooling for Tomorrow" events were held in the Netherlands: in Scheveningen (April 1998) and Rotterdam (November 2000). These were organised with OECD by the Ministry of Education, Culture, and Science and, for the latter conference, by the Rotterdam municipal authorities. Our thanks are extended to all these organisers, with a particular acknowledgement of the contribution made by the Netherlands Ministry officials, Jan van Ravens and Marceline Engelkes.

Table of Contents

Part I
REPORT BY THE SECRETARIAT

Part II
THE EXPERT PAPERS

Part I

REPORT BY THE SECRETARIAT

Chapter 1

The Wider Environment of Schooling: Deep Trends and Driving Forces

Introduction

This report begins with a broad survey of the major trends that set the environment in which schools will be shaped into the future. The trends reviewed are drawn from a number of the fields – economic, social, political, cultural, environmental – that are closest to the world of schools and schooling. Such a presentation is not meant to imply that these wider trends define agendas to which the educational world must simply react. Yet impact they undoubtedly do on the world of education, shaping its nature, outcomes, and the agenda of aims for tomorrow.

The features and trends presented are necessarily selective from the manifest complexity of the world of today and tomorrow. The complexity is compounded as not all trends point in the same direction, and sometimes conflict in terms of their impact on, and the agenda they set for, schooling. On some aspects, countries share similar basic developments, on others there are clear differences, even growing divergences. The aim in this chapter is to identify the "deep" factors and driving forces, rather than the more short-term aspects that tend to grab media attention.

The discussion of the wider environment of schools, together with the educational issues and trends of Chapter 2 are essentially historical as they are based on visible developments. Certain questions they raise for the future are identified. The trends in turn inform the scenarios for schooling presented in Chapter 3, where the perspective shifts from past and present to possible futures. The Secretariat report concludes in Chapter 4 with a recapitulation and discussion of the key emerging points, the policy questions and dilemmas these give rise to, and conclusions about avenues for further exploration in clarifying the school of the future.

Childhood, generational issues and the ageing society

Childhood in the 20th and into the 21st centuries

Too often, discussion about schooling for the future is divorced from consideration of the nature of childhood and youth in today's societies. Social historians at least since Aries (1973) have shown how the very nature of "childhood", far from being a given across time and cultures, is shaped by the particular circumstances of each era. This is easy to overlook, because our ways of organising childhood seem so natural.[1] Another reason for overlooking the nature of childhood may be the perception that it changes so slowly as to be, in effect, a given for the foreseeable future. This would be an unwise assumption as the status of childhood is currently subject to powerful pressures on a number of fronts.

Schools at the core of structures for childhood

Schools lie at the heart of these arrangements and of modern notions of "childhood", even if other sources of influence – TV and computer games perhaps, or the peer group – seem to exercise a more attractive pull for large numbers of young people. Organised schooling is in essence the compulsory cloistering of young people from a very early age into specialist educative institutions, characterised by their distinctiveness from adult life. The benefits of compelling this experience on all young people – benefits that are seen to accrue to society and to the young person and their families, now and in the future – are widely agreed to justify any costs incurred by the loss of freedom that compulsory attendance entails. Norms for staying on in education have continually been pushed back to older and older ages, delaying the onset of recognised "adult life" and extending the cloistering process.

The distinctiveness of "childhood" as a phase has been reinforced by other long-term trends, regulating, for instance, the ages when paid work, sexual activity, and family formation can begin, each strongly justified in terms of personal protection and the avoidance of exclusion. Early pregnancy/childbirth, far from being regarded as a norm, has come to be seen as a major social problem to be rectified. The long-term employment shifts, particularly the shift away from agriculture and other primary industries with its concomitant impact on communities, have served to distance work from the lives of the young, though some return to home-based work may in part reverse this trend.

The delayed process of entering fully into adult life can be described as "extended adolescence". The analysis prepared for the 1998 meeting of OECD social policy ministers described young people "deferring both marriage and childbirth until they can achieve economic autonomy – and this is taking longer" (OECD, 1999a, p. 16). The OECD work on transitions from school to working life has analysed the rapidity of this set of changes to suggest that between 1990 and 1996 the duration of young people's initial transition to working life grew by an average of nearly two years (OECD, 2000d). This is indeed very rapid and substantial change, raising the question of the limits of its continuation. How far are more flexible mixes of learning and work already emerging, especially as broader developments in the economic, society and lifelong learning argue for greater flexibility instead of an increasingly rigid age segmentation into different life phases? However desirable, the facts underpinning "extended adolescence" warn that such flexibility cannot at present be assumed.

"Extended adolescence"

With the extension of childhood and adolescence, tensions are introduced that may prove substantial enough to force new departures. For instance, the delay in acquisition of adult status, reinforced by the deteriorating labour market position of young people, stands in contrast to the earlier onset of puberty and sexual activity [around a third of 15-year-olds in a number of countries participating in a recent WHO survey report to having had sexual intercourse (WHO, 2000)]. Another example is that children and young people have become extremely powerful forces in the "adult world" as consumers, and are being carefully targeted

Tensions and pressures for change

15

in corporate marketing strategies. This is occurring at the time that their acquisition of full autonomy over their own resources is being delayed. A related set of concerns arises in relation to disaffection, even violence, within schools that have been designed for children yet must cater for young people with greater maturity and a wider range of out-of-school experiences. Prout (2000) advances the hypothesis that a growing gap is emerging in which public institutions are increasingly concerned with the control of children, while the private sphere is where children are more allowed to "express choice, exercise autonomy, and work at their individual self-realisation". To the extent that this gap is growing and that the school belongs firmly in the public domain, it may prove increasingly difficult to maintain legitimacy and student motivation.

Ageing societies

The "greying" of OECD societies

However, some of the most important pressures are being exerted from changes taking place at the other end of the age spectrum; questions relating to intergenerational relationships and segmentation cannot be understood apart from the ageing of societies. By 1999, the proportion of under-15s has fallen to less than 1 in 5 of total national populations in as many as 22 of the OECD countries, with only Mexico and Turkey significantly above this level. In 1960, in no OECD country was it as low as this. For the first time, the proportions of over 65s are beginning to approach those of the under-15s, and had reached 15% or more in 13 OECD countries (Figure 1.1). In short, our societies are "greying".

The "dependency ratios" – the numbers in the economically "non-active" to "active" populations – continue to go up linked both to ageing populations and to "extended adolescence". One proxy for this is in the comparison of the 15-64 age group with the combined numbers of under 15s and over 65s.[2] Over the longer term, the ageing of populations and rising "dependency" are set to continue:

"Population ageing means that OECD countries are at the end of a period which saw a steady increase in the share of 15-64 year-olds in the total population. Dependency

Figure 1.1. Age structure of OECD countries under 15 and 65 and over, 1960 and 1999

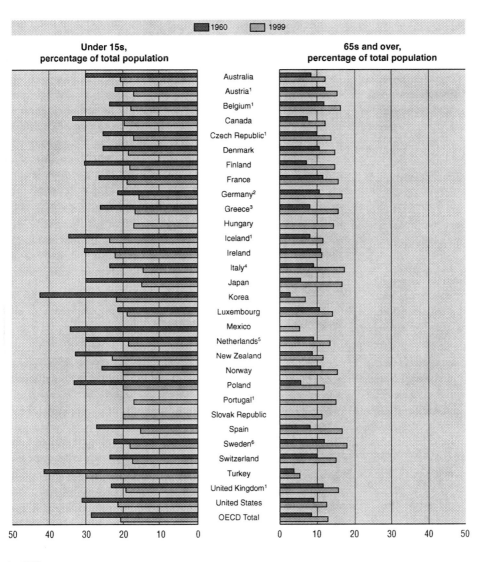

1. 1998.
2. Former West Germany only.
3. 1996.
4. Under 14.
5. 1997.
6. Under 16.
Source: OECD (2001*b*).

ratios in most countries are set to rise over the next 30 years, with some countries showing particularly sharp increases after 2010. In countries which are relatively young (*e.g.* Mexico), dependency ratios are still high but are projected to fall (OECD, 1999*a*, pp. 13-14)."

Growing "dependency ratios" and pressures for change

The growing dependency ratio could well be influential in leading to re-thinking the squeeze of the "active" generation into an ever-tighter age range in the middle of people's lives. The impact on public finances – increased calls on the expenditure purse unmatched by growth in the tax-paying base – could add to the social and/or educational arguments for re-examining the wisdom of the continued extension of adolescence. The evidence suggests that these are long-term changes, as it is only by 2020 and especially 2030 that very significant differences will be apparent from today. When those years are reached, however, the changes promise to be on such a scale as to have been anticipated by policy strategies well before then (see Visco, 2001).

New inter-generational relations?

The generation gap, a perennial – but new inter-generational forces at play

It is a perennial of educational and social debate that each "older" generation regards the habits of youth as a worrying break with the past. Kennedy in this volume (Chapter 10) describes this as a tradition to be traced back at least to Plato, and appearing with regularity over the past century. Habits of speech, dress, and social activities by the young contain an element of "shock value" that often do just this, and help to establish independence from parents and schools while reinforcing peer-group inclusion. Yet, the aims of many of the young tend to be very conventional, with similar aspirations to their parents – so much indeed that a common complaint from the ageing baby-boom generation is that younger adults are altogether too conventional.

If these tensions are perennials, is there any evidence that the current generation of young people has entered into qualitatively different relationships with their elders than in the past? There are certainly some grounds for reflection about generational relationships to inform thinking about schooling in the future.

One reason for this lies in the nature of learning and knowledge experienced by the "Nintendo Generation". A new argument is that this sets them increasingly apart from the world of schools and adults in terms not only of culture but of cognitive development. On this view, many young people have developed competences and approaches through their facility with ICT that find such poor reflection in their schooling as to reinforce distance and disenchantment. Michel in this volume (Chapter 11) also expresses concern about "zapping and surfing rather than the search for knowledge". As yet, however, firm evidence is lacking on the extent to which new cognitive processes are being developed through computer games etc., and, to the extent they are, whether this is a matter of urgency either for the young or for schools. There is thus a host of unanswered questions relating to the "Nintendo Generation" calling for more profound reflection.

The "Nintendo Generation"

Further grounds for reflecting whether inter-generational relations are entering new waters lie in the "contracts" that bind schools, parents and students. Over the latter decades of the 20th century, compulsion and regulation for the young have given way on many fronts to negotiation and consensus-seeking. The abolition of corporal punishment in many countries – in schools and, to an increasing extent, in homes as well – is one tangible indicator of this change. The establishment in some countries of rights for children to sue their own parents can equally be seen as a step of significance in recasting relations between the generations. Changes in discipline and rule-enforcement would be among the most noticeable shifts in school life and socialisation to strike someone revisiting today's world from the past. A question arising for the future is how far traditional organisational models and school ethos will prove untenable because of these broader cultural shifts.

Negotiation with young replacing compulsion

A third possible "generational" shift concerns the lack of engagement by many young in the civic fabric of society.

Lack of civic interest

Kennedy describes one international study and the pessimism expressed by the researchers in the results:

> Hahn (1998) investigated students' political values and understandings in Denmark, Germany, the Netherlands, the United Kingdom, and the United States.[3] Students were asked to report on their levels of political trust, experiences and interest, their confidence and views on political efficacy and their future civic participation. The researcher's own words are unambiguous: "the questionnaire responses are quite dismal... the depth of students' political cynicism (...) is troubling" (p. 31).

Individualism and sustainability – the role of schools in fostering sustainable experiences and values

Robert Putnam's most recent analysis of social capital (2000) – the "Bowling Alone" thesis about individualism, fragmentation and isolation in modern society – contends that there has been a clear generational shift. In his view, recent cohorts are less inclined to join, volunteer, engage politically or socially, or trust others than did earlier generations. This is not specific to the the young in school as it refers equally to their parents. This is a recent and controversial analysis, and the OECD/CERI work on human and social capital has concluded that, outside the US and Australia, the evidence is not compelling that engagement has declined in quantitative terms. It may well be, however, that the terms of that engagement are shifting to more individualistic and transient activities (OECD, 2001*d*). A question that then needs addressing is whether the spread and depth of individualism means that at some time the very sustainability of society will come into question. If it might, an obvious question for schools as key social institutions is what role they might play to foster more sustainable experiences and values.

The power of the retired as a political force – supportive of schools?

A final generational issue for this section concerns the growing numbers and relative prosperity of the retired in OECD societies. Söderberg in this volume (Chapter 9) summarises Swedish data on attitudes held by different age groups towards schools, and finds that a qualitative break in attitude occurs between the over- and under-65 year-olds (as this is the case in Sweden, with its strong tradition of support for public services, even greater age differences might be found elsewhere). In judgements of how well

20

schools succeed in reaching their objectives, the youngest age group with the most recent experience of schools was the most, and the oldest age group the least, positive. Not only is distance from schools' activities greater for the elderly, and their perceptions of relevance lower, but the importance of other public services, particularly health, understandably receive a higher priority.

Clearly, such a summary is far from conclusive for OECD societies in general, and in itself holds no surprises. What is noteworthy, however, is the numerical – and hence political – importance of the older sections of the population and their new-found general affluence. Taxpayer and voter attitudes on decisions relating to school investments are likely to be increasingly shaped by an older constituency who may question the case, to greatest effect in systems which allow the most room for voter/taxpayer influence on educational decisions. It suggests for Söderberg the "need in ageing populations for stress to be placed on intergenerational solidarity and support for investments in services essential for children". He does not maintain that ageing necessarily brings a decline in intergenerational solidarity, but that this becomes a new issue in the light of the changing numerical strength of the different generations and the political clout now exercised by older citizens.

Gender and family

Radical changes in the position of women in society

Of all the manifest changes to have occurred over the past century, one of the greatest has been the transformation in the position of women in many OECD societies. Some of the most substantial aspects of this have taken place in education itself; others include the public "visibility" of women and their importance, for instance, as consumers in today's affluent societies. Of particular note are two fundamental trends relating to women's lives that serve to define the wider environment for schools and the lives of their students.

Major transformation in the position of women

The first is the major shifts in fertility and birth rates. The facts themselves are dramatic across the OECD. Of the

Plummeting fertility rates

21

Table 1.1. **Total fertility rate[1] in OECD countries, 1998**

Australia	1.8[2]
Austria	1.3
Belgium	1.5
Canada	1.6[3]
Czech Republic	1.2
Denmark	1.7
Finland	1.7
France	1.8
Germany	1.3
Greece	1.3
Hungary	1.3
Iceland	2.1
Ireland	1.9
Italy	1.2
Japan	1.4[3]
Korea	1.6[2]
Luxembourg	1.7
Mexico	2.7[2]
Netherlands	1.6
New Zealand	2.0[2]
Norway	1.8
Poland	1.4
Portugal	1.5
Spain	1.2
Sweden	1.5
Switzerland	1.4
Turkey	2.7[4]
United Kingdom	1.7
United States	2.1[4]

1. Average number of children per woman aged 15-49.
2. 1996.
3. 1997.
4. 1994.
Source: OECD (2001*b*).

29 Member countries for which there were data, fertility rates[4] had fallen by 1998 to below 2.0 in 24 of them, and of these to 1.5 or less in Austria, Belgium, the Czech Republic, Germany, Greece, Hungary, Italy, Japan, Poland, Portugal, Spain, Sweden, Switzerland (Table 1.1). The age at the birth of the first child has risen steadily, associated closely with the increased employment trends discussed shortly. Between 1970 and 1995, the average across the OECD had risen from 24.2 to 26.6. It stood at over 28 years of age in Australia, Germany, the Netherlands, New Zealand, and Switzerland (OECD, 2001*o*). (There has also been a sharp increase in single parenthood, discussed further below.)

The implications of such substantial changes in fertility are far-reaching. They impact on women in ways affecting schools and raise questions such how many women are now having children at all? What are childcare needs? In what period of their adult lives are women having young (pre-primary and primary age) children and how is this affecting their experience of work, education and family? Fertility trends impact on the numbers coming into employment and the future labour supply in OECD countries, and in turn on the issues of dependency and "who pays?", as well as on international population movements and the ethnic diversity of societies. All these are key matters for schools. Fertility rates impact very directly, of course, on the numbers of children and young people coming through school doors each year. It cannot now be assumed that, after dramatic change, fertility rates will remain fixed into the future at the levels of the late 1990s. It is expected that numbers of 5-14 year-olds will drop by 9% of 2000 levels by the end of the decade across OECD as a whole. These numbers are foreseen to fall by the very large measures of 15 to 25% of 2000 numbers in the Czech Republic, Germany, Hungary, Poland, the Slovak Republic, and Sweden (OECD, 2001*c*, p. 36).

Rising female employment

The very marked shifts in women's employment are the second major set of changes to be highlighted. Across the OECD as a whole, the labour market participation rate of women aged 15-64 stood at over 6 in 10 (61.3) in 2000, still well below the same figure for men (81.1) but nevertheless a very clear majority of working age women (Figure 1.2. Taking the prime age group 25-54 years, these labour market figures are higher still: over two-thirds for women (68.2%) albeit compared with over 9 in 10 for men. In the Nordic countries and the Czech and the Slovak Republics, they stand at over 80% and largely approaching those of men, and at three-quarters or more in another nine countries (Austria, Canada, France, Germany, Poland, Portugal, Switzerland, the United Kingdom, the United States) (OECD, 2001*e*, Table C).

Again, such trends are linked to a range of on-going developments of significance both for students still in school and for the future world that today's girls and boys will live in

Figure 1.2.   **Labour force activity rates for persons aged 15-64 by gender, 2000**

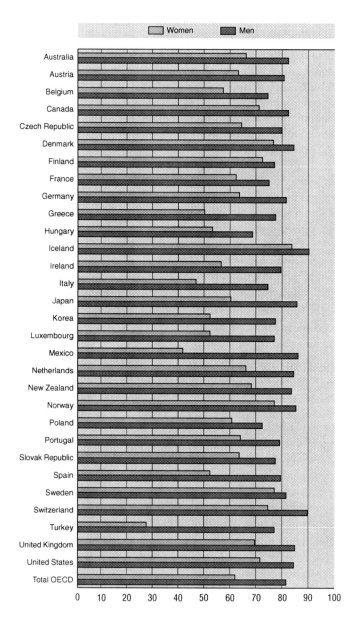

Note: The figure refers to persons aged 15-64 in the labour force divided by the working age population.
Source: OECD (2001e), Table B.

as adults. In addition to the fertility and child-rearing impacts of working life changes already been referred to, further important aspects include the numbers combining work and family responsibilities, the rise of dual-earning families, and the growing gulfs between "work-rich" and "work-poor" households. Much job growth over the past couple of decades has typically been in fields of high female employment, while the areas suffering most dramatic decline have tended to be in the "heavy" male-dominated primary[5] and manufacturing sectors. Some of the most important impacts of women's working lives have been on female educational ambitions and attainments. These have risen dramatically over the past 20-30 years, and are described in the next chapter as representing perhaps the "most remarkable educational trend of the recent period".

Focusing on the extent of change should not be to ignore continuing problems and stubborn inequalities. Women's earnings on average remain consistently well below those of men,[6] employment discrimination is still rife, as is the male domination of the higher reaches of management, the professions, and decision-making in most countries. While female employment has been more buoyant than men's, many of the jobs are in low-pay jobs and sectors, with limited rewards and prospects for further learning. Women who are combining paid work and family responsibilities find themselves under the intense time and energy pressures of "dual careers" at work and at home, as the patterns of household duties change much more slowly than do patterns of employment. Issues of childcare continue to be major preoccupations, despite the long time period during which working mothers with young children have become the norm in OECD countries, with continuing lack of coherence between many enterprise and school practices, on one side, and the demands of working parents, on the other (OECD, 2001*h*). And, the growing precariousness of marriage and rise of single parenthood bring risks of exclusion that are felt most acutely by women.

Stubborn inequalities alongside positive change

Yet, whether the focus is on the problems or on the positive transformations of women's life-styles, these changes have been fundamental and are likely to continue.

Carnoy, in his contribution to this report (Chapter 5), is clear as to their profundity. Alongside globalisation, he describes the "second major force behind world-wide social change" as the "rapid transformation of family life, driven in turn by a profound revolution in the social role of women".

Changing family lives and structures

Many affluent families in OECD countries

Changes in family structures – the immediate environments in which young people are raised – have been dramatic in their scale and swiftness, closely linked to the rapid developments in fertility and female employment discussed above. Some are generally positive. Falling numbers of children, combined with continuing growth in overall standards of living and consumption, mean that many young people have access to goods and services as a norm that would have been unimaginable even 2-3 decades ago. As with other trends reviewed in this section, however, the changes are complex and characterised by tensions.

But also "time-poor" and more family breakdowns

Improved material lifestyles often depend on double incomes, leading to the phenomenon of families being "work-rich" but "time-poor". Even such a basic family experience as the shared meal is being eroded for many – with longer adult working hours and the preferences of the young to "graze" – raising new questions about the nature of socialisation.[7] More obvious tensions still are raised by marital dissolution and fragmentation. The culture of modern family life, of providing an environment of affection and self-expression for children, stands in marked contrast with the conflicts of marital disintegration. Very large numbers of the marriages now being entered into will end in divorce. By the mid-1990s, the overall OECD divorce figure stood at 4 out of every 10 marriages. In Belgium, Sweden, Finland, the Czech Republic, the United Kingdom and the United States, the rates were significantly higher at between half and 70% (OECD, 2001o). More in schools are growing up as single children, or with the different types of sibling relationships formed through delayed family completion, re-marriages, or new partnerships.

More single-parent households

Whether because of marital dissolution or through rising numbers of children born outside marriage, the numbers of single-parent families are growing – another key trend in schools' wider environment. Even by the early 1990s, single-parent families were around a fifth in many OECD countries, and well over a quarter in the US (OECD, 1999a, Table 1.3). While not everyone will experience marital breakdown as a disaster, it leaves few unscathed and the risks of social exclusion can be acute among single-parent families, particularly those of vulnerable labour market status. Even when entrapment in poverty is avoided, the subjective impact on the young through a heightened sense of insecurity and risk may be no less real.

It is a truism in education that supportive family environments are critical for students, learning, and schools. Yet, it is also clear that such beneficial conditions cannot just be assumed. Van Aalst's review in this volume (Chapter 8) of studies and enquiries into the future world for schooling in a number of countries shows that there is a widespread perception of the weakening role for the home and family. The partnerships offered by schools to families in socialisation and investment through learning thus take on heightened importance. For such partnerships to be really effective to provide a balance to the individualism and fragmentation of contemporary societies, they will need to be accorded a high priority among the aims of schools rather than be regarded as incidental spin-offs. This issue helps to define the "reschooling" scenarios outlined in Chapter 3.

Strengthened family/school partnerships

Knowledge, technology and work

The knowledge and learning economy

OECD economies can now accurately be described as "knowledge-based", a matter of obvious importance to schools, given their unique set of educational responsibilities. The implications of these changes for education, and the extent to which schools are characterised by the organisational features typically found in knowledge-intensive sectors (these aspects are discussed in Chapter 2), have recently been addressed in a major OECD/CERI report (OECD, 2000a).

Knowledge-based economies, learning societies

This report summarised some of the key indicators of the developing "knowledge-based economy":

"Many indicators show that there has been a shift in economic development in the direction of a more important role for knowledge production and learning (...). Moses Abramowitz and Paul David (1996) have demonstrated that this century has been characterised by increasing knowledge intensity in the production system. The OECD's structural analysis of industrial development supports their conclusion. It has been shown that the sectors that use knowledge inputs such as R&D and skilled labour most intensively grew most rapidly. At the same time, the skill profile is on an upward trend in almost all sectors. In most OECD countries, in terms of employment and value added, the most rapidly growing sector is knowledge-intensive business services (OECD, 1998a, pp. 48-55).

Coping with rapid change

These observations have led more and more analysts to characterise the new economy as "knowledge-based", and there is little doubt about relative shift in the demand for labour towards more skilled workers (OECD, 1994). However if the knowledge intensity of the economy were to increase permanently, the destructive aspects of innovation and change might take on greater importance. In an alternative interpretation of the change in the composition of the labour force, Carter (1994) pointed out that the main function of most non-production workers is to introduce or cope with change. The rising proportion of non-production workers may thus be taken as the expression both of the growing cost of change and of an acceleration in the rate of change.

An acceleration in the rate of change implies that knowledge and skills are exposed more rapidly to depreciation. Therefore the increase in the stock of knowledge may be less dramatic than it appears. An alternative hypothesis is that we are moving into a 'learning economy', where the success of individuals, firms, regions and countries will reflect, more than anything else, their ability to learn. The speeding up of change reflects the rapid diffusion of information technology, the widening of the global marketplace, with the inclusion of new strong competitors, and deregulation of and less stability in markets (Drucker, 1993; Lundvall and Johnson, 1994; Lundvall, 2000)." (*op. cit.*, pp. 28-29)

This analysis identifies the importance of speed of change, which brings costs as well as benefits, and the premium this places on abilities to learn. It also raises profound questions for the kinds of knowledge students are being equipped with, and ought to be equipped with, by schools. This is especially because the actual deployment of knowledge by professionals, workers, scientists and so forth takes place well after they have left school, perhaps many years later, by which time most of what they were taught within the school curriculum is forgotten. This is the case for the highly skilled and still more for those in low-skill work environments who are up against the "use it or lose it" principle (OECD, 1997*b*, Chapter 3). The questions of the knowledge and skills that schools should focus on in preparing students for future lives within tomorrow's learning society are rendered still more complex as the pathways and destinations that students will later follow are far from identical. Not all will pursue professional careers in the dynamic sectors of the "new economy" – indeed most will not – so that curriculum cannot be designed as if all are on an identical high-flying track. The knowledge that many will use in work, society or leisure may be far from advanced.[8]

Despite – or because of – very diverse needs, attention comes to focus on generic skills and competences in addressing these questions. The four-way typology of knowledge presented in the knowledge management analysis is useful in distinguishing between "know-what", "know-why", "know-how", and "know-who" (Lundvall and Johnson, 1994; OECD, 2000*a*, p. 14). While "know what" is important, in its own right and to anchor concretely the latter three, the implication of rapid change and "knowledge decay" is that schools must lay a very sound foundation on which the other three forms of knowledge can be developed and maintained. How well they succeed in this in all countries is still an open question, especially where the traditions of factual knowledge transmission and recall remain dominant.

Implications of rapid change for school knowledge?

"Know-what", "know-why", "know-how", and "know-who"

The "technological paradigm"

"A common feature of new general-purpose technologies is that it takes a long time before they are implemented and use to their full potential across economies (…). It took several decades before manufacturing enterprises, having already invested in steam engines, introduced electricity. Thereafter, it took a long while before they implemented the organisational changes, in particular the assembly line, and developed the skills required to use the electro-motor to its full potential (…).

ICT is an example of a general-purpose technology that has pervasive effects on practically all sectors of economic activity. In line with other general-purpose technologies, reaping its full benefits calls for comprehensive structural and organisational change. However, the importance and all-purpose characteristics of ICT should not lead to lose sight of the more general dynamics of innovation in OECD economies. These are driven, *inter alia*, by the evolving relationships between science and industry and the impetus for better exploitation of knowledge."

Extracts from OECD (2000e)

Technological change as a driving force – opportunities and risks

The message from this analysis [and the recent final report from the OECD Growth Project (OECD, 2001k)] is thus both that technological change is a pervasive driving force in OECD countries and that its impact depends critically on its general context, including the opportunities for innovation and for the production, mediation and use of knowledge. Technology does not deterministically drive wider change, a point reinforced by Miller in his contribution to this report (Chapter 7). The high-level OECD forums on 21st century transitions analysed this inherent openness by distinguishing between opportunities and risks. There is agreement that technological advances in train now could be as significant as the earlier radical shifts associated with the steam engine, electricity, and the car, whether referring to ICT, bio-technology, or new materials technologies. But, there are also risks, including that possible schisms and divides will grow – between haves and have-nots, risk-takers and risk-avoiders. Addressing such divides defines important challenges for education, including schools.

So marked have been the shifts towards the integration of ICT into work, and the key economic role of knowledge and learning, that the term "new economy" has entered the policy and media lexicon. It is a term given to loose and exaggerated application, as implied by the title of the recent report from the OECD Growth Project *The New Economy: Beyond the Hype* but it points to possible new forces and relationships. For instance, productivity growth through technology might continue apace without running up against standard "old economy" constraints like rising inflation, facilitated by widespread organisational changes, the decline of hierarchical structures, and the powerful use of the networking possibilities of ICT. An important feature as identified by Miller is the blurring of the supply and demand sides of the economy, so that consumers enter more directly into the production process before output is actually created. How far such "new economy" characteristics are typical of the OECD as a whole is still debatable, especially in the light of recent economic downturns and the loss of confidence in the technology sector in particular. By the time current school students are active in the job market, however, such cautions and caveats may well be long forgotten.

The "New Economy"?

Changing nature of work and careers

There have been massive changes taking place in the structure of work and the economy over the long term. Since the beginning of the 20th century, the countryside has been transformed in many countries, with urbanisation and the widespread exit from agriculture. Even the factories that lay at the heart of jobs and economic strength within living memories are now declining as the place of employment. There has been a massive shift to services – the "tertiarisation" of work. With the possible dawning of the "new" economic age, these major movements are far from over.

The shift to service sector employment

Service employment has continued to grow in OECD countries, and now accounts for three-quarters of employment in several countries. The overall OECD average stood at 65% in 1999 (OECD, 2000*b* and 2001*e*). As recently as the mid-1980s, there were marked national divergences in the service share across countries but by now patterns have converged. Services are associated with a different profile of jobs from manufacturing. Of people working in the goods-producing sector, 65% occupy blue-collar jobs; this stands at less than 13% in services. While the ratio of women to men is only a third in the "goods-producing" sector, they are a slight majority (ratio of 1.04 OECD-wide) in the "service sector". In the latter, employment growth has been most rapid in producer and social services.[9] More generally, there has been a process of "up-skilling", revealed most convincingly in "within-industry" and "within-occupational" shifts, rather than the larger sectoral movements referred to above (OECD, 2001a, Chapter 4).

Up-skilling but many jobs not highly skilled   While it might be tempting to interpret these figures as sign that all now participate in the "new economy", they should be put in perspective. While among services, distributive jobs have grown least they still account for very large numbers, and typically double those in business services. Many work in the personal sector of hotel, catering, entertainment, domestic service and the like, very often in low-skill jobs. The social services sector is more dynamic with clear divergences across countries but even here, the ratio of unskilled to skilled jobs could well increase as social service jobs expand (Esping-Andersen, in Chapter 6 of this volume). At the same time, part-time working has increased in most OECD countries, sometimes very rapidly, associated on average with lower hourly earnings and less training (though such generalisation admits many exceptions) (OECD, 1999b, Chapter 1; approximately a quarter of female employment is part-time and 1 in 13 male jobs across OECD as a whole). And, while unemployment levels have been falling in recent years, it still represents a critical problem. Across the OECD as a whole, unemployment as a proportion of the labour force (men and women) stood at 6.4% in 2000, rising to nearly 9% (8.8) for the OECD European area.[10] The overall picture is therefore complex, with many problematic, as well as positive, developments.

Recognition of the importance of the knowledge economy should therefore be tempered by acknowledgement that a great many jobs remain outside very high-skill, dynamic sectors of the job market, and many people are outside the job market altogether. There is a general trend towards "up-skilling" but only as a central tendency. Demand for the most unskilled jobs has fallen – and hit hard the prospects facing the unqualified – but large numbers still occupy them. It is most plausible to assume that very wide differences in skill demands will remain a feature of tomorrow's employment world.

Consideration of skills trends can usefully be complemented by those relating to insecurity. The main trend is towards greater insecurity at all levels, but especially among blue-collar workers and the unqualified for whom job stability has clearly dropped. In part, security is a subjective matter: "a widespread and, in some countries, very sharp increase in numbers perceiving employment insecurity took place between the 1980s and 90s" (OECD, 1997a, Chapter 5). Even where job instability does not appear to have increased, the expected loss from job separation has as it becomes more difficult to find a satisfactory new income or security match in the event of job loss. This ties in with the "consumer society" trends discussed later in this chapter, bringing greater pressures to maintain income and lifestyles for individuals and families.

Insecurity

The more general conclusion to draw from these manifold changes is that linear hierarchical concepts of "skill", closely correlated with qualification levels, do not well apply to the jobs of today and tomorrow. More dynamic relationships are in play, with possibly far-reaching implications for how educational credentials will function in the labour markets of the future. This theme is developed in the scenarios presented in Chapter 3, where the consequences are discussed of futures in which schools are "liberated" from the very powerful grip they exercise over the credentialing and certification process. Already, the degree of change and flux has undermined the model of the lifetime career engaged in until retirement after an initial training period, which is one powerful argument in favour of universalising lifelong learning. It is difficult to be precise on how many major job shifts

Changing concepts of skill and career

33

people already in employment will make throughout their working lives; still more is precision impossible about futures for students still in school. The safest assumption is that all can expect unpredictable and changeable careers. This alone presents considerable challenges to schools, especially those which hold on to traditional assumptions about educational and work careers.

Rising adult educational attainments – towards the "expert society"?

Adults becoming better qualified

With the major post-World War II expansion of educational provision, attainments of adult populations have naturally risen, too. These trends are set to continue into the foreseeable future. For the whole 25 to 64 year-old age group – which includes those in their fifties and sixties who were in school too soon to profit from the more recent periods of educational expansion – as many as 62% have attained at least upper secondary education across the OECD as a whole rising to 8 in 10 or more in a number of countries[11] (Figure 1.3). Even for tertiary education attainment, many adults now have reached this level. Just over a fifth (22%) of all aged 25-64 across the OECD as a whole have attained tertiary level education, which is hardly a small elite group as in earlier times, and in many the figure stands at around a quarter of working-age adults. In Canada (39%), Finland (31%), Japan (31%) and the United States (35%), it is around a third or more.

Especially younger adults, today's parents

For younger adults who have not long left initial education the figures are naturally higher again and the overall OECD average now approaches the three-quarters mark (72%) of 25-34 year-olds who have attained at least the upper secondary level of education. In 13 countries, this figure is 80% or more, and even over 90% in the Czech Republic, Japan, Korea, and Norway. Among the next youngest 35-44 age group, as many as two-thirds across the OECD have attained this level of education, and is much higher than this in a number of countries. At the same time, around a quarter of younger adults have had a tertiary education – 25% in the 25-34 age group and 35-44 (23%) age groups. A third or more of the

Figure 1.3. **Population having attained at least upper secondary and tertiary education, 1999**

25-64 and 25-34 age groups

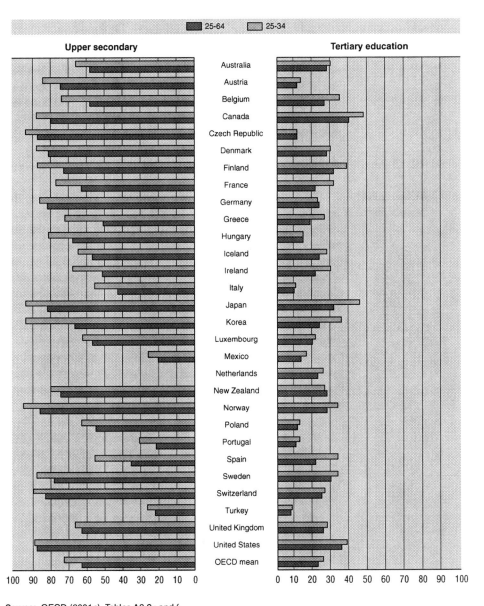

Source: OECD (2001*c*), Tables A2.2*a* and *b*.

youngest adults up to their mid-thirties have had a tertiary-level education in a number of countries, and in some cases it is approaching one half (Canada and Japan). These higher attainments of younger adults up to their mid-forties, together with those of students now coming through the system, will mean that attainments will continue to rise at least over the medium term. These younger adults in the 25-44 age groups also correspond broadly to the cohort of parents of school students in school; their rising "expertise" could well be exerting a diffuse but significant impact on schools, as discussed below. On the strength of this form of evidence, then, OECD countries seem well embarked to become "expert societies".

Problems and paradoxes: adult literacy

But still poor adult literacy levels   Such a conclusion might, however, be premature. The aggregate attainment figures are not very revealing about the spread of lifelong patterns of learning as they largely reflect the expansion of "front-end" provision in schools and colleges for the young. Hence, they tell us little by themselves about continued learning thereafter. More specifically, OECD analyses carried out with Statistics Canada have exposed an apparent paradox to qualify images of the "expert, high-skill society". Despite the rapidly increasing levels of educational attainment, there are serious literacy problems among the adult population of many countries. Indeed, certain of the countries enjoying among the highest levels of measured educational attainment are also those having outstanding adult literacy problems.

> "In 14 out of 20 countries, at least 15% of all adults have literacy skills at only the most rudimentary level, making it difficult for them to cope with the rising demands of the information age (...) low skills are found not just among marginalised groups but among significant proportions of the adult populations in all countries surveyed. Hence even the most economically advanced societies have a literacy skills deficit. Between one-quarter and three-quarters of adults fail to attain literacy Level 3, considered by experts as a suitable minimum skill level for coping with the demands of modern life and work." (OECD and Statistics Canada, 2000, p. xiii)

In part, of course, the "paradox" is explained because the high educational attainment and low literacy data refer to different populations. The analysis does indeed show that educational attainment is the strongest single predictor of literacy: an extra year of education is associated, on average, with an extra ten points on the IALS literacy test. Yet, the "fit" between the two is far from tight and many other factors are involved. In some countries, significant proportions of those who had apparently attained well in the education system got only the low literacy scores. There are very large differences between countries in the measured literacy scores of those who had less than upper secondary education.[12] In some, there is a clear gap between the literacy scores of those with upper secondary and tertiary level attainment, in others little discernible difference.[13] These variations warn that substantial skills problems in many societies have not been resolved with rising educational attainment levels.

Some with poor literacy are the unqualified – but by no means all

The world of the school

The rising general attainments of the population have other more diffuse impacts on the world of the school, particularly of reducing the distance between schools and teachers, on the one hand, and the general public, on the other. Many are now very familiar with the world of education, and are themselves qualified to levels at or greater than teachers. In the process, schools inevitably lose some of the "mystique" they enjoyed in earlier times. Parents and others are articulate and demanding. Pressures for greater accountability to render schooling more transparent can be linked *inter alia* to this factor, as can the problematic standing of teachers as a professional group, discussed in Chapters 2 and 3.

Declining school "mystique"

Söderberg in this volume (Chapter 9) suggests on the basis of Swedish data that higher levels of parental education foster critical attitudes that might actually weaken the standing of schools: "The general conclusion might thus be that a rise in educational level leads to more critical thinking about, and higher demands on, the educational system. It is possible that a well-functioning school system in a paradoxical sense contributes to weakening its own position." Much depends on what "weakening" and

Educated parents mean more critical attitudes

lower measured satisfaction levels mean. On the one hand, critical attitudes could be a sign of robustness as rising expectations and a desire for improvement find expression in educational action and investment.[14] On the other, they might express genuine dissatisfaction leading increasing numbers to retreat towards alternatives such as home or specialist schooling (as outlined by Hargreaves, 1999). More in-depth international evidence could usefully illuminate the issue of public attitudes and expectations. It is an important area and defines one dimension of the scenarios presented in Chapter 3.

Declining authority of expertise and ethical signposts?

An element of the declining "mystique" and distance between schools and societies also stems from the more diversified sources of knowledge in today's society. As populations become more highly educated and as the means of accessing knowledge become more diversified, the standing of school knowledge and the curriculum is increasingly problematic. Some refer to a general "decline in the authority of expert knowledge" (Prout, 2000), accompanying the erosion of cultural absolutes. Michel, in Chapter 11, also describes the problems, as well as the appeal, of the new "managerial paradigm" characterised by flexibility rather than more clear-cut cultural and ethical signposts. Schools can respond in different ways. They might try to "keep up" by seeking to reflect all the rapidly changing sources of knowledge in their curriculum. Alternatively, greater flux and diversity of knowledge, far from confusing their mission, may force greater clarification of what it is that schools are best placed to focus upon.

Lifestyles, consumption and inequality

The consumer society and sustainability

Massive rise in consumption in OECD countries

Consumption levels define a major aspect of life in OECD countries, in particular the trends and scale to which they have grown. To anyone arriving from a century ago, they would be a source of incredulity. There have been enormous changes experienced in average lifestyles and what many children today expect to be their standard of living in the future. The sheer scale of the change was one of the basic facts that introduced a joint Environment/CERI Workshop on education, learning and sustainable consumption held in OECD in 1998:

> "The scale of human consumption has risen dramatically and unequally over this century. The 1998 *Human Development Report* documents this: from $1.5 trillion in 1900 to $4 trillion in 1950, and then a trebling to $12 trillion in the 25 years to 1975, followed by another doubling to $24 trillion in 1998." (OECD, 1999*d* and UNDP, 1998)

There are undoubtedly massive benefits lying behind these stark figures, representing liberation from privation and drudgery. Unless there is a cataclysmic change brought on by, say, global conflict, it is perhaps safest to assume that the world of tomorrow for most OECD school students today will continue to have very high levels of consumption.

Yet, contained in these high and growing consumption levels are challenging aspects of the school's environment. A growing concern is that such high consumption has strengthened materialism as a defining value in itself, to the detriment of a range of other civic and cultural values that are needed for the future health of societies. This, and individualism more generally, may be eroding the "social glue" that is essential not only for individual and social development but even for economic development. (The relationships between social capital, human capital and sustainability are explored in a recent OECD analysis, see OECD, 2001*d*.) Nor, contrary to what might be expected, have individuals' subjective feelings of well-being kept pace with growing personal resources and their ability to consume (Inglehart, 1997). The opposite may even be the case: "(...) the proportion of people in the US describing themselves as 'happy' peaked in 1957 even though consumption rates have increased considerably since then. The US Index of Social Health has decreased by 52% in the last two decades despite a rise in consumption of nearly 50%." (OECD, 1999*d*, p. 12)

Given the role of schools in socialisation, it is not surprising that their potential for educating for a more complete range of human endeavours and outcomes should be

But problems too

39

appearing increasingly on educational agendas. An ambitious approach has been developed as part of a Pacific region project on "multi-dimensional" citizenship, which suggests the need for all to be sensitive to a variety of dimensions – the personal, social, spatial, and temporal – that defines their lives (Cogan, 1997). Such agendas are inherently controversial, whether through fear that devoting greater attention to values and civic attitudes risks indoctrination or that further extensions of schools' tasks, particularly beyond cognitive learning, will only exacerbate existing school overload. There are powerful economic and political interests with a stake in high consumption so that schools confront an ambivalence in the societal messages they receive in relation to consumption.

Not all share affluent lifestyles...

Concerns relating to the "consumer society" derive also from the disadvantage then suffered by those who do not enjoy access to high levels of consumption and material well-being. The more affluent become larger sections of OECD societies, the more sharply is the disadvantage experienced by those who still miss out. Still more glaring than these within-country inequalities, are the divides between the rich countries and the poor. The 2000 *World Development Report* shows that, despite major indications of progress over the past half century: "Of the world's 6 billion people, 2.8 billion live on less than $2 a day, and 1.2 billion on less than $1 a day" (World Bank, 2000). For these enormous numbers, the notion of a "consumer society" is largely meaningless.

... especially in the developing world

Such stark differences between the rich and poor in the world become a growing part of society's consciousness, particularly through the immediacy of media attention. Many of the young are acutely aware of such glaring inequalities and the environmental issues with which they are intertwined. In his contribution to this report (Chapter 8), van Aalst describes how the importance of these issues to young people is perceived as a driving force in schooling in the 21st century in a number of countries. It is less clear how consistent are these environmental concerns with the consumption habits of many in society, including young people who are among those with the highest material expectations.

Sustainability lies at the heart of these questions. At least since the Earth Summit in Rio in 1992, there has been recognition of just how unsustainable many contemporary production and consumption practices are. Though ambitious objectives for change are in place, actual progress is still painfully slow. While the issues of sustainable production and consumption are intertwined, those relating to consumption are much nearer to the lives of school students and provided the focus of the 1998 Environment/CERI Workshop. (For a recent summary of the environmental situation in OECD countries see OECD, 2001*i*.)

Slow progress towards sustainable consumption

It is natural to suggest that sustainability concerns should be reflected in new programmes that "teach" children about the environment. Yet, new programmes jostling for room into already-crowded school curricula are unlikely to make a significant impact, and moreover environmental information campaigns have been shown to be singularly ineffective in changing consumption habits or deeper-held values. Instead:

> "Among the most important learning that schooling provides of relevance to sustainability are the attributes of critical thinking, self-reflection, media analysis, personal and group decision-making and problem-solving. These capacities and skills abound in countries' official definitions of educational aims, but are often far less in evidence in the actual teaching and learning that take place. The successful acquisition of precisely these capacities, however, might represent a much more significant step towards an education for sustainability than relatively small-scale examples of curriculum innovation, no matter how valuable these are." (OECD, 1999*d*, p. 20)

A key question then is how well school systems in OECD countries really do develop the more general, critical higher-order competences that are horizontal across subjects and disciplines, building capacity in the young to become informed and responsible in the world of the 21st century. How well they do provides a valuable yardstick of the quality of education provided by schools, but as yet firm evidence is elusive. Such competences closely match those required in the labour market and organisations, including the capacity of each person to design their

Calling for critical, informed, responsible young people

41

own lifelong learning agendas and negotiate their way through complex, individualised pathways of professional development. They are less matters to be taught as part of the manifest curriculum, more embedded in the culture and everyday practice of working schools. They are inimical to the most traditional approaches and ethos of schooling, already out-moded by the second half of the 20th century.

Incomes, poverty and life-chances

Earlier long-term trends towards narrowing gaps...

In OECD countries, the long-term trend had been for income inequalities to diminish, even while the disparities between the top and bottom remain large, this alongside the massive rises in consumption already described (*e.g.* OECD, 1993, Chapter 5). More recently, however, changes have been occurring. On wealth, Wolff (1987, p. 1), taking a very long-term view, observed: "Perhaps the most important finding is the gradual but persistent decline in the degree of wealth inequality among households during the 20th century". The World Development Report (World Bank, 2000, p. v) also observed positive changes over the past century: "The 20th century saw great progress in reducing poverty and improving well-being. In the past four decades life expectancy in the developing world increased 20 years on average". At the same time, the inequality between the rich and poor countries of the world has been widening at an alarming rate as summarised by Jolly (2000). He refers to modestly growing inequalities over the first half of the 20th century, that quickened and then soared after 1960: "from 30 to 1 in 1960 to 60 to 1 in 1990 and 74 to 1 at present".

... but not between rich and poor countries

More recent signs of growing inequalities

Within the OECD countries since the 1970s inequality trends have been disturbed. They have widened in some countries in the 1980s, continuing into the 1990s. The more recent trends on incomes and poverty are presented in the box below in the form of "stylised facts" (OECD, 1999e). Such trends help to define the broader environment in which students live and, more specifically, highlight that schools are particularly affected in terms of groups hardest hit.

Widening gaps in some countries

Important messages for schooling emerge from these "stylised facts". The first is that the very long-term trends towards a narrowing of resource differentials among individuals and households have not continued as before. In many countries, the gaps are now widening, though this should be understood in the context of the overall rise in affluence, health and consumption levels. When all the caveats have been entered, however, and in the light of the well-established links between home background factors and educational attainment, schooling is confronting the situation where critical social inequalities remain. Enthusiasm for the "new economy", "knowledge society", etc., should not disguise this. Indeed, such developments may well be exacerbating the problems of those who are unable to participate fully in them.

Extracts from the "stylised facts" on income inequality and poverty in OECD countries

There was no generalised long-term trend in the distribution of disposable household incomes since the mid-1970s. However, during the more recent period (mid-1980s to mid-1990s), income inequality has increased in a greater number of OECD countries, *i.e.* in over half of the observed countries.

In those countries where inequalities increased, this happened mostly among the working-age population, whilst there were less changes among the retirement-age population. However, average incomes of the elderly increased towards the average of the population in most countries.

Changes in income distribution in the past ten years generally favoured the prime-age and elderly age groups, in particular those around retirement age. Persons living in multi-adult households have seen their income shares rise somewhat, especially in households without children, or when there are two or more earners present. On the other hand, young age groups lost ground, in particular those aged 18-25. Relative income levels of single parents and persons in workless households tended to weaken further.

The increased dispersion from gross earnings and other market income was the main contributor to widening inequality at the household level: increased inequality in earnings themselves; increased income differentials between households with different degrees of employment attachment; and a trend towards "employment polarisation" in many countries, leading to a simultaneous increase in "work-rich" and "work-poor" shares of households.

This increase in market income inequality was not, or not entirely, translated into higher inequality of disposable incomes for the working age population, as both transfers and taxes off-set the effects of earnings and capital/self-employment income on the distribution. In most countries, this effectiveness increased.

43 |

**Extracts from the "stylised facts" on income inequality
and poverty in OECD countries** (*cont.*)

Apart from income taxes, public transfers also played an important role in the redistribution of incomes to lower-income segments, in particular among the working-age population (...). Moreover, public transfers are a more important source of income for lower income groups. The part of non-pension transfers in the incomes of poorer working-age adults increased in a majority of countries.

Relative poverty rates remained broadly stable over the last ten years, with some countries experiencing declines (in particular Belgium and Denmark) and some others increases (in particular Italy and the United Kingdom) (...). The share of both elderly and children in the poor population decreased over the last ten years in most countries. However, poverty rates of children increased somewhat in a number of countries, while poverty rates of the elderly decreased.

Joblessness is a key factor in explaining why poverty often increased for those aged 18-25 and single parent families (...). For the working age population, poverty rates on a pre-tax and transfer basis rose in all countries, on average by 4 percentage points. Post-tax and transfer poverty rates fell or increased by less in all but two countries. This indicates an increased effectiveness of tax/transfer systems in alleviating poverty in a majority of Member countries.

---

*The young
and single-parent
households
slipping back*

A second main message is that different population groups and countries have fared differently. Lack of a universal trend is nevertheless consistent with growing inequalities in some countries, and, for market incomes, in the majority of countries. Some trends are even more clear-cut, especially concerning the socio-demographic groups whose fortunes have improved and others whose fortunes have slipped. Of particular relevance for schools is that the most gains have been experienced by older members of populations, and those well-established in employment while younger people (including children) and those with precarious labour market positions have done relatively badly. Households with children headed by young parents have lost out. Especially vulnerable are single-parent households, which have grown throughout the OECD, and those described as "work-poor". In short, problems have been aggravated precisely among those for whom schools are most responsible and have diminished among those furthest from the school gates.

There are wide variations between countries regarding the concentration of exclusion and poverty among children (UNICEF, 2000). In some countries, these rates are very low at only 5% or even less (Nordic countries, Belgium and Luxembourg). In others, as many as a fifth to a quarter of children live in poverty (Turkey, the United Kingdom, Italy, the United States, Mexico).[15] Compound disadvantages set up compound barriers as described by Esping-Andersen in Chapter 6 when he refers to the "bundling" of low pay or unemployment in couples, families or communities, causing people to become stuck in these situations, nurturing concentrated deprivation, and hardening the sense of social failure. He also draws attention to marked variations in the prevalence of terms such as "underclass", "social exclusion", "two-speed"/"two-thirds" society, etc., in everyday debate and discourse. Such terms, he suggests, are found rarely in Mediterranean Europe, where family institutions and protection remain strong, or in the Nordic countries with highly developed equity attitudes and anti-poverty policies.

Child poverty very marked in some countries

An extreme result of exclusion and insecurity is suicide. Kennedy in Chapter 10 compiles youth suicide figures to show that several countries have recently recorded steep rises. He links this to a broad range of factors, including the lack of inclusion, opportunity and social capital, and the experience of hardship. Many more young males commit suicide than young females – by a factor of 3, 4 or 5. However these gender differences should be accounted for – whether linked forward to the employment insecurities brought by the disintegration of staple male manual job opportunities, or connected back to the consistently higher numbers of boys than girls in special education, or to some other cause – these represent a stark indicator of contemporary malaise.

Growing youth suicide, especially among young men

45

Key role of the state

A third main message from the "stylised facts" is also relevant to the world of education. The role of the state through taxation and social transfers has been a critical one in modifying the inequalities that exist from the operation of the market in the absence of government action. This impact has, if anything, become greater and more effective in latter years. Thus, while it is commonly observed that "welfare state" structures and assumptions have been eroded since their immediate post-World War II heyday, there remains a critical state role in redistributing access to resources. The school is often an active partner in public policies to combat exclusion (the issue of co-ordination of services has been extensively studied by OECD/CERI; see OECD, 1998*e*).

The geo-political dimension – International, national, local

Globalisation

Polarised views on globalisation

Globalisation refers to a diverse set of important changes, often highly controversial. Viewpoints differ sharply on whether they are positive and to be encouraged, or grudgingly accepted, or else to be fiercely resisted. For some, globalisation represents the opening of national barriers, allowing the passage of knowledge, trade and culture for prosperity to flourish for the benefit of humankind. It embraces the Internet, travel, exchange and similar cross-border developments. For others, it encompasses a raft of mainly reprehensible developments – from international corporate power to growing international inequalities between rich and poor, to cultural and political hegemony. Viewpoints tend thus to be polarised between extremes, divided less over the facts of globalisation than over its benefits and costs.

The economic dimensions...

Globalisation has a strong economic base in growing interdependency across countries and between enterprises, involving increased and more liberalised trade, flows of finance, persons and services, the "borderless world" of rapid electronic communication and exchange, and a range of other on-going developments. It refers politically to the internationalising changes introduced by governments and NGOs as well as the prominence of international bodies/associations of varying statuses, powers, and memberships. In the world of today and tomorrow, such international bodies are inevitable in some form – even curbing the "excesses" of globalisation would ultimately depend on co-ordinated international action – but they attract growing controversy and are criticised variously for the approaches/philosophies they espouse, the volume of resources they control, or their apparent distance from the democratic process.

... the political...

The cultural dimension is equally controversial. There are very positive developments that have quickened over the past half-century: the major growth in travel and awareness of other cultures, the explicit pursuit of multiculturalism in education and societies, including awareness of the critical role of languages. Again, however, there are countervailing trends. Many worry about the impact of globalisation on language and cultural diversity. There has been a very clear shift towards English as the international lingua franca, as well as the questionable benefits from ubiquitous anglophone TV series. Even the apparently benign expansion of travel, broadening minds and economic development, is not without cost – analysed with prescience by Hirsch (1977) a quarter of a century ago – as high-volume tourism eventually threatens the very magnet sites that so attract. More problematic still are the effects described by Michel in Chapter 11 in Part II:

... and the cultural ones

> "Globalisation, because of the risk it brings of soulless standardisation, can lead to fragmentation and a reduced sense of belonging to a wider community. The excesses of unbridled markets, in which prices and the market are more important than social and cultural relationships, are being met with an excess of nationalism, regionalism and parochialism. These threaten peace and raise the spectre of resurgent racism and intolerance."

In all, therefore, the globalisation issues are far-reaching indeed.

47

Knowledge, learning and education are intertwined through all these dimensions. As expressed by Carnoy:

> "Even our cultures are globalising. One effect is that activities, including how we relate to our family and friends, are rapidly becoming organised around a much more compressed view of space and time. This extends to children in school or watching television who are re-conceptualising their 'world', in terms of the meanings that they attach to music, the environment, sports, or race and ethnicity."

Learning to deal with "hyper-complexity"

Education bears a heavy responsibility in equipping young people with the means to deal with the complexity – the "hyper-complexity" – these trends represent. The profound ethical and values questions call for discerning competences and a broad understanding of contemporary culture and life. These are formed through education in all its settings, formal and informal, but schools clearly have a potentially key role. In some specific instances, such as second- and third-language teaching, schools have the lead responsibility.

Opening educational boundaries, for good or ill...

There are charged decision-making and knowledge issues that also increasingly arise for education through the impact of globalisation. A world in which schools very actively use ICT and the Internet is a very different one from the situation at the other end of the spectrum where school knowledge is very tightly controlled through nationally- or locally-agreed syllabuses, textbooks, and materials. While at present schools mostly operate somewhere in the spectrum between the extremes, the trend is clearly moving towards the ICT scenario. This is on-going, not just about possible futures. In tertiary education in particular, there are already many examples of cross-frontier distance education programmes and diplomas, some public, some private. Increasing school use of Internet and educational software raises questions about who produces materials and where, in the process recasting traditional relationships and notions of sovereignty (see OECD, 2001*j*).

Forms of educational globalisation impact on schooling in other ways. National political debates are increasingly shaped by international comparisons, particularly of matters such as class sizes or student scores. Some systems have already been shaken by the so-called "TIMSS effect" after publication of comparative scores (and there may soon be similar "PISA effects" when the first results of the OECD/PISA surveys are published).[16] Certain countries have had to dip well into the international teacher labour market in the face of shortages, as such advanced-skill markets are becoming increasingly global. In short, education is an integral element of globalisation, as well as being profoundly affected by it. It features prominently as one dimension of the scenarios presented in Chapter 3.

... and creating challenges for national decision-making

The international movements of populations

An important aspect of globalisation is the greater movement of populations from one country to another. It is plausible that these flows will increase substantially in the years ahead though current trends are mixed. If increases materialise, they would enhance still further ethnic and cultural diversity and, in some cases, the socio-economic and educational problems experienced by minority populations. These present major challenges to the place called school. They sharpen issues concerning how well schools are able to deal with, even promote, diversity. They increase the range of family expectations and aspirations regarding what schools should achieve. They raise acute equity questions – when are educational differences the laudable expression of cultural diversity or instead the unacceptable face of social inequality?

Sharpening diversity and equity issues

OECD countries had already become places of net immigration by the beginning of the 1990s, including in the Southern European area that before had been an important sending region (OECD, 1991). Regarding the scale of population movements, migration flows have tended to increase since then but it is difficult to generalise, particularly on the basis of relatively short-term trends. Even over the course of 1990s, there were up- and down-turns in numbers, significant differences across

Net immigration into the OECD countries

Illegal migration

countries, while the nature and source of migration vary substantially. The phenomenon of illegal and irregular migration, by its nature, is impossible to chart with any precision but it is clear that it continues in large numbers. Those concerned are among the most excluded in OECD countries, lying outside even the most basis welfare provisions open to others.

Much within-OECD movement

Very different patterns of population flows emerge depending on whether they are expressed in absolute or relative terms: the former indicate the scale of world-wide movements whereas the size of flows relative to national population is what matters particularly to each country, including their schools. In absolute terms, by far the largest inflows of foreigners are recorded in the United States and Germany, followed by Japan, Canada and the United Kingdom. A striking feature of inflows for each country is that they tend to be dominated by a very small number of sending countries. These reflect a pattern of "regionalisation" and sometimes continuing ex-colonial links. They belie the notion that population flows are predominantly from poor to rich countries for a very large amount of the movement goes on between the OECD countries themselves. Some of this takes the form of the highly-skilled personnel who now participate in international labour markets.

Population growth outside the OECD area leading to intense worldwide pressures

Demographic projections suggest that pressures are set to intensify. Of the expected population increase of 2 billion over the first quarter century, only 145 million are foreseen for the OECD area, and much of this dominated by a small number of countries (Mexico, Turkey, Canada, the United States and Australia). The relative share of the OECD countries among the world population is expected to decline by 2025 to around 16% from current levels just under 20%. With 93% of the additional 2 billion humankind to be born outside the OECD area, the pressures "pushing" people to the richer countries could well intensify. At the same time, the very low birth rates in the OECD area might themselves be "pulling" in inflows, especially in the context of continuing labour shortages. These could be especially marked in Europe and Japan where the impact of ageing will be greater (OECD, 1999c). Whatever their source, an important trend already visible is for the numbers of foreign and foreign-born members of OECD societies to rise.

The "push" and "pull" factors will likely involve different profiles of foreign populations – those looking to escape poverty by moving to one of the world's rich nations contrast with the highly-skilled being targeted by OECD enterprises seeking workers internationally. Such differences and the demographic pressures combined, in the context of the markedly growing inequalities between the affluent and poor countries of the world, create conditions that may turn out to be far from stable.

Communities and regions

If the importance of a supportive family and home background to attainment is an educational truism, the role of close links between schools and their communities can be counted as another. Increasingly, however, questions arise about what those "communities" are. The extent of geographical mobility reduces lifelong connections to particular neighbourhoods and the density of social interactions that this brings. The radical decline of industries such as agriculture, mining, fishing, and steel production brought devastating decline to the residential communities that depended on them. There are other equally problematic development challenging established notions of "community": new patterns of urbanisation and sub-urbanisation; the individualisation of lifestyles (including the central place occupied by TV and other ICT media); the decline of established religions in many societies, as well as of other community-based institutions (local retailers, cafés, etc.).

The importance of the community – but what are communities today?

Evidence relating to the "social capital" of social and civic engagement (OECD, 2001d) suggests complex patterns. In some countries, there are signs of a decline in social engagement, membership of different bodies and other associational activity (Australia, the United States), in others, the picture is less conclusive. There does appear to be a shift towards individualised leisure and community activities, with more informal and transient forms of engagement, as well as a

Mixed evidence on levels of social engagement, with new forms of leisure and informal "connectedness"

51

growth of single issue politics. Our levels of trust in each other may not have declined significantly, but they have in relation to a range of public institutions. These are complex developments and the temptation should be resisted to romanticise about mythical "golden times" – new forms of communal activity, including virtual communities, develop as others decline. Yet, there do seem to be new trends in train relating to the nature of our connections to society and each other that are fundamental to grasp for schools and the young.

Without romanticising about a lost "golden age" of community, there are problems to be addressed. One affecting children very directly is lack of public spaces devoted to play. Such is the profound sense of unease about the security of young people, itself linked to the loss of the sense of protection offered by stable residential communities, that play space may be under-utilised even when it is available. Less established residential communities can lead to the deterioration of the social capital in the form of norms and values supportive of education, as analysed by Coleman a decade or more ago (Coleman, 1988). Schools can less readily turn to the "community" as an educational partner where it has become elusive, transient or virtual. These problems contrast with a widespread agreement on the need to devote particular attention to the socialisation of the young. In situations of problematic community support and social capital, individual schools, parents, and immediate families are placed under more intense pressures and responsibilities.

Community and socialisation role for schools

One way forward is to reinforce the socialisation functions of schools, and to recognise more explicitly their nature as communities in their own right, where, for instance, contacts, friendships, and play are valued as essential not incidental. Such an emphasis does not necessarily conflict with a strong focus on cognitive development but it suggests acknowledgement of a comprehensive set of educational outcomes going beyond measurable standards. This broader understanding of the school is developed particularly in Scenario 3 of Chapter 3, which itself draws on the arguments developed by Carnoy:

"The functional separation between residence, work, and urban services, the increasingly lower density of new urban forms, and increased geographic mobility have made it increasingly difficult to build social communities on a neighbourhood basis (...). The central organising point in our society at the neighbourhood level is the school – elementary and secondary, as well as child development centres. Because schools' location patterns are pervasive and residence-based, and because sociability is made easier through children's connections, schools could become the platforms for a variety of neighbourhood issues."

Of particular interest in this analysis is not only the concept of the school "with" or "for" or "instead of" the community but the school as community. In this analysis, the school becomes perhaps the leading community institution.

Learning cities and regions – "geography matters"

There is further reason why the locality and region are important. An over-individualised view of education, aptitude and society can neglect the importance of the geographical configurations in which we live. These configurations help to shape cultures and infrastructures for learning. From this derives the interest in the concept of "learning cities and regions" (OECD, 2001f). Building on the critical lesson that "geography does matter", the aim of this family of strategies is to create dynamic synergies and partnerships, to which schools contribute. Conversely, without recognition of the local dimension, opportunities for such synergies and partnerships may not be grasped, to the detriment of school learning.

Learning by interacting

A strong focus on the local level is justified not only by the need to create effective partnerships but from the very nature of knowledge and learning:

"Most significantly, however, both the production and the dissemination of 'know-how' is facilitated by what has been termed 'learning-by-interaction'. Quite simply, individuals are able to build significantly on what they learn through 'learning-by-doing' by communication and exchange with others – colleagues both in the workplace and outside (for example, Rubenson and Schuetze, 1995). Recent evidence from the UK suggests, moreover, that individual 'learning-by-interacting' is especially important where people perceive them-

53

selves to have exhausted the learning potential of 'learning-by-doing' on their own account (Eraut *et al.*, 1998)." (OECD, 2001f, pp. 16-17)

Again, there is need for new balances to be struck from an over-individualised view of the nature of education and schooling.

The changing nature of governance

Governance changing...

The environment of schooling embraces the broad nature of governance, which impacts on education either indirectly or directly through different forms of educational decision-making. Common challenges are now confronting governments across the different realms of public policy, as they explore new approaches to decision-making, account-ability, social responsiveness, and citizenship. In some, this is taking place against a history of powerful "welfare state" arrangements that have been modified over the recent period into increasingly complex, mixed policy models. Globalisation is one major factor spurring the search for new models.

... but governments not withering away

As a result of these changes, some suggest that govern-ments are in a state of terminal decline, overtaken by new players exercising private corporate, consumer and NGO power, or by configurations of policy-making undermining traditional sources of sovereignty and influence. Challeng-ing questions about government effectiveness are implicit in the analysis of declining of social capital, insofar as it sug-gests serious public disengagement from political institutions and tears in the social and community fabric. Mulgan's analysis for the OECD's International Futures Programme, while acknowledging the extent of change and the difficulties some governments have found to adapt to greater complexity, networked forms of organisation, and huge increases in information flows, questions the "terminal decline" thesis:

"The share of tax in GDP actually role across the OECD from 34% in 1980 to 38% in 1996. Contrary to many pre-dictions the demand for government and the capacity to supply this demand both remain strong. On the demand side, electorates have signalled clearly that they want public services, the security afforded by governments in health care and pensions, as well as common goods like clean air and safe streets. Business too has rediscovered its dependence on government to maintain social order, education and infrastructures." (Mulgan, 2000, p. 146)

As regards education and schooling, with the enhanced role for the exercise of citizen choice, rather than regulation, a growing premium is placed on the individual's capacity to exercise choice in the face of complexity. This in itself defines a demanding agenda for learning and an important criterion for judging the outcomes of schooling. As with the earlier discussion of sustainability, the conclusion may be less that students need more civics programmes – that might anyway be learned through a variety of channels – but more the critical faculties that will allow them to be active citizens. This is one pillar of preparation for lifelong learning.

Active choices in a complex world

Indeed, the major societal project of "lifelong learning for all" (OECD, 1996a), by its sheer ambition and diversity, is characterised by a complexity of forms, stakeholders, partnerships, and funding that epitomises the new context of governance in the 21st century. As an integral element of the overall strategy, schooling is thereby brought into quite new forms of organisation and decision-making.

Lifelong learning implies complex governance and partnerships

55

Notes

1. For discussion of how some of the most important aspects relating to schooling can remain "invisible" through their very familiarity, see Hutmacher (1999).

2. This understates the extent of "dependency" to the extent that economic activity is being delayed well beyond 15 years of age, which has been a powerful trend. It would also understate it if more are taking early departure from the labour market pre-65 years but on this there has been no clear trend over the 1990s. Partly, growing female participation rates offset falls for older men, but even for the latter there has been no consistent downward trend across countries (OECD, 2001e, Table C).

3. A study using the same instruments in Australia confirmed Hahn's results (Mellor, 1998).

4. Average number of children per woman aged 15 to 49 years.

5. Agriculture, mining, fishing, forestry, etc.

6. While the percentage gender gap for full-time earnings has narrowed to 10-15%, as a proportion of men's earnings, in Belgium, Denmark, France and Australia, it remained between 25 and 30% in Austria, Ireland, Canada, Spain and Portugal, and was around 40% in Japan and Korea (OECD, 2001o).

7. Not all countries could be so described, and those in the South European area in particular appear to be characterised by strong family institutions. These are singled out by Esping-Andersen in this volume (Chapter 6) as countries that have avoided the extreme marginalisation of social exclusion, as strong families offer protection and inclusion even in the absence of resources, though Carnoy reflects whether even in these cases traditions will be strong enough to resist the pressure leading to fragmentation.

8. This point has also emerged from work in the OECD International Futures Programme: "The key to a thriving learning society is the capacity of most people to produce relatively simple living knowledge, even if such knowledge is not new or a 'first'– either historically or worldwide" (Stevens et al., 2000, p. 14).

9. The "service sector" comprises producer, distributive, personal, and social services.

10. Of these, nearly a third (31.4%) had been jobless for a year or more across OECD, with the corresponding European figure at 43.2%.

11. The Czech Republic (86%), Denmark (80%), Germany (81%), Japan (81%), Norway (85%), Switzerland (82%), the United States (87%).

12. For example, in Sweden and Germany more than half the adults who had not completed upper secondary education scored at 3 or more on the document literacy scale. Less than 20% did so in the United States, Poland, Portugal, Hungary, Slovenia, and Chile.

13. "(…) the benefit of a completed tertiary education compared with secondary education differs dramatically across countries. In the Netherlands, for example, the difference in scores between those with only secondary education and those with tertiary education is very small, particularly when compared with the difference between these same educational groups in the United States. In Germany, the link between educational attainment and average literacy skills is weak at all levels of education. This contrasts with the pattern observed for a country such as Slovenia." (OECD and Statistics Canada, 2000, p. 24)

14. Söderberg also suggests on the basis of Swedish data that parents may operate as an articulate but in general "conservative" force – wanting results in terms of the tried and tested and avoiding any radical change that might be seen as risky.

15. Children defined as less than 18 years of age, poverty as less than 50% of median disposable household income, and the child poverty rate as the proportion of children living in households with incomes falling below this threshold.

16. TIMSS: Third International Mathematics and Science Study; PISA: Programme for International Student Assessment.

Chapter 2

Schooling Developments and Issues

Introduction

The broad canvas of Chapter 1 is complemented in this chapter by a closer look at education systems themselves, particularly schools. The chapter aims less to summarise trends and instead to identify some key developments and questions informing the scenarios in the following chapter, though any set of issues will fit differently each country's particular traditions and situation. How different are countries' education systems is now a moot question – will schooling continue to express largely national cultures or is there now a process of convergence in train, reflecting broader globalisation? The answer to this question influences whether the scenarios outlined in this report are alternative futures for countries or instead whether all are being pulled increasingly into the same main broad model.

Robust school systems

The universality of the "place called school" across OECD countries is a more notable fact than might at first sight appear. Only a century ago, universal secondary education was not established in some places and compulsory elementary attendance still in its infancy. Now, they are among the most established features of our societies. From this observation potentially opposing conclusions can be drawn as regards the future of schools. On the one hand, their historical recency is a reminder that they are less permanent than they seem, and may be subject to further important change in the future. On the other, that so many countries of such diverse cultures have arrived at a generally

The universal schooling model: relatively recent but firmly established

common arrangement for their young indicates the power of the schooling model. It means, following Hutmacher (1999) that: "There are aspects of what schools do that really 'work'. If they were totally dysfunctional, as some critics have supposed, they would not have survived for so long, still less to have expanded markedly over recent decades." (p. 33)

Extended participation, blurring the distinction between compulsory and non-compulsory attendance

Part of schools' universality is that education for the young is everywhere compulsory, with convergence apparent in that countries that had relatively late starting ages are introducing obligatory attendance for younger children, while those marked by early departure have sought to extend it. The obligatory period, that used to define the main boundaries of educational participation for most, is now extended so much in the pre-primary, upper secondary and tertiary phases that the very significance of compulsion has become blurred. In many countries, over 90% of the age group are enrolled in education for 12 or more years, and in some it is higher than this. In Sweden, the figure is 13 (from ages 6 to 18), in Japan and the Netherlands (between ages 4 and 17) it is 14 years, rising to 15 in Belgium and France (between ages 3 and 17) (Table 2.1; see also OECD, 2001*h*). Over three-quarters of the 15-19 population across the OECD (76.9%) are now students (though not all in places called "school"), and in a number of countries more than 85% are enrolled: Belgium/Flanders (90.6%), France (87.2%), Germany (88.3%), Netherlands (87.7%), Norway (86.1%), and Sweden (86.2%). Even the proportion of 20-29 year-olds who are students stands at 1 in 5 for OECD as a whole (20.7), and is a third or more in Finland (36.1%) and Sweden (33.7%) (OECD, 2001*c*, Table C1.2). Despite the intense policy attention being devoted to the lifelong reorganisation of learning, this evidence is strongly indicative of the substantial strengthening of "front-end" initial education.

Stronger "front-end" education

Growth in female attainments – a remarkable educational trend

A major extension in educational participation is accounted for by rapidly rising female attainments, and this from a position of disadvantage within the past 20-30 years (OECD, 1986). Across the OECD as a whole, women can now expect to attend education for nearly an additional half year (0.4) compared with men, and the gap is widest in

Table 2.1. **Years during which 90% are enrolled and enrolment rates for 15-19 year-olds, 1999**

	No. of years when over 90% of age group enrolled	15-19 year-old enrolment rates
Australia	11	80.3
Austria	12	76.7
Belgium	15	90.6
Canada	12	75.3
Czech Republic	12	74.8
Denmark	13	80.4
Finland	11	84.5
France	15	87.2
Germany	12	88.3
Greece	12	82.0
Hungary	12	78.1
Iceland	12	78.7
Ireland	12	79.8
Italy	12	70.7
Japan	14	m
Korea	12	81.2
Luxembourg	12	73.8
Mexico	7	39.3
Netherlands	14	87.7
New Zealand	12	72.5
Norway	12	86.1
Poland	11	83.0
Portugal	10	76.3
Spain	12	76.3
Sweden	13	86.2
Switzerland	11	83.6
Turkey	4	30.5
United Kingdom	12	72.5
United States	10	78.1
Country mean	12	76.9

m = missing data.
Source: OECD (2001*c*), Table C1.2.

those countries where the female strides have been greatest. In 17 out of 21 countries with data, female graduation rates from upper secondary education exceeds that of young men, and by 10 percentage points or more in the Czech Republic, Denmark, Finland, Greece, Ireland, Italy and Spain (OECD, 2001*c*). With school systems often characterised as painfully slow to change, this is indeed rapid and represents perhaps the most remarkable educational trend of the recent period. Certain distinctive gender paths and educational choices do remain and, as discussed in the previous chapter, these female educational gains are far from matched in corresponding earnings (see OECD, 2001a, Chapter 3). The extent of female educational progress is indicated by the concern now expressed instead in some countries for male under-achievement, linked in part to the decline in low-skill entry-level jobs that once were the destination for many unqualified young men.

And more "non-traditional" students

A further aspect of the extension of schooling has been the retention of many "non-traditional" students who before would have left, or been left aside by, school. Such a broad range of aptitudes and backgrounds increases the challenges facing schools, teachers and education authorities.

Massive school systems...

From the universality of schooling, and the growing participation in both compulsory and non-compulsory programmes, derives another key fact: OECD countries have massive systems of schooling, with millions of students and teachers in thousands of schools. Many more again are involved in organising education – administrators, decision-makers and inspectors; specialist support, ancillary and training staff; researchers; parents; etc.:

> "The education sector comprises a significant proportion of the labour market in all OECD countries. On average, 5.4% of the total labour force work in education including teachers, teachers' aides and research assistants, professional support personnel, management and administrative personnel, and other personnel who support the maintenance and operation of schools. The vast majority of these educational personnel are teachers [and] account on average for 3.5% of the total labour force. Combined primary and secondary teachers account for 2.6% of the total labour force, while those at the tertiary level account for 0.6%." (OECD, 2001c, p. 213)

... with far-reaching implications for reform

The sums of money involved are enormous – around 6% of GDP on education, and some 4% specifically on schools (though these magnitudes vary widely). To this can be added substantial additional outlays of time and money made by households and others. There have been very large investments made in school premises, which represent enormous collective monetary value in terms of property, buildings and equipment some of which are very longstanding.

The sheer scale of the school enterprise risks being overlooked when the focus falls, as it often does, on individual schools. It can render change aimed at large sections of the teacher or student body cumbersome and slow. Given the numbers involved, effective education reforms can prove very expensive. Such scale also influences teacher status, given that it is much more difficult for very large numbers to command prestige compared with smaller professional groups. The importance of these considerations is reflected in the next chapter where one of the "status quo" scenarios is described in terms of robust bureaucratic systems.

Having noted common aspects of school systems, there are important differences. Some systems maintain selection whereas many others have adopted comprehensive models. At the same time, simple classifications of models become harder to apply in the face of the specialisation of schools, the role of parental choice, and the contribution of the private sector. These vary widely across countries, as do the relative powers of the state, religious groups, and the community. Some countries maintain strong apprenticeship systems, whereas in others the institutionalised links between education and the labour market are much less well developed.

Despite common features, very wide diversity in structures, traditions, and roles

There are other important variations across countries. While all countries report a minority of "school failure", the relative scale of the phenomenon varies considerably (OECD, 1998d). This underlines that "failure" is not a constant impervious to policy action, but a social and educational variable. Large differences also exist between countries in those counted as having special educational needs (OECD, 2000g). There are major variations visible in student-to-teacher ratios. In primary education, student/teaching staff ratios, expressed in full-time equivalents, range from a high of 32 students per teacher in Korea to lows of 11 in

63

Denmark and Hungary, around an OECD mean of 18. There is also large variation between countries at the secondary level, "ranging from more than 21 students per full-time equivalent teacher in Korea and Mexico to below 11 in Austria, the Flemish Community of Belgium, Greece, Hungary, Italy, and Luxembourg." (OECD, 2001c, p. 240) These and other characteristics that vary across countries are certainly consequential for the organisation of teaching and learning. Behind the shared label "school" there exists a wide range of experiences and organisational characteristics.

Towards schools as learning organisations?

Moving away from the "factory model" and towards the "learning organisation"

Despite the many changes that have taken place in schools over recent decades, the concern remains that too little has changed about the place called school in its basic structural, organisational and behavioural characteristics. Many of the buildings are the same as in the first half of the 20th century or before – welcome continuity in some respects but raising the question of how well adapted to the learning needs of the 21st century. Some have referred to the "factory model" of schooling, that grew out of the industrial societies of the late 19th and earlier decades of the 20th century. This is characterised – perhaps caricatured – as a school mirroring the mass production methods of the industrial era that produced it, turning out a future workforce for the most part with basic skills and compliant attitudes.

Schools: vital in making the transformation to the knowledge-based societies of today and tomorrow, but must be revitalised

The question is then whether this remains the dominant model or whether instead schools have moved on to become the "learning organisations" appropriate for the knowledge-based societies of today and tomorrow. To what extent are schools and school systems willing to break the moulds of traditional classrooms and didactics? How far have they moved to become "learning organisations", concerned with knowledge-creation as well as knowledge-transmission (see OECD, 2000a, and Hargreaves, 1999). The importance of making these changes was underlined by former Swedish Education Minister Ylva Johansson, the Chair of the Netherlands/OECD "Schooling for Tomorrow" Rotterdam conference, in her conclusions:

"In sum, schools have been very important and, in many respects, successful institutions. They were integral to the transformation from agrarian to industrial societies. They represent a very important investment for our countries in making the further transformation from industrial to the knowledge-based societies of today and tomorrow, but for this they must be revitalised and dynamic."

In moving beyond the long-established models, the prevalence of the single-teacher classroom unit is in some cases being modified through the adoption of more complex, collaborative teams of teachers, though it is still hard to gauge how widespread this is. Such models of teaching and the organisation of learning are in general more demanding professionally and call on a wider range of skills and competences. In-service and initial training should play a major part in preparing for, and realising, these approaches. The creation and application of professional knowledge on the scale and in the time-frame demanded by "schooling for tomorrow" make demands at the individual and system levels:

"At the level of the individual teacher, there needs to be a psychological transition from working and learning alone, with a belief that knowledge production belongs to others, to a radically different self-conception which (...) sees the co-production of knowledge with colleagues as a natural part of a teacher's professional work. At the system level, ways have to be found to bring teachers together in such activity". (OECD, 2000a, p. 74)

From individuals to networks, from knowledge transmission to knowledge creation

Further modification to single-teacher classroom models comes with the introduction of parents and others into school teaching and learning. While an OECD/CERI study conducted several years ago found numerous positive examples relating to consultative governance and active parental involvement in homework schemes, there is far less evidence of such involvement in school-based teaching and learning (OECD, 1997c). At the same time, many countries are working with different forms of work experience programmes, integrating elements of non-school learning with their conventional coursework, which means that school students come to learn with a range of adult professionals. How

New roles in school for other adults and experts?

65

to open professional school roles for adults with different forms of expertise, while at the same time avoiding the assumption that teaching requires no specialised knowledge and training – the "bright person myth" (Darling-Hammond, 1997, p. 309) – defines a challenging agenda.

Flexible use of facilities and buildings

Considerable attention has also been given across OECD countries to ways of using existing educational facilities more flexibly (OECD, 2001m; OECD, 1996b). Greater flexibility involves addressing established educational aims more effectively through imaginative uses of educational facilities and creative design; in part, it is about opening schools to new uses, learners and schedules; in part, it is about creating alternative forms of schooling beyond conventional locations.

Overhauling educational R&D

The educational R&D system, as in other sectors, ought to be a major source of new insights, innovation, and improvement. But, it struggles to fulfil this role and its potential remained largely under-developed. The level of such investment is far lower than any other sector of comparable size, with an average of less than 0.3% of total education expenditure allocated to research so that the educational knowledge base tends to be seriously under-funded. It is unlikely, however, that just more funding of traditional research is sufficient, given the fragmentation of much educational R&D, and the difficulty of ensuring that it informs and is informed by practice. It suggests the need to address more profound questions relating to the nature, organisation and outcomes of R&D, focusing on development – "D" – just as much as research – "R" (OECD, 2000a).

ICT in schools*

Major educational ICT investments, especially in hardware and connectivity...

Perhaps the factor most identified as heralding fundamental change in the structure and organisation of schooling is the spreading impact of ICT on learning. There has been major growth in the use of computers and in access to the Internet, which opens up burgeoning opportunities for

---

* This section draws substantially on the report prepared for the ICT Forum held in Paris on the occasion of the meeting of the OECD Ministers of Education, April 2001 (OECD, 2001l).

research, sharing materials and networking among teachers and learners. Governments, the private sector, families and individuals are making very large investments in ICT for education. In the 1999 *Education Policy Analysis* (OECD, 1999f, Chapter 3), this was estimated at an annual figure of US$16 billion for OECD countries across primary, secondary and tertiary education, which could well have grown significantly since. The bulk of this to date has been spent on hardware and connectivity, far less on software, and relatively little on teacher training, though the balance has begun to shift recently in recognition of unmet needs. But despite high expectations and growing use, the evidence is not yet compelling that much impact has been made on the teaching and learning taking place in schools or that a significant learning return can be seen for the major investments undertaken.

Teachers and learners are the core elements in the education process and they need to embrace the potential of ICT for these benefits to be realised. In general, this is still not the case, however, even though many schools are well equipped with computers and access to the Internet, albeit not necessarily in every classroom. Mostly the technology use reflects traditional classroom methodology, though affording some increased attention to the individual learner. It still depends too much on highly motivated, pioneering principals and teachers (see OECD, 2001c, pp. 254-264; and Pelgrum and Anderson, 1999).

Hence, more important even than the investments in equipment, connectivity and materials are the human and educational aspects – training, professional development, and the reorganisation of education, schools and classrooms on a sufficient scale to realise the potential of ICT to make a real difference to learning. This means to focus on the skills possessed by individuals and teams of teachers, on the attitudes and learning environments so that the imaginative and discerning use of ICT is possible, and on the incentives for teachers to develop new approaches and competence in their day-to-day teaching. Far from ICT's active use diminishing the role of the teacher, as some have expected, it calls for a more diverse curriculum and a demanding repertoire of teaching and organisational skills.

... but insufficient investments in skills, organisations, and people

Mismatches between conventional organisation of education and effective use of ICT for learning

ICT offers manifold opportunities to develop the skills of communication, analysis, problem-solving, information management and retrieval – in short, the lifelong-learning skills which are increasingly valued in contemporary society. The Internet opens up access to public information and opportunities for dialogue in unparalleled ways. Yet these skills and ways of working sit uneasily with the existing school curriculum, and are not reflected in the leaving examinations used for certification purposes. The educational potential of ICT cannot be fully realised whilst these imbalances remain.

The "learning digital divide"

Attention has also come to be sharply focused on the "digital divide". In national debates and international initiatives, much of the attention has been on access to technology, especially in less-developed countries. But the telling divides concern education and competence with ICT as much as the technology itself (see OECD, 2000c). The term learning digital divide signals these problems, which form in fact a complex of divides. Given that within OECD countries the gaps in home ICT access and use are much wider than exist in education, there are important equity responsibilities to be discharged by schools in tackling this form of learning divide.

Enormous potential alongside profound questions

The scale of the educational investment in ICT has provided a powerful influence for innovation and reform. It implies a changed relationship between learners and teachers, and for both it opens up opportunities for a more collegial approach. But it also raises profound questions: for the nature of schools as learning organisations and for the routines of educational systems, for teachers and their professional roles, for schools as cultural and socialising institutions, for languages and cultures, and for relations between the generations.

Evaluation, assessment and certification

The influential role of evaluation and assessment – matching it to 21st century needs

What is assessed in education, especially quantitatively, powerfully shapes policy debate and practice. Hence, it is important that assessments are appropriate for the 21st century, reflecting demanding, dynamic concepts of educational quality. What once were considered highly advanced cognitive and attitudinal competences, beyond the reach of most, are increasingly expected as the norm. Similarly with what is expected of schools and teachers: the criteria by which they are judged need to reflect increasingly demanding definitions of education and professionalism. Evaluations and assessments are key elements in the decision-making process. They provide the information on which many accountability judgements are made and the means for steering in systems that are increasingly decentralised. How adequate this information is depends largely on how comprehensively it covers the key dimensions of system and institutional performance rather than just a selection of the most readily measurable.

One major purpose for assessment and evaluation is to take stock of what has been attained, whether in absolute terms or through comparisons – "summative" assessment. New surveys and indicators have made a major contribution to this but in most countries, examinations and certification represent its most influential form. The question arises of whether the traditional examination system that still dominates in many countries exercises an altogether excessive influence, diverting massive volumes of energy into the credentialling rather than learning process. Yet, even if most can agree that examinations dominate excessively, they do perform a critical sorting and selection function. This is expected and readily understood by students, teachers, parents and the wider public. If schools do not do this, other ways will need to be found to meet this function.

"Summative" assessment

Significant change will call for new departures in methods and systems for competence recognition. It is scarcely imaginable that significant progress can continue towards the knowledge-based, lifelong learning society without major changes in the systems for recognising and accrediting competence. This in turn will inevitably have an important impact on the formal education system, especially schools. As monopolies over certification are broken and recurrent opportunities for competence recognition change perceptions about different educational pathways, it can be expected that education systems will put up fierce resistance to the perceived loss of power. Declining monopoly

Competence recognition and certification – a declining educational monopoly?

may in the end turn out to be a source of liberation, however, permitting them to focus much more on learning and less on sorting and credentialling. These possibilities and options enter into the delineation of the scenarios below – futures where schools continue to be dominated by the requirements of standardised examinations and tests are clearly different from those driven by individual learning and development.

"Formative" evaluation at the heart of educational progress and individualised learning

The other major purpose of evaluation and assessment – the formative – is to provide frequent feedback as the means of building further learning progress. Schools, teachers, and students alike require such information to identify attainments made and to expose needs. Often, the assessments involved are informal. They do not offer the newsworthy judgements of summative assessments, but these forms of evaluation lie at the heart of educational progress and are integral to concepts of learning organisations. In general, it remains a badly neglected field. Supportive policies could be taken further in many countries, for instance, through the development of teacher skills in incorporating formative evaluation into day-to-day teaching. The thorough-going individualisation of learning depends on such strategies.

Teachers and teacher policies

Teacher quality to the fore, as a result of rising expectations...

The quality of learning and the success of reform and innovation depend crucially on teachers. Teacher quality, of individual professionals and of the force as a whole, has risen in profile and priority as a result of a number of diverse factors. Partly it is a reflection of the rising expectations towards education in general which perforce finds expression in what is expected of teachers. Ambitions for what education can achieve have grown sharply over recent decades in many countries, and the stakes involved have correspondingly risen. This might well be preferable to indifference but it brings its own tensions, and as demands grow so do criticisms. These may unduly fall on schools when the relevant learning settings are often elsewhere, whether other forms of post-school education or homes, communities, workplaces or the media. Justified or not, searching questions come to be asked about teachers' professional activity, their organisation and abilities, and their quality in general.

A second reason for increasingly intense focus on teacher quality is readier acknowledgement in many quarters of how teachers are the linchpin of schooling success. To plan for educational change in the absence of a close focus on what teachers do, how well they are prepared, and how they are organised, is to miss a – many would say the – crucial factor. The effectiveness of curriculum or evaluation policies, for example, or new drives to raise standards or to meet the needs of particular groups of students, will only produce significant change if they are well understood and energetically applied by teachers. They are in the vanguard of innovative approaches to teaching and learning. This has always been true but political consensus seems to be shifting towards a better understanding that they are an integral part of the "solution" rather than of the "problem".

... of recognition of teachers as the linchpin of schooling success...

This is well illustrated in relation to the integration of information and communication technologies into school and classroom life discussed earlier. At one time, technological applications and computer-assisted instruction were even promoted as a misguided means for making education "teacher-proof". But, without the skilled and imaginative use of ICT by teachers, its potential as a powerful vehicle for learning will remain unrealised. Indeed, in the wake of the major educational investments in ICT, many countries have turned to teacher professional development strategies as essential if such significant expenditures are to yield returns.

Teacher quality is a high priority today not only because teachers are central to the success of education – which has always been true – but because the demands on them are also rising. The more complex and uncertain the world in which we live, the more that alternative sources of knowledge and influence are available to students, the more open schools become to diverse clienteles, and the more varied

... and of greater professional demands

71

the organisational and pedagogical strategies that teachers should deploy, the greater become the levels of professional skill needed to meet them. There are growing expectations that they can operate in new organisational structures, in collaboration with colleagues and through networks, and be able to foster individual student learning. These call for demanding concepts of professionalism: the teacher as facilitator and knowledgeable, expert individual and networked team participant, oriented to individual needs and to the broader environment, engaged in teaching and in R&D. Not least, teachers are in the spotlight with the expectation that schools are expected to develop the competences and motivation that will serve students on a lifetime basis, a significant change from the view of school education as a self-contained process.

Diverse national conditions and variables affecting the attractiveness of teaching

The importance of teachers to the future of schooling finds them as one of the defining dimensions of the scenarios presented in the next chapter. This relates to their professionalism and organisation, and to their conditions and the overall attractiveness of teaching. These factors are closely inter-related – the nature of professionalism shapes, and is shaped by, attractiveness of the work and teacher motivation. Were teacher shortages to emerge on a large scale it might well threaten the demanding notions of quality outlined above. One of the six scenarios in the next chapter imagines a "worst case" where shortages reach crisis proportions leading to system "meltdown". In avoiding such a future, salary levels are certainly relevant but by no means determinant:

> "Whilst improved salaries, better physical facilities and lower class ratios have important impacts, the critical features required to raise the image and self-esteem of teachers in the immediate future include more relevant professional training for individual teachers and improved working conditions and work organisation in schools." (ILO/UNESCO, 1997, p. 10)

Salaries vary widely for novice and experienced teachers

Recent OECD analysis in fact shows how varied across countries are the different variables relating to teachers and their conditions. Starting salaries, and those reached well into the career after 15 years' experience, are both relevant to the standing of teaching, including the ratios of teacher salaries to country GDP per capita, which take account of varying national wealth. On this latter indicator, the starting salary of primary teachers is highest in Greece (1.3), Korea (1.5), and Spain (1.3), and after 15 years' service, in Greece, Portugal, and Switzerland at around 1.6, New Zealand (1.8), and Korea (2.5). In contrast, even after 15 years, the ratios are still clearly less than 1.0 in a few cases (the Czech Republic, Hungary, Iceland, and Norway). Comparable figures for lower secondary teachers are, for starting salaries, highest at around 1.4-1.5 in Germany, Korea, Mexico, Spain, and Switzerland. After 15 years, the highest are in Korea (2.5), Mexico (1.8), New Zealand (1.8), Spain (1.7), and Switzerland (1.9). The same countries have the lowest relative salaries as for primary teachers (OECD, 2001*c*, pp. 203-204). Some regional patterns can be discerned as they tend to be relatively high in the Pacific area, Southern Europe and the German-speaking systems, and low in Scandinavia and Central Europe.

Teacher ageing, often mentioned as a critical problem confronting OECD countries, actually varies widely as well as shown in Table 2.2. Four in ten teachers are aged 50 years or more in Germany (at primary and lower secondary levels), Italy (lower secondary), and Sweden (at all levels, and nearly half are this old in upper secondary schools). In contrast, figures under 20% for the over-50s are found in Austria and Korea, and, among primary teachers, less than a quarter are in this age bracket in Belgium, France, Iceland, Ireland, Luxembourg, the Netherlands, New Zealand, Switzerland, and the UK. Hence, the ageing problem is one affecting particular countries and types of education far more than others.

Ageing in some countries and levels and not others

Teaching is often labelled a "feminised" profession, though this also varies considerably both by country and by level of education. Women dominate the teaching service in pre-primary and primary schools in most countries, but at secondary level the sexes are in fairly even balance or are even in the minority in some countries (see OECD, 2001*c*). Poor relative pay and status may be associated with

Women in teaching...

73

Table 2.2. **Age distribution of teachers by level of schooling, 1999**

	Primary			Lower secondary			Upper secondary		
	Under 40	40-49	50+	Under 40	40-49	50+	Under 40	40-49	50+
Austria	46.7	38.0	15.3	40.1	43.2	16.8	34.9	40.5	24.6
Belgium (Fl.)	51.4	27.9	20.7	x	x	x	36.4	35.9	27.7
Canada	36.2	38.7	25.1	36.2	38.7	25.1	36.2	38.7	25.1
Czech Republic	42.1	24.6	33.3	42.0	25.4	32.6	35.7	30.6	33.8
Finland	46.3	28.4	25.2	36.1	31.4	32.6	31.1	34.4	34.5
France	41.3	37.6	21.1	36.5	30.8	32.6	37.3	31.5	31.2
Germany	21.5	38.1	40.4	13.7	40.7	45.7	25.2	39.9	34.9
Iceland	45.9	31.8	22.3	x	x	x	30.8	34.4	34.8
Ireland	41.8	33.6	24.7	36.5	34.9	28.7	x	x	x
Italy	31.7	39.7	28.6	9.0	46.4	44.6	17.9	45.0	37.1
Korea	53.2	29.8	17.1	63.4	23.1	13.5	54.3	30.9	14.9
Luxembourg[1]	47.8	29.4	22.9	34.9	32.3	32.8	x	x	x
Netherlands	35.2	40.1	24.6	x	x	x	25.8	39.7	34.5
New Zealand	40.6	36.0	23.5	38.3	36.4	25.2	34.7	37.8	27.5
Norway	x	x	x	37.8	30.3	31.8	26.1	34.1	39.8
Slovak Republic	47.1	27.5	25.6	33.8	37.1	29.1	44.2	33.0	22.8
Sweden	26.1	32.9	41.0	33.2	25.1	41.6	23.4	28.0	48.7
Switzerland[1]	46.3	33.6	20.1	37.9	34.9	27.3	31.9	35.1	33.9
United Kingdom[2]	40.5	36.9	22.5	39.5	38.6	21.9	39.6	38.5	21.8
Country mean	41.2	33.6	25.2	35.5	34.3	30.2	33.2	35.8	31.0

x = data included under other columns in the table.
1. Public institutions only.
2. Only general programmes at the upper secondary level.
Source: OECD (2001c), Table D2.1.

a high degree of feminisation, but as women's employment expands throughout many professional fields such associations will tend to break down, bringing perhaps still more serious consequences for the future supply of teachers. Concerns of a quite different kind arise from the absence of men teachers. This has become an issue of growing concern in relationship to the socialisation of the young, and especially in situations of children growing up in single-mother families and/ or where there is manifest educational under-achievement by boys.

... and men

The importance of continuing professional development is just as critical for teachers as for any other professional sector subject to rapid change. It is equally important for young teachers as for ageing staff. It is at the core of school innovation and dynamism. Networking can be understood both as a means of reorganising teacher work away from individual isolation and as a form of professional development. Opportunities for professional development are an important aspect of attractiveness and conditions in their own right. Despite its importance, the 1998 OECD review was critical of the overall state of teacher professional development, many exemplary cases notwithstanding:

Professional development for all teachers, young and old, but not yet systematic

> "There is, of course, no shortage of in-service training in many of the member countries of the OECD. There is also some evidence of an emerging paradigm shift from individual to whole school development, driven partly by decentralisation and by increased responsibility on schools to decide their own needs. However, much of what passes for professional development is fragmented and fleeting. All too often it is not focused sufficiently and is too 'top-down' to give teachers any real sense of ownership. It is rarely seen as a continuing enterprise for teachers and it is only occasionally truly *developmental* (OECD, 1998c, p. 17)."

This is not only about classroom teaching. As responsibility devolves increasingly to those at the local level to make decisions and manage resources, so do the needs multiply for training to discharge these new management tasks. This applies to a wide range of professionals within

Training for school management: a high priority with decentralisation

75

school organisations and in the wider coalition of stakeholders which makes up the school decision-making environment. There is now a major challenge to organise preparation for management at all levels, and especially for school leaders and other educational professionals when responsibilities are being extended into new and unfamiliar territories (see OECD, 2001n).

Chapter 3

Scenarios for the Future of Schooling

Introduction

The chapter presents six scenarios constructed through the OECD/CERI programme on "Schooling for Tomorrow". Their purpose is to sharpen understanding of how schooling might develop in the years to come and the potential role of policy to help shape these futures. While this does not exhaust approaches to forward-looking policy thinking, scenario development is a particularly effective way of bringing together the "big picture" of strategic aims, the long-term processes of change, and multiple sets of variables. Perhaps surprisingly, forward thinking of this kind has been relatively little developed in education compared with other policy sectors, despite education's fundamental characteristic of yielding benefits over very long time spans. Former Swedish Education Minister Ylva Johansson, in her conclusions as Chair of the Rotterdam conference described forward-thinking approaches in education as "woefully under-developed". A major challenge for policy-making in this field is both to make it more genuinely long-term in vision and to integrate more effectively knowledge about education and its wider environment into the process of reflection and governance.

Need for policy reflection on long-term future of schooling...

Proposing several scenarios underlines that there is not one pathway into the future but many, and they should not be expected to emerge in a "pure" form. Distilling the infinite range of possible futures into a limited number of polar "types", however, stimulates consideration of the strategic choices to be confronted and the principal dimensions of change. The scenarios invite the questions: *a)* how probable, and *b)* how desirable, each is. These questions have been analysed by Hutmacher in this volume (Chapter 12) using

... and for clarifying the desirable and the possible

77

earlier versions of these scenarios. The task for policy thinking is to consider what might be done to bring the probable and desirable as closely as possible into alignment, making the more desirable futures more likely, and *vice versa*.

The OECD schooling scenarios

The OECD "Schooling for Tomorrow" scenarios combine different elements – trends, plausible inter-relationships between clusters of variables, and guiding policy ideas. They are thus neither purely empirical (predictions) nor purely normative (visions). They have been constructed as alternatives for schooling per se rather than as educational extrapolations based on scenarios developed for other fields – the social, economic, technological, environmental, cultural, etc. – though, of course, education is strongly influenced by such factors.

These schooling scenarios have been constructed in a time frame of approximately 15 to 20 years – long enough for significant change to occur beyond immediate political cycles, but not so far off as to be remote to any but futurists and visionaries. The interest is as much in the intervening processes of change as in the fully-fledged scenarios themselves. They may be considered either as stable "steady-states" or as more volatile, and hence likely to set further cycles of change in train. The scenarios are bounded in age terms, covering organised learning from birth up to around completion of secondary education. It is for children and young people of this age range that public responsibility for education is most highly developed in OECD countries, raising a distinct set of policy issues compared with later learning for adults organised through highly diverse arrangements. The six scenarios are not specific to the primary or secondary phases, though it can be expected that certain aspects would apply more directly to one or other of these cycles.

Two OECD scenarios extrapolating the status quo, two describing "re-schooling" futures, two "de-schooling"

Two of the scenarios are posited on the continued unfolding of existing models (The "status quo extrapolated"), two describe the substantial strengthening of schools with new dynamism, recognition and purpose (described as "Re-schooling"), while the two final scenarios portray future worlds that witness a significant decline in the position of schools ("De-schooling").

The "status quo extrapolated"	The "re-schooling" scenarios	The "de-schooling" scenarios
Scenario 1: "Robust bureaucratic school systems"	Scenario 3: "Schools as core social centres"	Scenario 5: "Learner networks and the network society"
Scenario 2: "Extending the market model"	Scenario 4: "Schools as focused learning organisations"	Scenario 6: "Teacher exodus – the 'meltdown' scenario"

To facilitate comparison, the scenarios have been constructed within a common framework of clusters of variables that were identified as critical dimensions in determining the shape of school systems: a) *Attitudes, expectations, political support*; b) *Goals and functions for schooling*; c) *Organisation and structures*; d) *The geo-political dimension*; e) *The teaching force*. Each scenario refers to the systemic "centres of gravity" of schooling arrangements rather than descriptions of particular schools or local cases. While, for instance, there will already be some examples of schools in OECD countries that fit the "re-schooling" features of Scenarios 3 and 4, these would only come about when the large majority of schools can be described as "key social centres" or as "focused learning organisations".

Scenarios referring to whole systems, not individual cases

The "status quo extrapolated"

Scenario 1: "Robust bureaucratic school systems"
- **Strong bureaucracies and robust institutions**
- **Vested interests resist fundamental change**
- **Continuing problems of school image and resourcing**

This scenario is built on the continuation of dominant school systems, characterised by strong bureaucratic elements and pressures towards uniformity. Despite education being to the fore on political agendas, robust schools and systems prove to be extremely resistant to radical change, because of the strength of the vested interests of the powerful stakeholders. Resource levels do not pass the thresholds that would allow longstanding criticisms of schools to be laid to rest or quality to be generally assured.

Scenario 1: strong bureaucratic systems resisting radical change...

New tasks and responsibilities are continually added to the remit of schools, in the face of the problems arising within the other core socialisation settings of family and community, causing schools' financial and human resources to be continually stretched. The norms of completed years spent by students in schools and initial education continue to go up, and the diplomas so gained are widely regarded as the main passports to the next stages of life (though in reality the links are more complex). Despite repeated policy initiatives, the educational inequalities that reflect unequal social and residential home backgrounds/environments prove extremely resilient.

... while performing fundamental tasks not always well recognised

While schools are continually criticised for being outdated and slow to change – accusations such as being excessively bureaucratic, with teachers wedded to traditional instruction methods – some inertia may simply be inherent in the nature of school systems. It may only be expected in societies that expect a great deal from schools, seeking to include all young people for ever-longer time periods with ever-fuller curricula, while being unwilling to invest on the very large scale that might bring about fundamental, as opposed to incremental, change. Societies,

Scenario I

Attitudes, expectations, political support	Education, especially schooling, is politicised, and to the fore in party politics. Despite continued grumbling about the state of schools from parents, employers and the media, most are basically opposed to radical change. More positive attitudes held towards local than overall provision. Possibilities for "playing the system" are important in ensuring the continued support of schools by educated parents resulting in pressure for the greater exercise of choice.
Goals and functions	Much attention focuses on the curriculum, with many countries operating a common curriculum and assessment system – aimed at enforcing standards or creating greater formal equality or both. Formal certificates seen as main passports to economic/social life – but while increasingly necessary are increasingly insufficient. Larger relative numbers and greater diversity of "older young" in initial education as the norm continues of staying on longer and longer. Continuing inequalities alongside policy endeavours to combat failure.

Strong bureaucratic character of schools and systems continues. Dominance of the classroom/individual teacher model, but some room for innovation and of developing schools as learning organisations. Increased ICT use in schools but not radical change to organisational structures of teaching and learning. Growing but patchy connections between educational and "non-educational" community uses of school facilities.	*Organisations and structures*
The nation (or state/province in federal systems) still the main locus of political authority but squeezed by: – decentralisation to schools and communities; – new corporate and media interests in the learning market and; – globalising pressures, including growing use of international surveys of educational performance.	*The geo-political dimension*
Highly distinct teacher corps, sometimes with civil service status. Strong unions and associations in many countries and centralised industrial relations. Professional status and rewards problematic in most countries. "Craft" models of professionalism remain strong. Growing attention to professional development (INSET), and efforts to retain teachers. This is partly in the face of major teacher supply problems, exacerbated by ageing.	*The teaching force*

including parents, may well prefer only gradual evolution in their schools. This scenario also recognises that schools perform many fundamental tasks (looking after children, providing protected space for interaction and play, socialisation, sorting and selection) that generally pass unnoticed compared with the obvious ones of imparting literacy, numeracy, disciplinary knowledge, and diplomas (Hutmacher, 1999). The question then is: "If schools systems were not in place for these purposes, what alternatives would serve them better?" Fragmentation in families and communities, the other settings in which children are socialised, reinforces the pertinence of this question (see Scenario 3).

Yet, even if school systems are excessively bureaucratic and slow to create such dynamism themselves, there may now be developments in train that will force disruption to the status quo. Among the most important of these factors are the growing power of learners and parents as "consumers"; the impact of ICT in eroding established school and classroom boundaries; and a potential crisis of teacher supply. (These factors are reflected in the scenarios outlined below,

New forces – such as ICTs or teacher crisis – may still break open the "status quo"

including "extending the market model", "learner networks and the network society", and "teacher exodus – 'the meltdown' scenario".) It remains to be seen whether schools can accommodate such pressures, as they have many times before, or whether there will be major ruptures with the past.

Scenario 2: "Extending the market model"

- **Widespread dissatisfaction leads to re-shaping public funding and school systems**
- **Rapid growth of demand-driven "market currencies", indicators and accreditation**
- **Greater diversity of providers and professionals, greater inequality**

Scenario 2: market approaches to schooling expanding significantly...

Trends towards more market-oriented schooling models – of organisation, delivery and management – are much closer to the experience and cultures of some countries than others. In this scenario, these trends are extended significantly in the face of widespread dissatisfaction with the performance of relatively uniform structures of public school systems and with existing funding arrangements to provide cost-effective solutions. In response to these pressures, governments encourage diversification and the emergence of new learning providers through funding structures, incentives and de-regulation, and discover considerable market potential, nationally and internationally. Significant injections of private household and corporate finance are stimulated.

... stimulating widespread innovation, but creating difficult transitions and widening inequalities

New market "currencies" of indicators, measures, and accreditation of both learners and providers flourish, while direct public monitoring and curriculum regulation decline. Public education, schools and the government role do not disappear, despite greater privatisation and more mixed public/private partnerships, though outcomes depend greatly on the funding and regulation regimes being introduced and may differ significantly between the primary and secondary levels. In an atmosphere of shake-up, innovation and imaginative solutions abound as do painful experiences of the transitions. Alongside the positive features of fresh thinking are the seriously

82

enhanced risks of inequality and exclusion and of the public school system being relegated to "residual" status.

The development of a much more market-oriented model for schooling is likely to depend on a number of factors. It would be fuelled by a substantial sense of dissatisfaction with established provision among "strategic consumers", especially articulate-middle class parents and political parties, combined with a culture where schooling is already viewed as much as a private as a public good. Wide differences of educational performance would add weight to the criticisms, while the significant development of the "market model" in schooling would itself be supported by a degree of social tolerance of inequality. The nature of the teaching force could be a determining factor. A crisis of teacher supply (see Scenario 6) might well quicken the search for market-based models as it would for other alternatives. And, while a fragmented teaching force might be conducive to such changes through its impotence to resist them, a monolithic profession resisting innovation could conceivably produce the same result.

Dissatisfaction by "strategic consumers": impetus for market solutions

The business environment is likely to be highly influential, but in which direction is not necessarily clear-cut. On the one hand, more aggressive entrepreneurial cultures might be best for identifying new markets and approaches that break with convention. On the other, highly developed traditions of human resource development, with a deep understanding of "soft skills" and learning, might be needed to generate successful demand-oriented approaches of competence development, measurement and accreditation. Political tradition and government action would clearly be critical – in setting market terms, encouraging alternative forms of supply, permitting the exercise of demand. Its role would also be important in managing what could be a painful set of transition processes. Such responsibilities notwithstanding, this scenario assumes a diminished direct government role in provision.

Entrepreneurial and political cultures' influence on schooling, but in which direction?

There is substantial interest in market approaches in some countries and quarters and many pertinent developments (hence this scenario is included in "The status quo extrapolated"). But, they cover a bewildering variety: the enhanced exercise of parental choice, including in some

Many existing market examples but how far should they be extended in schooling?

83

Scenario 2

Attitudes, expectations, political support	Significant reduced belief in the value of public education overall. Possible funding "revolts" by taxpayers. Divergent and conflicting positions expressed. Teachers' associations unable to resist moves to greater privatisation. A political culture develops that supports extended competition across many areas of social, employment, and cultural policy. The stability of new market solutions highly dependent on how well they meet perceived shortcomings.
Goals and functions	Different indicators and accreditation arrangements become basic to market operations; "efficiency" and "quality" are prominent criteria. Decline of established curriculum structures defined in terms of programmes and delivery, re-defined as outcomes. Alongside strong focus on knowledge and skills, values and attitudes – such as attitudes to risk, co-operation and hard work – may be prominent and hence recognised as outcomes. Market-oriented schooling may also, in response to demand, allow greater reflection of cultural/religious beliefs. Stronger emphasis on information, guidance and marketing – some publicly organised, much private. Substantial tolerance of wide inequalities and exclusion. Possible tendency for greater homogeneity of learner groups. Lifelong learning becomes the norm for many. Clear boundaries for "staying on" in school lose meaning in the face of diversified educational careers.
Organisations and structures	Privatisation, public/private partnerships, voucher systems, and diverse management are the norm. Individualisation and home schooling flourish. Greater experimentation with organisational forms. Many existing programmes disappear. Possible big differences emerge between the primary and secondary sectors, with market models more strongly developed at secondary level. Markets develop in childcare and culture, not just employment-related learning. ICT is much more extensively and imaginatively exploited for learning. Networking flourishes where tangible gains perceived by all parties; otherwise competition inhibits co-operation. Copyright issues acute.
The geo-political dimension	Substantially reduced role for central providers and public education authorities. They still oversee market regulation, but much less traditional "steering" and "monitoring". International providers and accreditation agencies become more powerful, but strong players, many private, operate at each level – local, national, international. Much more diverse set of stake-holders involved in educational governance. Funding arrangements, including absolute levels of resources, are critical in shaping new learning markets.
The teaching force	Less distinct teaching force, a wide range of new professionals with diverse profiles – public, private; full-time, part-time. Potential quality issues. The new "teaching professionals" in ready supply in areas of residential desirability and/or learning market opportunity. Otherwise, problems of shortages and speed of market adjustment. Flourishing training and accreditation for professionals to operate in the learning market. Transition problems until new markets become embedded.

cases through vouchers; the involvement of the private sector in the running of schools or parts of systems; substantial household contributions for supplementary private tuition as in Japan or Korea, or for attendance at private schools (such as the oddly-named English "public schools"); the public funding of "private" institutions organised by particular cultural, religious or citizen groups; the corporate promotion of the e-learning market, and others. Is education a frontier on the point of being breached by the profit motive or is it so distinct that it will continue to resist? Much might turn on the *level* of education in question. Flourishing corporate initiatives in the ICT learning market at tertiary level, for example, stand in contrast with modest growth in schools. The further question then is about where the main boundaries will be drawn in the applicability of this scenario – between secondary and tertiary (in which case it would not be a schooling scenario as such)? Between lower and upper secondary? Between primary and lower secondary?

The "re-schooling" scenarios

Scenario 3: "Schools as core social centres"

- **High levels of public trust and funding**
- **Schools as centres of community and social capital formation**
- **Greater organisational/professional diversity, greater social equity**

In this scenario, the school comes to enjoy widespread recognition as the most effective bulwark against social fragmentation and a crisis of values. There is a strong sense of schooling as a "public good" and a marked upward shift in the general status and level of support for schools. The individualisation of learning is tempered by a clear collective emphasis. Greater priority is accorded to the social/community role of schools, with more explicit sharing of programmes and responsibilities with the other settings of further and continuing education/training. Poor areas in particular enjoy high levels of support (financial, teaching, expertise and other community-based resources).

Scenario 3: schools as high status, community institutions providing bulwark against fragmentation

85

Greater resource equality, experimentation, school autonomy, and shared roles...

Overall, schools concentrate more on laying the cognitive and non-cognitive foundations of knowledge, skills, attitudes and values for students to be built on thereafter as part of lifelong learning. Norms of lengthening duration in initial schooling may well be reversed, and there is greater experimentation with age/grading structures and the involvement of learners of all ages. Schools come to enjoy a large measure of autonomy without countervailing central constraints, as levels of public/political support and funding have been attained through a widespread perception of high standards, evenly distributed, thereby reducing the felt need closely to monitor conformity to established standards. Strong pressures for corrective action nevertheless come into play in the face of evidence that any particular school is under-performing. There is more active sharing of professional roles between the core of teachers and other sources of experience and expertise, including different interest, religious, and community groups.

... help schools contribute to the development of social capital

Scenario 3 describes a strengthened, creative school institution available to all communities, meeting critical social responsibilities while silencing critics. This scenario fits a longstanding tradition advocating that closer links be forged between schools and local communities. More recently, such arguments have acquired an added urgency and relevance with the fragmentation occurring in many family and community settings, raising new concerns about the socialisation of children. In response to these concerns, the school could thus become a much-needed "social anchor" and constitute the fulcrum of residential communities (Carnoy and Kennedy respectively in Chapters 5 and 10 in this volume). In Chapter I, we have seen that some analyses suggest that "social capital" may be in a process of erosion in a number of OECD countries to the detriment of individual well-being, society and the economy. In this scenario, the school is instrumental in arresting this trend, benefiting in the process from the positive impact on educational achievement of strengthened infrastructure and belief in the values upheld by schools.

Scenario 3

Wide measure of party political and public agreement on goals and the value of public education; funding increases.	*Attitudes, expectations, political support*
High-trust politics with extensive co-operation between authorities, teachers, employers, and other community groups in relation to schools.	
The role of schools as centres of community activity/identify is accorded widespread recognition.	
Educated classes and media supportive of schools, giving them greater freedom to develop their own pathways as centres of social solidarity/capital in different partnerships.	
The role of schools continues in transmitting, legitimising and accrediting knowledge, but with greater recognition and focus on a range of other social and cultural outcomes, including citizenship.	*Goals and functions*
More diverse forms of competence recognition developed in enterprises and the labour market liberate schools from excessive pressures of credentialism.	
The lifelong learning function is more explicit.	
Possible reversal of trend to longer school careers, but less clear-cut boundaries between school participation and non-participation.	
Inequalities reduced but diversity widens and social cohesion strengthened.	
Strong distinct schools reinvigorated by new organisational forms, less bureaucratic, more diverse.	*Organisations and structures*
General erosion of "high school walls". Wide diversity of student body; greater inter-generational mixing and joint youth-adult activities.	
Sharp divisions between primary and secondary levels are softened; possible re-emergence of all-age schools.	
ICT is strongly developed, with particular emphasis on communication (by students, teachers, parents, community, other stakeholders). Networking flourishes.	
The local dimension of schooling substantially boosted, supported by strong national frameworks, particularly in support of communities with weak social infrastructure.	*The geo-political dimension*
New forms of governance are developed giving various groups, enterprises, etc., a bigger role.	
International awareness and exchange is strong, but supra-national control is not, encouraging local diversity.	
A core of high-status teaching professionals, but not necessarily in lifetime careers.	*The teaching force*
More varied contractual arrangements and conditions, but significant increases of rewards for all.	
A prominent role for other professionals, community actors, parents, etc.	
More complex combinations of teaching with other community responsibilities.	

This future for the place called school would call for very major changes in most countries – more than would normally be feasible even over a 15-to-20-year time period. The scenario is predicated not only on important *The scenario's demanding pre-requisites may be unrealistic* re-definitions of purpose, practice and professionalism, but also on the new definitions being widely endorsed by the main stakeholders throughout society. Generous resourcing would probably be called for, given the need for very even patterns of quality learning environments across all communities and for establishing high esteem for teachers and schools, though some of this might be attained through more cost-effective resource use. Greater flexibility of action would also be needed. If schools could rely on the existence of universal opportunities for continuing education and the certification of competences outside education, this would be a major step in liberating them from the excessive burdens of credentialism; in these circumstances such flexibility might well be more attainable. However desirable any of these prerequisites to this scenario may be, they are not necessarily very likely in the foreseeable future.

Closer ties to communities may widen not narrow inequalities

Furthermore, the problems relating to communities and social capital that make this scenario attractive could equally be the very factors that prevent it being fully realised. Far from equalising the effect of different socio-economic environments, the strategy of linking schools very closely with their communities might only serve to exacerbate the gaps between the vibrant and the depressed. Hence, without powerful mechanisms equalising resources and status, and without a strong sense of common purpose, the risk is that scenario would reflect, even exacerbate, existing inequalities between different communities [discussed in relation to "educational priority zones" (ZEPs) by Michel in Chapter 11]. These problems would need to be overcome if the future is to lie with this radical form of "re-schooling".

Scenario 4: *"Schools as focused learning organisations"*

- **High levels of public trust and funding**
- **Schools and teachers network widely in learning organisations**
- **Strong quality and equity features**

In this scenario, schools are revitalised around a strong "knowledge" agenda, with far-reaching implications for the organisation of individual institutions and for the system as a whole. The academic/artistic/competence development goals are paramount; experimentation and innovation are the norm. Curriculum specialisms flourish as do innovative forms of assessment and skills recognition. As with the previous scenario, all this takes place in a high-trust environment where quality norms rather than accountability measures are the primary means of control. Similarly, generous resourcing would probably be required, though there would be very close attention to how those resources are used in pursuit of quality. Professionals (teachers and other specialists) would in general be highly motivated, learning groups are small, and they work in environments characterised by the continuing professional development of personnel, group activities, and networking. In these environments, a strong emphasis is placed on educational R&D. ICT is used extensively alongside other learning media, traditional and new.

Scenario 4: most schools as "learning organisations" with strong knowledge focus...

In this scenario, the very large majority of schools merit the label "learning organisations". They are among the lead organisations driving the "lifelong learning for all" agenda, informed by a strong equity ethos (thereby distinguishing Scenario 4 from the two "status quo" scenarios in which quality learning is distributed much more unevenly). Close links develop between schools, places of tertiary education, media companies and other enterprises, individually and collectively.

... and high levels of support, trust, and flexibility, and advance equity aims

This differs from the previous scenario by its stronger "knowledge" focus that is well understood by the public and avoids the risk of ever-widening social remits making impossible demands on schools. It assumes strong schools, enjoying very high levels of public support and generous funding from diverse sources, as well as a large degree of latitude to develop programmes and methods. The teacher corps remains a more distinct profession, albeit with mobility and using various sources of expertise, than in the "school as social centre" scenario.

But not typical of today's practice and with conditions hard to create

89

Scenario 4

Attitudes, expectations, political support	Wide measure of party political agreement on goals and on the value of education as a "public good". Very high levels of public support for schools, including through funding where this is judged necessary. Care taken to ensure the gaps between more and less endowed schools does not widen learning opportunities. Educated classes and the media are supportive of schools, permitting an environment of freedom to individualise their programmes. High-trust politics. Schools work hard to maintain their supportive constituency and generally succeed in lowering "school walls".
Goals and functions	Highly demanding curricula are the norm for all students. More specialisms catered for (arts, technology, languages, etc.) but a demanding mix of learning expected of all students, including specialists. School diplomas continue to enjoy major currency, albeit alongside other forms of competence recognition. Innovative developments of assessment, certification and skills recognition for broad sets of talents. The lifelong learning function is made more explicit through clarification and implementation of the foundation role for lifelong learning. Extensive guidance and counselling arrangements. A major investment made in equality of high quality opportunities – overt failure considerably reduced by high expectations, the targeting of poor communities, and eradication of low quality programmes.
Organisations and structures	Strong schools as learning organisations with distinct profiles. Flatter, team-oriented organisations with greater attention to management skills for all personnel. Team approaches are the norm. Intense attention to new knowledge about the processes of teaching and learning, and the production, mediation and use of knowledge in general. Major new investments in R&D. Wide variety in age, grading and ability mixes, with more all-age and school/ tertiary mixes. ICT is strongly developed, both as a tool for learning and analysis and for communication. Links between schools, tertiary education, and "knowledge industries" are commonplace – for INSET, research and consultancy.
The geo-political dimension	Strong national framework and support, with particular focus on communities with weakest social resources. International networking of students and teachers. Countries moving furthest towards this scenario attract considerable international attention as "world leaders". Substantial involvement of multi-national as well as national companies in schools (but close attention given to widening gaps).
The teaching force	A high status teaching corps, enjoying good rewards and conditions. Somewhat fewer in lifetime careers, with greater mobility in and out of teaching and other professions. More varied contractual arrangements but good rewards for all. Major increase in staffing levels, allowing greater innovation in teaching and learning, professional development, and research. Networking the norm among teachers, and between them and other sources of expertise.

Many in education would regard this "learning organisation" scenario as highly desirable but at least two related sets of problems stand in the way of transforming the desirable into the probable. First, OECD analysis has shown that this model is very far from typical of practice in schools across different countries (OECD, 2000a). The scenario would thus call for radical breaks with established practice especially by and among teachers that, as discussed in relation to Scenario 1, could be extremely difficult to realise on a broad scale. Second, as with the previous scenario, the formulation begs questions of how to create a very supportive media and political educational environment, ensure such generous funding levels, and capture high status for schools and teachers where these do not already exist. Such conditions are far from being met in most countries at present, implying concerted strategies and investments to turn this situation around. Similarly, this scenario's equality assumptions are highly demanding, at the same time as socio-cultural and educational inequalities remain firmly entrenched. In short, this scenario remains a good way off, whatever the progress in particular schools and pockets of excellence.

The "de-schooling" scenarios

Scenario 5: "Learner networks and the network society"

- **Widespread dissatisfaction with/rejection of organised school systems**
- **Non-formal learning using ICT potential reflect the "network society"**
- **Communities of interest, potentially serious equity problems**

Whether schools are criticised for being too reflective of unequal social and economic structures, or insufficiently reflective of diverse cultures, or out of tune with economic life, in this scenario these very different sources of criticisms take firm root. Dissatisfaction with available provision leads to a quickening abandonment of school institutions through diverse alternatives in a political environment supportive of the need for change. This is further stimulated by

Scenario 5: institutions and systems dismantled...

Scenario 5

Attitudes, expectations, political support	Widespread dissatisfaction with the institution called "school" – its bureaucratic nature and perceived inability to deliver learning tailored to complex, diverse societies. Flight out of schools by the educated classes as well as other community, interest and religious groups, supported by political parties, media, multimedia companies in the learning market. New forms of private, voluntaristic and community funding arrangements emerge in tune with general developments towards the "network society".
Goals and functions	The decline of established curriculum structures with the dismantling of the school system. Key role for different values and attitudes. New attention comes to be given to "childcare" arrangements with the demise of schools. Some of these are based on sports and other cultural community activities. Hard to predict how far various measures of competence become the driving "currency". To the extent that they do, strong emphasis on information, guidance and marketing through ICT, and on new forms of accreditation of competence. Possibly wide inequalities open up between those participating in the network society and those who do not.
Organisations and structures	Much learning would take place on an individualised basis, or through networks of learners, parents and professionals. ICT is much more extensively exploited for learning and networking, with flourishing software market. If some schools do survive, hard to predict whether these would be mainly at the primary level (focused on basic knowledge and socialisation) or at secondary level (focused on advanced knowledge and labour market entry). Some public schools remain for those otherwise excluded by the "digital divide" or community-based networks – either very well-resourced institutions or else "sink" schools.
The geo-political dimension	Community players and aggressive media companies are among those helping to "disestablish" schools in national systems. Local and international dimensions strengthened at expense of the national. While international measurements and accountability less relevant as systems and schools break up, new forms of international accreditation might emerge for elites. Bridging the "digital divide" and market regulation become major roles for the public authorities, as well as overseeing the remaining publicly-provided school sector. Groups of employers may become very active if these arrangements do not deliver an adequate skills base and if government unwilling to re-establish schools.
The teaching force	Demarcations between teacher and student, parent and teacher, education and community, blur and break down. Networks bring different clusters together according to perceived needs. New learning professionals emerge, employed especially by the major players in the network market. These operate via surgeries, various forms of "helpline" and home visits.

the extensive possibilities opened up by the Internet and continually developing forms of powerful and inexpensive ICT. The result is the radical de-institutionalisation, even dismantling, of school systems.

What takes their place is part of the emerging "network society". Learning for the young is not primarily conferred in particular places called "school" nor through professionals called "teachers" nor necessarily located in distinct residential community bases. Much more diverse cultural, religious and community voices come to be reflected in the day-to-day socialisation and learning arrangements for children in the "network society". Some are very local in character, but there are also extensive opportunities for distance and cross-border learning and networking. The demarcations between the initial and continuing phases of lifelong learning come to be substantially blurred. While these arrangements are supported as promoting diversity and democracy, they may also bring substantial risks of exclusion especially for those students who have traditionally relied on the school as the mechanism for social mobility and inclusion.

... and replaced by diverse learning networks as part of "network society"

Scenarios based around these ideas are among the most commonly proposed as "visions" for the future of schooling. They have the appeal of offering, for those in search of change, a clear alternative to the more school-based models outlined above. Scenario 5 can be understood as a feature of already-visible developments towards the "network society" (Castells, 1996), building on the potential of ICT to provide the means for learning and networking beyond time and place constraints. It is in tune with those messages of the broader lifelong learning agenda stressing flexibility, individualisation, and the role of non-formal learning. In relation to school-age learning, home schooling is growing and some predict this will quicken into the future, even if it is still relatively small-scale in most countries (Hargreaves, 1999). While sharing some common features with the "market model" of Scenario 2 , the driving force in this scenario is co-operation rather than competition, again appealing to those in search of alternative "post-industrial" paradigms.

Common ideas among futurists as a clear alternative to school-based approaches

93

But is this scenario feasible or sustainable?

Yet, it also raises serious questions of feasibility and sustainability. How well would such arrangements meet the range of critical "hidden" functions, including of socialisation, that has made the school such a universal model and so resilient (as discussed under Scenario 1)? What would happen to those individuals and communities who are not active participants in the "network society" and who have low social capital? It is possible that this scenario would actually deepen the "digital divide" (OECD, 2000c). This scenario, therefore, also runs into potentially severe inequality problems, raising the prospect of government intervention in ways that would undermine the very distinctiveness of this scenario. Does it really provide a feasible scenario for the 21st century or is it instead proposing a return to 18th/19th century educational arrangements (plus the Internet)? Along with such questions about feasibility are those to do with stability/volatility – does it describe a "steady-state" future or a transition point calling for further transformation?

Scenario 6: "Teacher exodus – The 'meltdown scenario'"

- *Severe teacher shortages do not respond to policy action*
- *Retrenchment, conflict, and falling standards leading to areas of "meltdown", or*
- *Crisis provides spur to widespread innovation but future still uncertain*

Teacher supply problems reach crisis proportions threatening "meltdown"...

This scenario can be regarded as an elaboration of a "worst case" in response to the question posed in conclusion of Scenario 1 – would the "status quo" survive were teacher shortages to turn into a real staffing crisis? This "meltdown" scenario comes about through the conjuncture of four main factors: *a*) a highly skewed teacher age profile resulting in outflows through retirement far out-stripping inflows of new recruits; *b*) a long period with very tight labour market conditions and general skill shortages resulting in severe difficulties both to recruit new teachers and to retain them in the profession; *c*) the upward shift in teacher rewards and/or staffing levels needed to make a tangible impact on relative attractiveness being viewed as prohibitively expensive, given the

Scenario 6

Widespread public and media dissatisfaction with the state of education in the face of the teacher recruitment crisis and growing sense of declining standards, especially in worst-affected areas. Relative political impotence to address the loss from the teaching force given the scale and long-term nature of the problem and/or deep-seated cultural barriers to changes needed to set in train another of the scenarios. The education political climate becomes either increasingly conflictual or leads to consensual emergency strategies.	*Attitudes, expectations, political support*
Established curriculum structures under intense pressure, especially in shortage subjects. Where main response is one of retrenchment, examinations and accountability mechanisms are strengthened in a bid to halt sliding standards. Where the teacher shortage instead stimulates widespread change, major revisions of curricula undertaken – much more outcome- and demand-oriented and less supply- and programme-centred. New forms of parallel evaluation and assessment methods developed. Inequalities widen sharply between residential areas, social and cultural groups, etc. Affluent parents in worst-affected areas desert public education in favour of private alternatives.	*Goals and functions*
Very diverse organisational responses to lack of teachers. In some situations, there is a return to highly traditional methods, partly through public pressure in response to declining standards, partly because of large classes In other situations, innovative organisational responses using different forms of expertise (including from tertiary education, enterprises, communities), and diverse mixes of lectures, student groupings, home learning, ICT, etc. Intensive use of ICT as an alternative to teachers; ICT companies very actively involved. Wide disparities again possible between highly innovative and traditional uses.	*Organisations and structures*
The position of the national authorities is strengthened in the face of crisis, as they acquire extended powers. It weakens, however, the longer the crises are unresolved. Communities with no serious teacher shortages seek to protect themselves and extend their autonomy from national authorities. Corporate and media interests in the learning market intensify. International solidarity improves between some countries where initiatives develop to "lend" and "borrow" trained teachers, including between North and South. Solidarity declines and protectionist responses increase the more generalised the shortages and where several countries are competing for limited pools of qualified staff.	*The geo-political dimension*
Teacher rewards increase as part of measures to tackle shortages. Conditions of teaching worsen as numbers fall, with problems acute in worst-affected areas, exacerbating the sense of crisis. Strenuous efforts made to bring trained – especially retired – teachers back into schools. Often only disappointing results, particularly where school politics and very conflictual and in areas of severe shortage. In some countries, the distinctiveness of the teacher corps and role of unions/associations increase in proportion to their relative scarcity. In others, established conventions, contractual arrangements, and career structures are rapidly eroded. As schools shorten teaching time, many posts created for semi-professional "child-minding". The market in home tuition flourishes, possibly with government subsidies to lower-income households.	*The teaching force*

95

sheer numbers involved; and *d*) even when measures are proving effective, they require long delays before a noticeable effect results in greater numbers of practising teachers, making it still harder to break into the vicious circles.

... despite concerted policy measures

The scenario posits a staffing crisis in a context that differs in at least two important respects from that of the "baby boom" of the 1960s. First, the quality demands and expectations of students for extended educational careers have moved on substantially in forty years. Second, the attractiveness of school-level teaching as a career has declined against a continuing upward trend in the share of advanced-skill posts throughout the economy as a whole, posts that often enjoy greater rewards. This combination of factors comes together in this scenario in the form of a very serious crisis for schools, rather than assuming that the problems will always be "muddled through".

Reactions to "meltdown" differ, from conflict and retrenchment to innovation and cohesion

As the teacher exodus takes hold and the scale of the "meltdown" crisis is recognised, potentially very different outcomes could be part of Scenario 6. At one extreme, a vicious circle of retrenchment, conflict, and decline sets in, exacerbating the inequalities and problems further. At the other, the teacher crisis provides the spur to radical innovation and change, with different stakeholders joining forces behind far-reaching emergency strategies. Even in that more optimistic case, "meltdown" would not necessarily be avoided. In between, a more evolutionary response to the crisis might be that rewards and attractiveness of the profession increase leading eventually to reconstruction. Whether actions taken would allow another scenario to take the place of "meltdown" would depend critically on the room for manoeuvre permitted by social and political cultures.

Proven resilience of school systems, but also signs in some countries give grounds for concern

There are many uncertainties in this scenario, therefore, and its value in some countries may lie less in its predictive power and more in sharpening awareness of the possibility of severe teacher shortages and their consequences. Some might judge it to be unlikely given the proven resilience and adaptability of school systems: they would argue that some matching of teacher supply and demand will always be achieved and "meltdown" avoided, though perhaps with costs to be paid in educational quality. Even in quantitative terms, however, the previous chapter showed patterns and trends that might prove highly problematic. In certain countries, teacher salaries remain well below average GDP per capita even after 15 years' service. Problems of an ageing profession are not universal but are acute in places. Where these, and other indicators of problematic attractiveness and recruitment, are found in combination, then indeed this form of "worst case" scenario may become much more likely.

Concluding remarks

As the methodologies for educational forward-thinking remain under-developed, there is much to be done in building up a "toolbox" of such approaches to inform the policy-making process. Scenarios, as presented in this chapter, are one vehicle for doing this. This is most effectively undertaken at the levels and among the stakeholders who are strategic in the change and decision-making process, stimulating dialogue among them. Used thus, they might well need to be reformulated in terms of the relevant realities for a particular country or setting. They might need to be distilled down still further from the reported six. This is to underline that these scenarios are not meant to be understood as a polished final of statements about the future but the starting point for a process of genuine engagement.

The scenarios: not polished final statements about the future but the starting point for dialogue and engagement

The OECD "Schooling for Tomorrow" programme has begun to use them in this way. These scenarios informed a major international conference held in Rotterdam towards the end of 2000, and were presented to the OECD Ministers of Education as part of their analytical material at their Paris April 2001 meeting. In the Rotterdam conference, participants completed a questionnaire on the desirability and likelihood of the different scenarios, and the results are reported and discussed by Hutmacher in this volume (Chapter 12). He has complemented this by repeating the exercise in a national (Swiss), as well as the international,

Such dialogue begun at international and national seminars, with broadly consistent results

seminar, as discussed in his chapter. He finds a broad measure of agreement across these different events. In general, the "re-schooling" scenarios receive the greatest endorsement. The Rotterdam participants in particular were sceptical about a future dominated by schooling markets. The bureaucratic "status quo" scenario is peculiar in being viewed as reasonably likely to occur but an undesirable future. With that exception, however, Hutmacher finds surprisingly little dissonance between what are judged to be desirable and expected futures – those perceived as preferable tend also to be thought the more likely to occur.

Broadening the consultation process and the methodologies

This finding clearly cannot be generalised. Hutmacher is the first to acknowledge that the numbers responding were small and drawn from a very particular group – the informed and influential "insiders" of education systems. To arrive at a more accurate picture of views about educational futures, many more would need to be surveyed and drawn from a wider cross-section of relevant stakeholders. It would be particularly useful to know the views of influential "outsiders". And, it would be valuable to move beyond surveying attitudes towards engagement in active dialogue. These directions are among those proposed by van Aalst in conclusion to his chapter in this volume (Chapter 8):

> "People drawn from outside education will need to be consulted. An interactive process of matching trends with specific educational measures requires the imaginative dialogue between those within education and key stakeholders in the trends: identification of those who 'carry' a trend is important as is establishing channels of informed communication."

He also argues for a range of approaches – rather than adherence to a single methodology based on scenarios or driving forces – including those "sensitive to weak signals about change". Future CERI work will be looking to expand its range of approaches to forward-looking policy thinking in education.

Chapter 4

Overview:
Policy Goals, Tensions, Questions

Overview of key points

The wider environment of schools

The natural starting point for examining the environment of schools in 21st century societies is the nature of childhood. While seemingly timeless, it has already changed markedly over the past half century and this looks set to continue. New relations are being established between the generations, altering the organisation and experience of socialisation into society and culture. The economic and cultural context is shifting rapidly, as is family life. These and other changes place onerous new responsibilities on schools – some look to them to provide a steadying "social anchor" amid fragmentation. At the same time, schools are integral to the "extended adolescence" that complicates matters as much as it resolves problems. And, some are concerned that an unrealistic burgeoning of demands on schools is bound to lead to disappointment and failure without greater focus in those areas where they enjoy specialist expertise and genuine room for manoeuvre.

Changing nature of childhood

A raft of indicators points to how far our economies have become knowledge-based, and the trends show no signs of slowing. The speed and direction of economic change places a growing premium on learning – one powerful impetus behind the widespread policy endorsement of lifelong learning. Yet, professional prospects differ markedly and many will continue to be employed outside the high-skill advanced knowledge sectors. This gives schooling a

Knowledge economy, rapid change, and globalisation

burdensome challenge – providing all the basis to develop their talents in a world of rapid change where students are entering highly diverse careers. The very speed of change calls too for a well-developed emotional and non-cognitive, as well as knowledge, basis with which student will be able to cope in the future. Economies and cultures are rapidly globalising: students' horizons need to be stretched, their discerning faculties developed, intolerance and parochialism avoided.

Affluence, diversity, and inequality

There are important social dimensions defining the wider environment for schools and young people. Longevity, affluence and consumption continue to rise, yet are offset by other factors. There is little evidence that indicators of "happiness" have risen in step and some suggest that social capital is falling. Affluence brings its own problems of sustainability, and also raises fundamental questions about dominant values, including (but not only) for schools. As the world becomes more global, so does the need for schools to address, even promote, cultural diversity. Social inequalities have become more, not less, marked in many countries, and young people are among those who have fared worst among the "winners" and "losers" of these trends. Even more glaring are the international inequalities, especially between the North and South.

School systems

Massive school systems – can they change?

School systems are enormous enterprises in all countries, employing very large numbers, deploying vast sums of money, providing occupation for millions of students. Despite the wide diversity of cultures and traditions across OECD countries, in all has "the place called school" become the dominant model for educating the young, even though schools and systems continue to reflect this international diversity. Increasingly, large, relatively bureaucratic systems are being asked to accommodate new directions and flexible models. Schools are being exhorted to become "learning organisations". Students are expected to create not just "receive" knowledge; teachers to abandon old-fashioned didactics and professional isolation. ICT alters the boundaries of knowledge and action, while new forms of competence recognition and accreditation erode traditional school monopolies over credentialling. It remains to be seen how well the tensions inherent in these different structures and developments can be resolved.

The scenarios

The OECD scenarios for future schools have been developed under three broad headings – the "status quo extrapolated", "re-schooling", "de-schooling". In the first scenario, large, bureaucratic systems continue as the norm, through the strength of the interests with a major stake in them and through the sheer difficulty of organising equally effective alternatives. In the second, market approaches are extended much more radically, bringing innovation and dynamism but also augmented risks of exclusion. In the third, schools are strengthened significantly by investing in them as focal centres for communities, giving them a range of important new tasks, responsibilities and partners. The fourth sees "learning organisations" for the young become typical of the very large majority of schools, based on demanding, flexible programmes for all. The fifth scenario presents schooling consistent with a highly developed "network society", heavily exploiting ICT's potential and leading to the widespread dismantling of school institutions. The final scenario addresses a future in which teacher shortages reach crisis levels yet prove largely resistant to the policy initiatives taken to rectify them.

Six scenarios for schooling

Scenarios help to clarify the main directions and strategic options for schooling over the long-term, as well as the policy issues that arise in shaping different futures. They are tools for reflection, not analytical predictions. The final section of this chapter considers some of the policy questions raised by these different futures.

Schools and competences for lifelong learning

The situation of schools needs to be understood in the broader context of overall learning, where the ambitious goal has become "lifelong learning for all". Despite agreement on the principle, it is not clear how far countries have actually moved towards generalised lifelong learning

Despite widespread policy endorsement of lifelong learning, progress is limited

Little fundamental re-think of schools' role to achieve this

opportunities. While there is a greater volume and range of participation in learning than there used to be, in most countries the ambitious goal of universal learning careers is still a long way from being implemented. And, despite much greater recognition that schools are fundamental to lifelong learning, rather than a separate set of provisions that precedes it, there is as yet little evidence of a more fundamental re-think of what the distinct role of schools should be to meet this challenge.

It will mean an end to a bureaucratic, status quo...

The scenarios can help the clarification process. So long as schools continue to adhere to the model and assumptions of Scenario 1 – bureaucratic systems continuing the status quo – their capacity to contribute systematically to laying foundations for lifelong learning is bound to be limited. For in this model, schooling is too closed and inflexible and its professionals and organisations themselves are insufficiently defined by lifelong learning characteristics. Moving towards one of the other scenarios is thus necessary, though the nature of the foundation laid will clearly be shaped according to whether this is in the direction of "de-schooling" or "re-schooling", and whether the latter would take the broader social remit or one more focused on knowledge. Which scenario is chosen also influences whether lifelong learning would be "for all" as the scenarios differ in their emphasis on inclusiveness.

... possibly in favour of "re-schooling" in earlier school years, and "de-schooling" later

It may be that lifelong learning would be best served by a judicious combination of scenario features for different phases of learning. To realise lifelong learning for all may well call for "re-schooling" in the earlier cycles, with both strong knowledge and social remits. But, it may also need more "de-schooling" in the later years, permitting powerful roles for markets, distance education, community networks and informal learning, as well as the public authorities.

Competences for the future

In this report, the growing demands on schools have been outlined, and the related knowledge, skills and values for students' future lives and for lifelong learning. What will today's students need to equip them for their life at school and afterwards as members of the workforce, community, family and polity? How to define these in general when individuals will confront highly varied future lives and careers, within structures and conditions that will themselves be constantly changing? The boxed list brings together the indications provided by the foregoing analysis, as an ambitious list that all might attain (even if in reality many will not).

Competences for life and for lifelong learning

- Students should have prose, document and quantitative literacy to the level "considered a suitable minimum for coping with the demands of everyday life and work in a complex, advanced society" (Level 3 in the international surveys). At present, between one-quarter to as many as three-quarters of adults in the surveyed countries do not attain this level.
- Familiarity and facility with ICT, as a source of information, a tool for learning and for communication/networking with others. "Digital literacy" as discerning ICT use.
- A sound basis of facts and understanding ("know-what" and "know-why"), to be continually extended through the lifetime for different professional and community contexts. A firmly-established capacity for learning and re-learning – "know-how" – and the motivation to do so.
- The capability to work and learn with others –team-working– as well as for independent learning. The ability to develop networking – "know-who".
- The cognitive and non-cognitive, including emotional, basis to function, even to thrive, in a world of complexity, "information overload", uncertainty, and rapid change.
- The human and social competences for community and civic participation, that will also find application in much of the "service" and "self-service" economy.
- Enquiring and critical faculties, with the ability to engage the major value and ethical issues confronting societies in the 21st century. Tolerance and an appreciation of diverse cultures.

Goals, functions and tensions

The goals which schools work towards are complex. Most systems have defined missions for their schools, with account taken of the varying needs and capabilities of students at different ages. As ideals to be aimed at, there is bound to be a gap with actual outcomes. Some countries have sought to tighten the link between ends and outcomes

Goals: complex interplay with each other, not equally attainable; functions: not all expressed as aims

103|

---

by target setting. In making missions, aims and targets more explicit, it is important to avoid an excessive focus on the readily measurable to the neglect of the less tangible, but often essential, aspects of a school's achievements.

Rotterdam framework for policy orientations and innovation

At the November 2000 Rotterdam conference, the chair, former Swedish Education Minister Ylva Johansson, drew up her conclusions for the framing of education policies in general and on fostering and disseminating innovation. She developed these under a number of guiding headings within these two areas. For "orientations for future policies", the key headings were: *i*) high ambitions, strong organisations; *ii*) schools as democratic agents for social cohesion; *iii*) well-resourced schools to meet demanding public responsibilities; *iv*) networks and partnerships are critical; *v*) from teaching to learning; *vi*) teachers and leadership; *vii*) ICT as a learning and development tool. For "fostering and disseminating innovation", the headings were: *i*) national standards, school autonomy; *ii*) bold experimentation, evaluation, and dissemination; *iii*) the key role of partnerships; *iv*) sustaining innovation and improvement. It is not expected, of course, that any particular framework of aims and principles will find universal consensus.

Tensions and paradoxes

Trying to resolve difficult tensions

Once all the different aspects of schooling are considered together, it becomes clear that they do not always sit easily with each other. Whereas goals are often proposed as if they fit neatly together into a grand schema, in fact they are replete with tensions. Even if they cannot be entirely resolved, clarification of the most obvious sources of tension can help to eliminate the most glaring contradictions and illuminate pathways to progress.

Autonomy vs control, stronger or weaker schools?

Many countries have decentralised but central control remains and may even be strengthened – on curriculum and assessment, for instance, or in new forms of accountability and standard-setting. Some reforms seek to strengthen schools *qua* schools – as dynamic organisations with powerful identities and ethos – while other reforms weaken them through extending alternatives. Thus can different reform endeavours neutralise each other? These competing, countervailing movements are expressed in the scenarios – in the same country, movements can be found side by side designed to maintain the status quo, build "re-schooling", and quicken "de-schooling".

In a number of countries, schools are under increasing pressure to conform to precise, standardised outcomes. The arguments are that education is far too important to be left to chance and that such large sums of public monies must be seen to give value. And yet, these pressures are being exerted at a time when most agree that flexibility in individuals and organisations is what is needed in the 21st century. To be an innovative learning organisation means being able to experiment and take risks, with the necessary corollary of occasional "failures". Greater institutional autonomy is being granted in systems that are typically "low-risk". This brings its own tensions as schools are forced to ask whether they can pursue much more diversified pathways without stumbling over powerful accountability pressures to standardise?

Conformity vs *experimentation. School systems as "low-risk"*

Many in society espouse strong views about what takes place inside schools and classrooms, usually based on little other than hearsay and their own past personal experiences, rather than any contemporary familiarity or knowledge. Parents have direct experience of their own children's schools and tend to be positive about them; they also hold much more negative opinions about the state of education in general on the basis of far less knowledge. This is not just a case of lamentable public ignorance as it is compounded, in some countries in particular, by the "height" and "thickness" of school walls. Pressures for greater accountability stem in part from the desire to make schooling more transparent.

Strong opinions on the basis of widespread ignorance

There is widespread agreement on the need to individualise learning, given the complexity of pathways to be followed and value of tailoring to individuals' needs. Most also agree, however, that among the skills and attitudes most needed are co-operation and team-work. Yet, countries still

Individual vs *collective approaches*

105|

tend to retain individual-based assessment methods, and diplomas and qualifications that are awarded on an exclusively individual basis. There are tensions between the individual nature of much teaching and learning, and the value of more communal forms of "learning through interaction" and teacher networking. Socialisation and learning for citizenship, by definition, cannot be done in isolation.

Diversity vs *equality of opportunity*?

Learning with, through and about others is to champion diversity. Multiculturalism is a norm of contemporary school systems. But, it brings its own tensions, especially as it relates to equity and equality of opportunity. Under what conditions does democratic diversity become unacceptable inequality? How far can schooling, which reflects communities and the broader society, be expected to attain much more equal and equitable outcomes, and up to what price are societies willing to pay to do so?

The mismatch between important functions and the recognised outcomes

This report has argued how important are the socialisation, and indeed "childcare", functions of schools, especially in the light of a series of on-going employment, family and community trends. Yet, the terms in which schools are judged in many countries are increasingly focused on their success in purveying cognitive knowledge. How can this mismatch be managed?

Are schools expected to do too much?

At the same time, one of the greatest tensions schools experience is between attempting to satisfy burgeoning demands of all kinds, particularly in social, cultural and pastoral fields, and maintaining focus on the teaching and learning functions by which they are most clearly judged. This is to ask about the distinctiveness or complementarity of the "re-schooling" Scenarios 3 and 4 – a social and communal focus, on the one hand, and knowledge-based, on the other. Can both be pursued with equal fervour, or must more of one mean some sacrifice of the other?

Policy questions and the scenarios

It has not been the aim of this report to produce a blue-print for the school of the future, or for policies that define the way ahead across the OECD countries as a whole. Those tasks more properly lie within the different countries, regions, and communities with decision-making responsibility for schools. It is useful nevertheless to elaborate some of the questions that need to be addressed in moving into the future, drawing particularly on the different implications of the scenarios presented in Chapter 3.

Cultural and political environment. Public attitudes, the degree of consensus or conflict over goals (dis)satisfaction with schools, and the level of recognition and esteem in which they and teachers are held, will all be critical in shaping the future of schooling. The broad environment becomes even more critical the more that schools are called upon to be autonomous, work in partnerships, and orient themselves to demand. Should this environment be viewed largely as a given and beyond the reach of educational policy? Or instead, should it be treated as an important target of policy strategies, with a view to setting in train virtuous circles on matters that are beyond the reach of regulation and administration?

Can the cultural and political environment be a variable of educational policy?

Accountability. This is an integral feature of all the scenarios, though Scenario 5 – learner networks and the network society – assumes a much-reduced degree of control. The mechanisms through which accountability is realised, however, differ widely across the scenarios: from those based on the close monitoring of performance and attainments, to the accountability generated by the exercise of "client demand", to that exerted by widely-shared norms of demanding quality standards. As demands on schools grow, and with it the costs of failure, how can the need for accountability be assured without its mechanisms undermining the very quality and flexibility they are intended to promote?

How can accountability be assured without undermining flexibility of action?

Diversity, uniformity, equality. One of the strengths of the systemic "status quo" model is its pursuit of a formally equal opportunity structure, even if this may come with excessive bureaucracy and continuing actual inequalities. In the other scenarios (except Scenario 6), major departures from standardisation are sought, though by different routes and approaches to inclusion/exclusion. Important

Need for greater diversity, but risk of widening inequality?

107

equity questions are raised by all the scenarios. How should the tensions between diversity, flexibility and equality of opportunity be resolved?

Sufficient resources or high ambitions – how will they be found?

Resourcing. Schooling requires numerous resources – finance, professional expertise, technical infrastructure and facilities, community and parental support. Outcomes depend partly on their levels, but also on how such diverse resources are combined, used, and managed. Certain of the scenarios – 2, 3, and 5 particularly – are consistent with diversification of the resource base, with or without a major change in educational spending. Scenarios 3, 4 and 6 may well call for significant increases in the total spending effort. Scenarios 2 and 5 in particular could well see widening inequalities in resources per student. Fundamental resource questions will arise. Are societies willing to invest sufficiently in schools for the tasks being expected of them? If resources are stretched too far to sustain high-quality learning environments, what redistributions are possible in a lifelong learning framework? Can existing resources be used much more effectively in schools and, if so, how?

New demanding models of professionalism – but how to recruit enough teachers?

Teachers. The human resources – the professionals working in schools – are clearly fundamental to the future. Teachers become still more critical to the success of schooling as expectations about quality increase – more demand-oriented approaches and less supply-determined; more active and less passive learning; knowledge creation not just transmission in schools. Responses to these pressures will often result in teachers having to operate in new organisational structures, in close collaboration with colleagues and through networks, facilitating learning and overseeing individual development. The profile, role, status, and rewards of teachers differ significantly between the scenarios, and some imply a degree of change both towards and by teachers that may well prove uncomfortable to them and to society. How to devise new models of teacher professionalism and organisational roles, in ways that enhance the attractiveness of the job, the commitment of teachers, and the effectiveness of schools as learning organisations? How to attract new blood into the profession?

Schools and lifelong learning. The principle of integrating school policy and practice into the larger lifelong learning framework is now widely agreed, for the benefit both of schooling and of lifelong learning strategies. It is less clear what this means in practice and the extent of change it implies. The scenarios suggest contrasting possibilities such as shorter, more intensive school careers compared with an extended initial education; diversified agencies, professionals, and programmes compared with highly focused knowledge-based approaches. Behind these choices lie further questions. Does the task of laying firm foundations for lifelong learning call for fundamentally different approaches by schools? Or instead, is it tantamount to a restatement of a demanding equality objective – ensuring that the quality resources and opportunities presently enjoyed only by the best-served are available to *all* students?

What way best for schools to lay foundation for lifelong learning?

References (Part I)

ABRAMOWITZ, M. and DAVID, P. (1996),
"Technological Change and the Rise of Intangible Investments: The US Economy's Growth Path in the Twentieth Century", in D. Foray and B-A Lundvall (1996).

ARIES, P. (1973),
Centuries of Childhood, Penguin, London.

BLOSSFELD, H.P. and SHAVIT, Y. (1993),
Persistent Inequality: Changing Educational Attainment in Thirteen Countries, Westview Press Inc., Colorado.

CARTER, A. P. (1994),
"Production Workers, Meta-investment, and the Pace of Change", paper prepared for the International J.A. Schumpeter Society, Munster, August.

CASTELLS, M. (1996),
The Rise of the Network Society. The Information Age: Economy, Society and Culture, Vol. I, Cambridge, MA.

COGAN, J. (1997),
Multidimensional Citizenship: Educational Policy for the 21st Century, an executive summary of the Citizenship Education Policy Study Project, Minneapolis, USA.

COLEMAN, J.S. (1988),
"Social Capital in the Creation of Human Capital", *American Journal of Sociology*, Vol. 94, S95-120.

CROS, F. (1999),
"Innovation in Education: Managing the Future?", in OECD (1999g), Chapter 4.

DARLING-HAMMOND, L. (1997),
The Right to Learn: A Blueprint for Creating Schools that Work, Jossey Bass, San Fransisco.

DRUCKER, P. (1993),
The Post-capitalist Society, Butter worth, Heinemann, Oxford.

ERAUT, M., ALDERTON, J., COLE, G. and SENKER, P. (1998),
"Developments of Knowledge and Skills in Employment", *Research Report No. 5*, University of Sussex Institute of Education, Brighton.

ERIKSON, R. and GOLDTHORPE, J.H. (1992),
The Constant Flux: A Study of Class Mobility in Industrial Societies, Clarendon Press, Oxford.

FORAY, D. and LUNDVALL, B-A. (1996),
Employment and Growth in the Knowledge-based Economy, OECD, Paris.

HAHN, C. (1998),
Becoming Political, State University of New York Press, New York.

HARGREAVES, D.H. (1999),
"Schools and the Future: the Key Role of Innovation", in OECD (1999g), Chapter 3.

HIRSCH, F. (1977),
Social Limits to Growth, Routledge and Kegan Paul, London.

HUTMACHER, W. (1999),
"Invariants and Change in Schools and Education Systems", OECD (1999g), Chapter 2.

ILO/UNESCO (1997),
"Joint ILO/UNESCO Committee of Experts on the Application of the Recommendation concerning the Status of Teachers", Special Fourth Session, Paris, September.

INGLEHART, R. (1997),
Modernisation and Post-modernisation: Cultural, Economic and Political Change in 43 Societies, Princeton University Press, Princeton.

JOLLY, R. (2000),
"Global Inequality, Human Rights and the Challenge for the 21st Century", in OECD (2000g).

KENNEDY, K.J. and MILLS, G. (1996),
"Curriculum Policy Developments in the Asian-Pacific Region: A Cross-country Analysis", paper presented at the 20th Annual Conference of the Pacific Circle Consortium, Sydney 12-15 May.

LUNDVALL, B.-A. (2000),
"The Learning Economy: Some Implications for the Knowledge Base of Health and Education Systems", in OECD (2000a).

LUNDVALL, B.-A. and JOHNSON, B. (1994),
"The Learning Economy", Journal of Industry Studies, Vol. 1, No. 2.

MELLOR, S. (1998),
"What's the Point?": Political Attitudes of Victorian Year 11 Students, Research Monograph No. 53, Australian Council for Educational Research (ACER), Melbourne.

MULGAN, G. (2000),
"The Prospects for Social Renewal", in OECD (2000f).

OECD (1986),
Girls and Women in Education, Paris.

OECD (1991),
Migration: The Demographic Aspects, Paris.

OECD (1993),
Employment Outlook, Paris.

OECD (1994),
The OECD Jobs Study: Evidence and Explanations, Paris.

OECD (1996a),
Lifelong Learning for All, Paris.

OECD (1996b),
Schools for Today and Tomorrow, Paris.

OECD (1997a),
Employment Outlook, Paris.

OECD (1997b),
   Education Policy Analysis, Paris.

OECD (1997c),
   Parents as Partners in Schooling, Paris.

OECD (1998a),
   Technology, Productivity and Job Creation: Best Policy Practices, Paris.

OECD (1998b),
   Human Capital Investment: An International Comparison, Paris.

OECD (1998c),
   Staying Ahead: In-service Training and Teacher Professional Development, Paris.

OECD (1998d),
   Overcoming Failure at School, Paris.

OECD (1998e),
   Co-ordinating Services for Children and Youth at Risk: A World View, Paris.

OECD (1999a),
   A Caring World: The New Social Policy Agenda, Paris.

OECD (1999b),
   Employment Outlook, Paris.

OECD (1999c),
   Trends in International Migration, SOPEMI, Paris.

OECD (1999d),
   "Education and Learning for Sustainable Consumption", report of a joint Environment
   Directorate/CERI Workshop, held 14-15 September 1998.

OECD (1999e),
   "Trends in Income Distribution and Poverty in the OECD Area", OECD Working Document
   DEELSA/ELSA/WP1(99)15.

OECD (1999f),
   Education Policy Analysis, Paris.

OECD (1999g),
   Innovating Schools, Paris.

OECD (2000a),
   Knowledge Management in the Learning Society, Paris.

OECD (2000b),
   Employment Outlook, Paris.

OECD (2000c),
   Learning to Bridge the Digital Divide, Paris.

OECD (2000d),
   From Initial Education to Working Life: Making Transitions Work, Paris.

OECD (2000e),
   "Is There a New Economy?", first report on the OECD Growth Project (Meeting of the
   OECD Council at Ministerial Level, 2000), Paris.

OECD (2000f),
   The Creative Society of the 21st Century, Paris.

OECD (2000g),
Special Needs Education: Statistics and Indicators, Paris.

OECD (2001a),
Education Policy Analysis, Paris.

OECD (2001b),
OECD in Figures: Statistics on the Member Countries, Paris.

OECD (2001c),
Education at a Glance: OECD Indicators, Paris.

OECD (2001d),
The Well-being of Nations: The role of Human and Social Capital, Paris.

OECD (2001e),
Employment Outlook, Paris.

OECD (2001f),
Cities and Regions in the New Learning Economy, Paris.

OECD (2001g),
Governance in the 21st Century, Paris.

OECD (2001h),
Starting Strong: Early Childhood Education and Care, Paris.

OECD (2001i),
OECD Environmental Outlook, Paris.

OECD (2001j),
E-learning: The Partnership Challenge, Paris.

OECD (2001k),
The New Economy: Beyond the Hype, Paris.

OECD (2001l),
ICT: School Innovation and the Quality of Learning – Progress and Pitfalls, booklet produced for the Forum on ICT held on the occasion of the meeting of OECD Ministers of Education, April, Paris.

OECD (2001m),
Designs for Learning: 55 Exemplary Educational Facilities, Paris.

OECD (2001n),
New School Management Approaches, Paris.

OECD (2001o),
Society at a Glance, Paris.

OECD and STATISTICS CANADA (2000),
Literacy in the Information Age, Paris.

PELGRUM, W.J. and ANDERSON, R.E. (1999),
ICT and the Emerging Paradigm for Life Long Learning: A Worldwide Educational Assessment of Infrastructure, Goals and Practices, SITES IEA and the University of Twente, Netherlands.

PROUT, A. (2000),
"Children's Participation: Control and Self-realisation in British Late Modernity", Children and Society, Vol. 14:4, September.

PUTNAM, R. (2000),
Bowling Alone: The Collapse and Revival of American Community, Simon Schuster, New York.

RUBENSON, K. and SCHUETZE, H.G. (1995),
  "Learning through the Workplace: A Review of Participation and Adults Learning Theory", in D. Wagner and D. Hirsch (eds.), *What Makes Workers Learn?*, Cresskill, N.J. Hampton Press.

STEVENS, B., MILLER, R. and MICHALSKI, W. (2000),
  "Social Diversity and the Creative Society of the 21st Century", in OECD (2000f).

UNDP (United Nations Development Programme) (1998),
  Human Development Report 1998, Oxford University Press, New York.

UNICEF (2000),
  A League Table of Child Poverty in Rich Nations, Innocenti Report Card Issue No. 1, June, Florence.

VISCO, I. (2001),
  "Tackling the Economic Consequences of Ageing", OECD *Observer*, No. 226/7, Summer.

WHO (CURRIE, C., HURRELMANN, K., SETTERBOBULTE, W., SMITH, R. and TODD, J.) (2000),
  Health and Health Behaviour among Young People, WHO Policy Series: Health Policy for Children and Adolescents Issue 1, International Report, Bielefeld and Copenhagen.

WOLFF, E.N. (1987),
  International Comparisons in the Distribution of Household Wealth, Clarendon Press, Oxford.

WORLD BANK (2000),
  World Development Report 2000/2001: Attacking Poverty, Oxford University Press, Oxford.

Part II
THE EXPERT PAPERS

Chapter 5

Work, Society, Family and Learning for the Future[1]

by

Martin Carnoy
Stanford University, United States

Introduction

Historic changes are transforming our everyday lives and are likely to transform schooling in the future. The transformation of work and employment under the impact of the information revolution and the globalisation of the economy have produced a major strain in the relationship between work and society. Though rooted in a common pattern of technological change and institutional rigidity, it has taken substantially different forms in Europe, the United States, and Japan, shaped by cultural contexts, business strategies and government policies. At the heart of the problems is the inability of social and economic institutions to adapt to the new, informational patterns of working in contemporary societies.

Changes in work and employment profoundly affect the network of institutions on which our societies are based: family, community, and the state. The difficulties experienced by these institutions amplify the problem and worsen its social impact. There is now need for a general overhaul of the relationships between work and society beyond piecemeal remedies and short-term policies. But, within these changes have been created the bases for reintegrating the individual into productive, more egalitarian social structures: *knowledge and information*. Knowledge and information have always been important, but they have become a primary commodity of exchange in the new global environment and will be at the core of the 21st century society.

Given their centrality, that there is a critical role to be played by learning, education and schooling is obvious. There is a crucial additional role for schools to play as key community institutions in societies that have lost so many of their traditional sources of social interaction. This chapter describes the crisis of the relationship between work and society, and then presents current problems and future solutions in the three key institutional settings: work, family and community. In each case, the learning and schooling implications are discussed. The chapter concludes with discussion of the particular part that government can play in addressing these issues.

Crisis in the relationships between work and society

We are witnessing the reversal of the trend towards salaried employment and socialisation of production that was the dominant feature of the industrial era. This amounts to the radical transformation of work arrangements in advanced societies. More intense competition on a world wide scale makes firms acutely aware of costs and productivity. Their "solution" to this has been to re-organise work around decentralised management, work differentiation, and customised products – individualising work tasks and differentiating individual workers in their relationship to supervisors and employers. This has made sub-contracting, part-timing, and hiring temporary labour much easier, since so much of work can be narrowed down to specific tasks, even as other "core" activities are multi-tasked and conducted in teams. Income profiles over work lives are becoming flatter, even for highly educated workers. And, wage labour is rapidly feminising, with enormous implications for the way work and families is organised.

The crisis does not take identical forms in all parts of the industrialised world. Europe as a whole still faces serious unemployment[2] and US-style deregulation has attractions as a means to resolve it. But, deregulation has serious downsides, and the United States is characterised by particularly marked inequalities and intense pressure to work. It could even be argued that its efficient "job creation machine" has created increasing numbers of dysfunctional families, individual stress, and deteriorating communities. Japan has in the past been highly successful in achieving rapid economic growth with full employment and low inflation by means of a "neo-corporatist" macroeconomic policy that brings labour and large industries together to agree on wage and price increases. But even Japan has been in the grips of recession, rising unemployment, and increased competition; its society and system are suffering a malaise from which it is still to emerge.

Worldwide, these changes are profoundly altering the way we live and relate to each other and the role of knowledge and information in work and personal interactions. A major force behind these changes is economic globalisation and the intensified competition it brings. A country's investment, production, and innovation are no longer constrained by national borders. Even our cultures are globalising. One effect is that activities, including how we relate to our family and friends, are rapidly becoming organised around a much more compressed view of space and time. This extends to children in school or watching television who are re-conceptualising their "world", in terms of the meanings that they attach to music, the environment, sports, or race and ethnicity. Our lives are being transformed by a massive diffusion of new information and communication technologies.

The second major force behind world-wide social change is the rapid transformation of family life, driven in turn by a profound revolution in the social role of women. They have gradually rejected "going it alone" on social cohesion. Smaller families earlier in the 20th century buttressed social cohesion, gave more time for community building, and allowed women to create a social life for themselves outside the family. But since the late 1960s there has been a profound shift in gender relations in family and work. Divorce rates have soared, first in the United States and then in all but a few developed countries. Masses of married women have come into the workplace, part-time and then full-time. The family can no longer be assumed to reproduce labour and knowledge as it has in the past. We cannot even assume that new family arrangements will produce *enough* labour.

While the individualisation of work undermines the importance of one of the most important social agencies in our life, *the workplace*, not all aspects of the changes are experienced negatively. The resurgence of the individual, with greater freedom and self-directed initiative, frees people from bureaucracies and from the often-excessive constraints of workplace relationships. But these can only be enjoyed if alternative forms of social organisation provide a web of social relationships that can serve as psychological support and a basis for interaction. The industrial revolution disassociated residential communities, workplaces, and social life, in an historical movement that classical sociologists such as Durkheim characterised as the substitution of "organic" for "mechanistic" solidarity. With the loss of the social relevance of the workplace, and of work-based forms of social organisation, a greater demand is placed on other forms of sociability.

Local communities and voluntary associations are foremost among such forms. Evidence in advanced societies, however, points to a possible serious erosion of membership in voluntary associations, as a result of individualistic values, time constraints, and dual-job families (Putnam, 1995). As for local communities, whose resurgence as social networks could provide a useful compensatory mechanism to individualism, urban research has also shown their limits and contradictions. By and large, residence-based communities have tended to fade away as forms of social interaction and collective undertaking in advanced societies. Could they be replaced by "virtual communities" organised around electronic interactive networks, as some envision (*e.g.* Rheingold, 1993)? Scattered observations from France and the United States suggest that such "virtual communities" may be only ephemeral forms of social relationships, except when they are anchored in professional activity or become the extension of family/friendship networks. Although it is still too early to assess the long-term significance of emerging forms of interactive electronic communication, it is likely that it will reinforce existing social networks rather than substitute for them (Benson, 1994).

121|

The *family* could be the social institution to temper the stress induced by the processes of desegregation of labour and the individualisation of social and economic life. In times of historical transition, the nurturing effects of family life can be critical for psychological support, social stability, economic security, and creative socialisation. The social disintegration and economic distress induced by unemployment and of the shrinkage of the welfare state have been attenuated in a number of countries by strong family structures.[3] For families to offer the fundamental mechanism through which the transition towards new forms of work and the de-institutionalisation of social protection can operate, it has to be redefined and strengthened under the new cultural and technological conditions. Not all societies have strong families, and it is unclear that even those that do will maintain them given current social trends. More will be needed as policy support than simply invoking family values if they are to survive the shocks of deteriorating living conditions, lack of child-care, stressful dual workdays, long commuting hours and downgraded schools.

Work, networks and learning

While the transformation of work and employment has resulted in a crisis of their relationship with society, it has also created the bases for reintegrating the individual into highly productive, more egalitarian social structures. These bases are *knowledge* and *information*.[4] The distinguishing feature of work in the information age is the centrality of knowledge, especially "transportable" general knowledge that is not specific to a single job or firm. The best jobs are those that require high levels of education, call for extensive general knowledge, and provide opportunities to accumulate more knowledge. The best firms are those that create effective environments for teaching, learning, and interchanging information. It is knowledge and information that create flexibility in work – the capacity of firms to improve product lines, production processes, and marketing strategies, all with the same workforce. It is these which enhance the capacity of workers to learn new processes, to shift jobs, even vocations, over the course of a work life, or to move geographically.

In the new knowledge economy, characterised by *flexibility* and *networking* there is a premium on a worker's ability to move from a job in one firm to another to learn new jobs in the same firm, to do different types of tasks in the course of the day or week, and to adjust quickly to diverse employment cultures and group situations (Capelli, 1993). The firms that promote and reward such flexibility tend to be the more successful (Derber, 1994, pp. 15-18, 107-108), creating yet greater demand for workers with these abilities. At the core of high productivity work in the information age is the complex interplay between more educated and flexible workers and best-practice firms.

Best-practice workplaces are *learning organisations.* New technologies, including the art of flexible organisation itself, make their maximum contribution to productivity when they are based on learning and teaching as an inherent part of the work process. The new compact between company and worker de-emphasises paternalistic relations in favour of self-reliance and co-operation. Management has to give up some power over decisions in order that employees have more; networking firms also have to give up some control over information in order to share in other firms' knowledge. Learning is accumulated in these arrangements, permitting innovation, the more productive uses of resources, and lower costs of production. Indeed, much of the new technology developed in firms, as they develop/improve processes or products, is the result of accumulated learning (Dosi, 1988; Rosenberg, 1982).

More knowledge and information do not, in themselves, create more jobs. Yet, a society organised around learning networks provides the basis for much higher productivity, greater equality, and the reintegration of individualised citizen-workers. Over the longer run, this pathway will create greater wealth and income, generate more or higher quality jobs, transform the nature of leisure, and develop the re-integrative activities that make life interesting and rewarding. Future working and employment policies will need to be organised around the *employability* of individuals and families, not permanent jobs. The social well-being that all democratically-elected governments aim for will depend as much on how well workers, individualised by flexible work organisations, are integrated into such learning networks as on the annual increase in the number of jobs.

Implications for education and the organisation of learning

As learning becomes the new focus of work in the information age, traditional concepts of education must change. The workers that do best in flexible, learning organisations are good both at solving problems individually – the higher-order skills normally learned by students going on to post-secondary education – and, as important, at group-working to innovate and motivate. The latter is a skill that is hardly touched upon in our present educational system, a rare example when co-operative skills are fostered is in management courses. Indeed, learning networks require workers to have a "management mentality", including knowing how to motivate individualised fellow workers to apply their knowledge for maximum efficiency and quality, and to learn – and teach others – how to do better (what might also be described as "people skills").

If education is to develop higher-order problem-solving skills *and* competence to be able to organise more learning, it suggests profound change in school curricula and in job training programmes. Standard forms of vocational education – specific skills for specific jobs – become largely outmoded, except insofar as they are effective in imparting problem-solving and organisational skills to those otherwise alienated from more academic programmes (Stern *et al.*, 1995). School learning should itself be co-operative in form – studying, learning and being assessed as groups. The curriculum should actively include the development of networking, and of motivational and teaching skills. In the information-age environment, the processes of, and motivations for, learning should become endogenous to curriculum itself.

General education during youth should be viewed as only the *beginning* of the learning process. In the past, young people went to school, got a job, which they often then did for much of the rest of their lives. In the information age, the worker is no longer defined in terms of a specific job but of accumulated learning and the capacity to apply it to different situations, within and outside the traditional workplace.

There remains the problem of ensuring reasonable-paying jobs for all those who want them. Nor does more education necessarily create new jobs, as seen in Europe. Without specific action to incorporate the young into the jobs, the result could simply be rising educational attainment levels among the unemployed. Nevertheless, keeping young people in school longer in itself holds advantages. It delays entry to the full-time job market, and it provides employers with a better educated and more flexible, trainable, employable, and potentially productive workforce. That workforce is more likely to view further education as a natural part of their working/learning lives later on if their initial school period has lasted longer. Together with best-practice workplaces organised around training and learning, this positive attitude sets the stage for higher productivity and lower unemployment in the long term. It can be the foundation for successful apprenticeship programmes, other school-to-work transition programmes incorporating job-site training, and national service experiences connected to work/training internships.

Perhaps the most difficult, but necessary, transformation for OECD countries is to organise schooling around *universal post-secondary education* that imparts self-reliance, rapid adjustment to change, and mobility. To now, educational systems have not only a manifest role of imparting cognitive knowledge and skills, but a latent one as social selectors (Bourdieu and Passeron, 1970; Carnoy and Levin, 1985). This may have worked reasonably efficiently in hierarchical industrial systems, however inequitable the outcome. They were stratified but could provide reasonable security and increasing wages even to those with basic education. Today, such stratification is socially counter-productive yet the systems that certify it remain largely untouched. Youth with only secondary education is increasingly at risk in the labour market, as both the education system and employers regard them as inadequately prepared for the higher-skilled, flexible jobs. To change this means to enhance expectations and compress the distribution of education by raising the social minimum.

Education and learning are not only central to employment in the information age but also to the family and community. These are examined in the next two sections.

The family and household

Far from losing its fundamental importance to work, the family will be even more crucial as the economy shifts to flexible, knowledge-based production. Its role is already changing from a "family consumption partnership" to a "household investment and production partnership", given the inherently close relationship between family and work and women's changing social role. What is new – and rarely discussed in analyses of the changing work system – are the potentially ruinous implications for the development of highly competitive yet socially stable knowledge-based societies should families not emerge reconstructed and healthy from the current transition. Learning, and investment in it, are at the heart of revitalised family structures.

In a seminal study, Young and Willmott (1973) characterise the family as having passed through three historical stages. Stage 1 was the "family as production unit", with all members working in the home/farm/small-scale home factory production. In Stage 2, this home-centred family broke down, with disastrous consequences particularly for women. Both men and women (and children) were employed outside the home, but when there were young children, women could not work and men controlled income. In Stage 3, the smaller family of the end of the 19th and early 20th century slowly led to married women going back to work after the years it would take to get all the children to around working age. The family increasingly became a centre of activity for men as well as women, they forming a *consumption* partnership around the home and the family. This stage reached its high point in the 1950s and 1960s, and gives us the model for the "traditional family" that conservatives are so often nostalgic for.

Young and Willmott, however, missed key aspects relating to the Stage 3 family. It has not only been a unit of consumption but also one of *investment*, especially in its children so that they could earn more than their parents and move up the consumption ladder. This investment role became increasingly important in the post-World War II period. A priority for welfare state support for families was to maintain and enhance the family's investment role in producing ever more productive labour for the flexible, competitive economy. By the 1980s, with flexible production patterns and the increasing importance of education in determining access to high-paying jobs, such investment became even more important. As it became commonplace for both parents to work even when the

125|

children were young, they came to consume all kinds of services that were only available to higher income families in the past. In the best of cases, such services embodied important investment components. In Europe and Japan, child-care, pre-schooling, and especially health care, are provided by the state and subsidised precisely because of concern to support the family's investment role.

Family life and conditions vary widely between America, western Europe, and Japan. In Japan, the traditional family is still the norm. Women often accept a sub-ordinate status as caretakers, providing a cushion for the labour market as many are part-timers without career perspectives and helping men's professional transition towards new forms of employment (Kamo, 1990; Nomura *et al.*, 1995). In Western Europe, participation of women in the labour force has substantially increased in recent years, but the network of supportive state institutions (accessible day care, good public schools and local transportation) and the persistence of family connections still tend to allow the family to play its supportive role. In contrast, the American family is in crisis, despite the value placed on it in the public mind. One quarter of US households is single. Only about another quarter of households corresponds to the classical married-couple-with-children model. The fastest growing household category is single-parent families, particularly those headed by women. At the same time, so much child-care is of such poor quality that it risks children's development. In some ethnic minorities, the crisis is deeper still, playing a major role in perpetuating the underclass status of a significant segment of the minority population (Wilson, 1987).

The crisis of the American family may seem extreme compared with other countries, but it may also presage a trend. In spite of its positive effect on the overall human condition, the transition towards more egalitarian forms than the patriarchal nuclear family also accentuates the crisis of work. If we add to this the growing cultural trend towards individualistic values in all societies, the already-visible American crisis may well be replicated elsewhere in the not-so-distant future. However, the combined effect of flexible production, women's determination for greater equality in the family and labour market, and the increased importance of the family as an investment unit, have not only eroded the *Stage* 3 family. They are now shaping the emergence of what could be the next stage of family life, and one that has learning at its core.

Learning and education decisions within families and households

In its ideal form, we envisage the family as an "investment-production partnership". Because the quality of upbringing has increased implications for future productivity and employability of the labour force, the investment choices made, and guidance offered, by the family are crucial to society's future. Since parents will spend much of their time working outside the home, the services available to them to invest in their children will be key to how well the family does in its child-rearing role.

There is a second part to the partnership that distinguishes it from the *Stage 3* 'consumption family". With two members of the family earning income, there can be periods of time when one is taking additional education or training, while the other earns; one member can also be the main support with employment income while the other starts up a business from home. In increasingly isolating social structures, families continue to be a source of psychic reward, as well as a site of increased stress. Whether psychic reward or stress dominates depends largely on the availability of community and state support networks. This is the subject of the next section.

The family in a flexible work system is therefore a central hub of productive and reproductive activity. When it is strong, it serves to hedge against the risks of unemployment. It can provide a source of child development for its offspring, of investment capital for adult and child education and job training, and of personal security and growth. Networked into larger information and communication systems, it can also become a production unit. Rather than just income, the main commodity of exchange in fixing and maintaining the variables of this family relation – the duration and the quality of the marriage, divorce, the number and the timing of the children – should increasingly be expressed in terms of learning. This commodity of exchange should be the opportunities available for adults and the capacity of the family to provide learning for children.

The high probability of single parenthood for women clouds the gender decisions around educational investment, both for adults and children. Young people are marrying later than their parents, largely because of the much greater labour market uncertainties. The greater possibilities of divorce and single parenthood for women also influence this choice; they feel compelled to take more education and develop a career precisely because, once married, their education/training opportunities decline relative to men. Divorce and single parenthood also play an important role in the investment in children. Not only is less income available to the single-parent family, particularly if the other parent does not pay child support. But it is much more difficult for one parent to provide the same kind of time, and to have flexibility in work and adult learning, as in a two-adult family.

The intense emphasis on learning as a commodity of exchange has already occurred in upper middle-income, highly educated family situations, where women are choosing to establish careers (achieving higher levels of education and taking jobs with high levels of learning opportunities) before having children. Such learning-driven behaviour as a dominant force shaping family formation, now more limited to educated young people sensitised to the implications of flexible labour markets, is spreading to the rest of the population and may well continue to do so.   127|

The reconstruction of community in the information age

As the workplace loses its central position in the information age, it becomes imperative for other spheres of social life to become supportive of integration interaction, and human development. Historically, communities structured around the place of residence have played this role. Contemporary conditions of urbanisation and the transformation of sociability, however, have considerably reduced the integrative potential of neighbourhoods. Spatial development in the last quarter of the century has been characterised by widespread territorial sprawl (Garreau, 1992; Dogan and Kasarda, 1987). The functional separation between residence, work, and urban services, the increasingly lower density of new urban forms, and increased geographic mobility have made it increasingly difficult to build social communities on a neighbourhood basis (Fischer, 1984).

There are, of course, community organisations throughout OECD societies But, research suggests (*e.g.* Castells, 1983; Borja, 1988) that many of these are defensive and parochial in character. They might well be described as agents of "collective individualism", oriented towards the preservation of the status quo in their neighbourhoods without much weaving of the fabric of supportive social relationships.

It is possible, and indeed necessary, to reconstruct communities, and to link them with the processes of flexible production, as one important means of rebuilding relationships between work and society. This means starting from the current state of existing communities and the extreme individualisation in the uses of space in order to design strategies adapted to contemporary technological and spatial characteristics. It is no easy task to preserve street life and encourage the public uses of space, even though these are stated goals of most cities. French policies have shown, however, that cities can be revitalised: neighbourhood feasts and public cultural celebrations staged by the city of Paris in recent years, have had substantial impact on the willingness of Parisians to use their beloved city Rome's anti-crime programme is based on the simple idea that streets filled with people and activities, including in the evening, will be relatively safe, while empty streets encourage crime, deteriorating urban sociability further in a vicious circle Thus, theatre, music, and youth festivals may well prove to be more effective forms of fighting crime than resorting to an over-worked and overwhelmed police service.

The re-conquest of public space is not enough. Neighbourhoods need to build institutions of sociability and self-reliance. Recent experiences with social services and community centres are not encouraging. They are instruments of social work and counselling, but hardly sites of stable social networks. The reconstruction of community also requires active, innovative local governments, based on decentralised resources and power. Local governments in Central-Northern Italy, or Germany or Catalonia, for instance, have taken major responsibility for connecting local life and the collective conditions for new economic development

Local centres for training, information, productivity development, and management counselling have been critical in revitalising a flexible network of small and medium enterprises. By so doing, they have also revitalised the local society.

The central role of the school in revitalising neighbourhoods

Without precluding the positive role of community centres in some cases, the central organising point in our society at the neighbourhood level is *the school* – elementary and secondary, as well as child development centres. Because schools' location patterns are pervasive and residence-based, and because sociability is made easier through children's connections, schools could become the platforms for a variety of neighbourhood issues. They could provide the material support for the formation of networks of solidarity between families of different types, all concerned with the future of their children. Children could thus act as the fulcrum around which family, community, and the future worker (the child) are brought together in a system of interaction, blending instrumental goals (child-care, development and education) with expressive, emotional, and social interaction. This requires an effort, both from government and from society, to transform the school, to make it more open to the community, and accordingly, to provide the public school system with better trained personnel, more resources, better physical facilities, and more innovative management.

Through the school, other social networks organised at the municipal level could come into contact with each other. For instance, the Municipality of Bologna has developed an interesting experience of social exchange between classrooms and associations of the elderly. Groups of children and of elderly adopt each other. The older people visit the school, tell their stories, thus transmitting oral history, while also baby-sitting children when their parents need such services. The individualisation of society, which gradually phases out the traditional role of grandparents in socialisation, could thus be counteracted with the organisation of inter-generational networks on a local basis. The education of the new generation would be more strongly rooted in an historical perspective and this will be especially important for the informational worker of tomorrow.

The development of electronic communication also offers the possibility of creating virtual communities, in a new form of spatial organisation, that Castells (1993) has called "the space of flows". At the historical beginning of this process, in the 1990s, such virtual communities are highly elitist and restricted to the most educated segments of the population and to the age groups that are culturally inclined to the daily navigation of "the net". Without recourse to science fiction fantasies, it is conceivable that in the early 21st century this form of communication could offer a platform for greater political participation and closer social interaction. United States evidence seems to indicate, for instance, that people are not

129|

very interested in paying more to select among hundreds of films or shows available on line, while in fact they are strongly attracted to the possibility of enhancing their information, education, and participation in public affairs (Tiller, 1994). The use of interactive, electronic communication to reconstruct social networks without depending on physical proximity, is indeed a new frontier of public policy and private initiative that deserves to be fully explored and exploited.

The key role of the state

The state as knowledge and information intermediary

The welfare state is in general in trouble financially, and seemingly unresponsive to the major economic and social changes taking place. Yet, the state is crucial to the building of new networks and to do that, it will have to reorganise and recast priorities. Because different societies have different tolerances for state activities and regulation, how it does so will vary from country to country. Such variations notwithstanding, the reorganised "knowledge and information" state would have several fundamental commonalties:

- It would focus a great deal of its activities on the nation's educational, training, and informational infrastructure.

- It would focus more government spending on support for families as centres of learning and production, rather than as consumption units.

- State spending and programme control would be highly decentralised, with many government services delivered by states, provinces, departments, and municipalities.

- Within the traditions of each country, the state would develop "solidarity" economic and social policies, focusing on equalising learning, employment, and self-employment opportunities for across population groups and regions. These would include income transfers, particularly in terms of who pays for particular learning and employment programmes.

OECD Member countries confront major constraints on their ability to reorganise their capacity to raise revenue, for instance, and their room for manoeuvre in shifting spending from present activities to those that would develop knowledge and information networks and a learning society. The political path to effect a shift will be easier where the state already enjoys legitimacy as a mechanism of social leadership and change – compare, for example, Northern Europe and Japan with Italy and the United States. But the successful transformation in all countries lies in making consistent choices that move them away from the predominance of service delivery towards a society organised around learning and more equal access to knowledge and information.

The state is the main provider of formal education in every advanced industrial society. Even in the United States, the large majority of post-secondary students attend public institutions. In the information economy, the state will need to expand this role, to give a higher proportion of young adults the chance to acquire professional and semi-professional degrees, and of older individuals the possibility to attend university and earn degrees during their working lives. Although improved and expanded education is probably the single best policy for governments to pursue to sustain more flexible production, a human resource strategy works best in the context of a state that takes an active role in building capacity at the local level to make lifelong education a community effort and to integrate individuals into community, national, and global networks.

Governments will continue to play a key role in preparing youth and adults for the workplace and in ensuring that information with high social benefits is widely accessible. They will also have to take responsibility for promoting more job training in private firms and for increasing young people's access to it. Public service programmes for young and old (including military service), may, in some countries, serve as major training and apprenticeship organisations for a wide range of occupations, especially for those young people with low levels of education. Municipal governments should provide training and marketing services, perhaps tied into local community college resources, for small-scale entrepreneurs who want to start their own businesses and need market and financial information. And, municipal and provincial governments would be strategically placed to build networks between public educational institutions, public and private community service organisations, and private firms to develop integrated work systems for higher productivity.

State support for the household partnership

The integration of households into learning networks is the linchpin of a flexible, knowledge-based work system. State family policies are fundamental to this integration, in providing a sufficient scale of material resources to support household investments in its members along with necessary political accountability. Policies need to enhance the household partnership's capacity to invest in learning without interfering in the privacy of its decisions. They can do this by a number of means: helping the family acquire education for its children even as parents work flexible schedules; giving parents new possibilities to take further education and training themselves; guaranteeing access to health care when family members are unemployed or studying; providing training to youth, prospective and existing parents on child care and development; providing fiscal incentives to reward families that invest in education; strictly enforcing laws to ensure that parents, whatever their domestic/residential arrangements, contribute financially to the support of their children.

131|

Knowledge acquisition depends heavily on early childhood development, and early childhood takes place in families. Those OECD countries that have been especially conscious of the welfare of children of working parents provide extensive opportunities for high-quality, subsidised day care. For instance, in the Nordic countries, France, and increasingly in Japan, family policy is a high priority and "day care" is state-organised around well-trained, certified teachers specialised in early childhood development. Going further still, child development centres are key to meeting the household's need for parents' job flexibility and young children's enriched learning. They are an expensive option, and, as in the case of higher education, parents who can afford to pay should do so. But, access must be on an equal footing. Otherwise, as too often happens now, the outcomes of the market model are highly unequal which is the opposite of what a flexible, knowledge-based society needs for sustained development. High quality health care needs to be assured for all children from the pre-natal phase onwards; again, the state role is critical. And, major investments should be made in education regarding the responsibilities and skills of parenthood.

Beyond early childhood development, governments need to make schools community learning centres, where parents can leave their children in a learning environment during the time they are at work or education, including during the school vacation period. The community learning centre should also be places where parents and seniors can come to engage in learning activities, whether related to their children's education or to other adult activities, including community-run business courses for the self-employed.

Currently, parents are supported fiscally in Europe and the US through family income entitlements, tax deductions for dependents, and welfare for mothers with dependent children. In the knowledge economy, fiscal incentives should more be tied to investment in education and training rather than simply to having children. Tax deductions for the costs of children's college education and for adult training are a step in this direction; similarly, deductions should be allowed for children's pre-school and parents' education toward a degree.

The focus on state support for families through education and training investment tax credits and the direct provision of high quality early childcare also suggests that the state needs to reconcile the way it views and delivers education. Local educational institutions – from primary and secondary schools to community colleges and universities – are the logical sites around which the state can build all-day, all-year, cradle-to-the-grave learning networks for households to hook into. These institutions will have to evolve to meet the varying needs of different communities. In low-income communities, for example, the need for full-day children's education and adult learning opportunities may be far greater than in high-income communities. The allocation of resources should be responsive to these differences. Educational systems are likely to have to become more all-encompassing to serve as a "public family" and a "community" as part of their expanded role in reintegrating workers and the children of lower-educated families more successfully into society and into flexible, knowledge-intensive work.

The emphasis on local governments must certainly be accompanied by mechanisms of redistribution of public revenues to avoid the reproduction of social inequality on the basis of segregated residence. But within the limits of prudence, societies would greatly benefit from a major shift of power, resources, and responsibility to the local level. Strong local government, active citizen participation, and the formation of networks of solidarity and reciprocity around the neighbourhood school are the mechanisms that would help to rebuild community, strengthen the new family, and contribute to educating the future, quality labour force.

State solidarity policies

Unregulated markets are marked by high levels of income inequality, as well as ethnic and gender discrimination (Danziger and Gottschalk, 1993; Levy and Murnane, 1992; Carnoy, 1994). At least part of this is a result of unequal access to learning, a product of family income/education differences and the unequal treatment of children by schools.

Markets also discriminate among ethnic and gender groups in hiring and job promotion. Even were the state to be effective in networking households into learning opportunities, equalising access to educational resources, and encouraging employers to be more equal in their training and pay for different ethnic and gender groups with comparable qualifications, there would still be some proportion of the working age population who would, if left unprotected, be poor. The continued existence of poverty can produce a permanent underclass, with high rates of unemployment, crime and social problems, and dysfunctional learning experiences for children. The state is the only institution able seriously to address the existence of such an underclass.

Equalising learning and reducing poverty represent high return investments for knowledge-based societies. Permanently poor households and communities cannot engage in the kind of learning and teaching needed by workers in flexible production, so, without intervention, they will always be at risk of dependence and alienation. Solidarity policies should be organised around the citizen/learning-worker/teacher rather than the job. Their underlying theme should be the enhancement of individual capabilities universally rather than providing universal entitlements. Most OECD countries provide some form of universal health care cover and public education. Yet, many do not do a good job of equalising access to learning, beginning with the early start in childhood and continuing right through the life-cycle.

133|

Notes

1. This chapter is based both on a paper delivered by Carnoy at the OECD/Netherlands seminar on "Schooling for Tomorrow" held in Scheveningen, Netherlands (April 1998) and on an earlier analysis prepared by Carnoy and Castells for the OECD (*Sustainable Flexibility: A Prospective Study on Work, Family and Society in the Information Age*, 1997). A more detailed analysis of the issues raised in this chapter is developed in Carnoy (1999).

2. Since Europe has an extremely low birth rate, present-day growth rates, should they continue into the future, could easily eliminate today's unemployment problem and replace it with a labour shortage filled increasingly by immigration from Eastern Europe, North Africa, and the Middle East, already well under way. This implies that northwest Europe's income distribution, work intensity, and social problems could become more like the United States' in the next generation.

3. For instance, the mystery of the calm and well-being of Spanish society in spite of such high unemployment rates in the 1990s (with only about 60% of the unemployed receiving unemployment insurance) can be explained by looking at the role of the Spanish family (Leal *et al.*, 1993). The large majority of unemployed are women and youth, who continue to live with their husbands and parents and are supported by them. All are supported by the social security system to whose benefits all family members are entitled because of their relationship to the one salaried worker in the family. Young people, on average, reside at home until almost 30 years old, often under conditions of total individual freedom (Zaldivar and Castells, 1992).

4. Knowledge can be defined as the *cumulated stock* of cognitive skills and information held by each individual, family, and community (including firms) related to the individual that can be applied to work, personal, and social situations. Information is the *flow* of usable knowledge available to individuals, families, and communities, including workplaces.

Chapter 6

A New Challenge to Social Cohesion?
Emerging Risk Profiles in OECD Countries

by

Gosta Esping-Andersen
University Pompeu Fabra, Spain

Introduction

The advent of welfare capitalism in mid-20th century in Europe was understood by many as the beginning of the end of the old *Arbeiterfrage*, of class polarisation. Social scientists coined a new vocabulary to describe the new era of social cohesion: the "affluent worker", the "waning of oppositions", the "end of ideology". Already, such catchwords seem anachronistic as new forms of segmentation emerge. The United States and Britain are preoccupied with their new underclass, the European Community with social exclusion. This is reflected in media language: in France the metaphor is of a "two-speed society", in Germany a "two-thirds society", while the Danes distinguish between the "A-team" and "B-team". Yet, two sets of countries are largely label-free: the Nordic group and Mediterranean Europe. While in the former case, the explanation might be simply that no acute marginalisation has yet surfaced, this would not apply to Southern Europe, which has experienced very high and long-term levels of unemployment, visibly concentrated among youth and women.

Several major trends underpin polarisation and marginalisation. One of the most important is technological change, which is eroding the position of low qualified workers and, more generally, those with low competence, cultural and/or social capital. But also, growing family instability means that children and youth confront material want or insecurity. Globalisation and the tertiarisation of the economy bring with them new forms of social risk, whereby some emerge as winners and others as losers. Despite the ubiquity of these "driving forces", they do not seem to result in convergent social and economic outcomes. Some countries seem to have no "B-teams", even if they suffer from high levels of unemployment; where they do exist they do not always share the same profile. In Northern America,

135

they are most likely to be single mothers or low-paid workers; in Continental Europe, youth predominate among those "at risk".

In assessing trends in inequality, a clear distinction should be made between static measures (such as poverty head-counts) and dynamics (entrapment in, or inter-generational transmission of, under-privilege). The available data tell us that low pay, child poverty, and inequalities are worsening in many economies, but how should this be interpreted? A spell of employment in a low-paid job, for instance, need not be regarded as a threat to life chances if avenues of mobility exist. We learn more about life chances from dynamics rather than static measures, but there is an unfortunate shortage of illuminating data.

The focus in this chapter is on three sets of questions. The first has to do with the "driving forces" of service-led economies: what are the emerging employment dilemmas? What will a labour market restored to full (or near full) employment look like? The second concerns the relationships between inequalities and the dynamics of social exclusion. The third, and least documented, addresses the institutional realities of social cohesion: what does it mean to experience unemployment or other forms of exclusion? How are they expressed and managed?

Services and employment

Discussion of technology's effect on jobs tends to focus excessively on manufacturing and the higher end of business services. These are both areas of the economy exposed to international competition, with a premium on skills, and with falling demand for low-level jobs. The bias resulting from this focus leads to a possibly exaggerated view of the centrality of education and skills for the future of employment. Today, virtually all net job creation comes from services. In the past, *distributive* services such as sales were the vanguards of the "tertiarisation" process, but they are no longer growing. Instead, most employment growth will come from *business, social* and, to a lesser extent, *personal* services. The potential dynamism of each is governed by different principles.

Business services are generally skilled and professionalised. They have enjoyed major growth over the past decades, driven by new technologies, globalisation, and the new structure of business demand. Many of the jobs have been exported out of the manufacturing sector, like accountancy, engineering, and marketing.

Social services also provide a substantial source of job growth. Their skill and occupational profile is more dualistic, with a high end of professionals and semi-professionals, and a low one of routine, poorly qualified jobs (home helps, hospital orderlies etc.). Social services will in all likelihood remain dynamic in the future, due to such factors as population ageing and the integration of women in labour markets. Yet, many families can ill afford these services unless they benefit from public subsidies or direct "welfare state" employment creation, most typically in the Nordic countries. (Good quality private day care, for example, costs around US$750-1 000 per month in most countries.) The ratio of unskilled to skilled jobs in this sector is likely to increase the more that social service jobs expand. The largest untapped sources of employment in this sector are the intensive care of the elderly and of children. These require only modest levels of certified skills and education, but they are nonetheless unlikely sources of openings for, say, redundant steel workers.

Proportionally, *personal services* have not grown much. They have received a boost in the de-regulated economies such as the United States because of low wages and heavy immigration, but high labour costs in Europe mean that these jobs have been stagnant and even declining – at least in the formal economy. In the United States, they account for about 10-12% of all jobs; in Europe, for 5% or, at the most, 7%. They are typically labour-intensive and low-skill – for instance, cleaning, laundering, or waiting. Like social services, they substitute for household self-servicing and are therefore vulnerable to the "Baumol syndrome" of being priced out of the market.

The eroding position of low qualified workers is most acute in the exposed economy. Many labour economists assess the impact of globalisation on low-skilled employment to be peripheral because most new jobs are created instead in the sheltered service sector. This is true to the extent that competition from developing countries – from immigrant maids or from Indian computer services – is marginal. But, while social and personal service jobs are likely to be important sources of mass employment, they face formidable competition from the *household economy*. The choices made by families between self-servicing or purchasing their childcare needs, laundry, ironing or cooking depend on relative prices. Here, there is a clear equality/jobs trade-off (see Table 6.1).

In sum, it may be true that technology factors are driving unskilled workers out from manufacturing and certain services jobs, but this is not necessarily the case for services directed at household consumption. Most research has been too narrowly preoccupied with emerging skill profiles in the former, and has provided

Table 6.1. **Long-term service employment trends: annual average change, 1970-1993**

	All employment	All services	Personal services	Social services	Business services
'Anglo" group	1.5	3.0	3.7	7.3	7.3
Nordic group	0.6	1.9	0.9	3.3	5.5
Continental Europe	0.5	2.4	n.a.	n.a.	4.3
Japan	1.2	1.6	n.a.	n.a.	3.5

Source: OECD data file on services statistics.

Table 6.2. **Annual average percentage change in low-skilled workers by service category, 1980-1990**

	Whole economy	Hotels, restaurants	Personal services	Social services
"Anglo" group	0.3	0.0	−0.6	4.8
Nordic group	−3.6	−4.5	−1.9	−1.5
Continental Europe	−1.6	1.8	−2.0	2.3
Japan	−2.6	−2.4	−3.0	−2.5

little firm evidence on the skills and human capacities required in services at the lower end of the spectrum. This lack notwithstanding, it is known that personal and social services, with their direct rapport between producer and client, demand very particular social and communicative skills. Possession of these skills is more likely to depend on childhood socialisation ("cultural capital") than on institutionalised training (Table 6.2).

Nowhere are unskilled workers enjoying a sellers' market, but the contrast between the "Anglo" low-wage economies and the rest is notable. The potential of labour-intensive social and personal services to furnish job growth may exist not only for low-skilled workers, but also for inexperienced new job-seekers. If so, this offers a counterweight to the prevailing pessimism that technology and globalisation necessarily erode less qualified jobs. Where such jobs do grow, it would also address a related dilemma. While it may be agreed that education and training strategies offer the single best long-term policy, there is still the immediate question of how to manage the skill deficit in the short-run.

This raises a final employment dilemma for discussion. The question of how to absorb an excess supply of low-qualified workers not only relates to unskilled adults. It also arises in relation to inexperienced first-time job seekers – even those with certificates of advanced learning – where there are burning issues to do with the passage from school to first jobs to careers. Previously, it was typical that young workers passed directly from school to a lifelong career. In the immediate post-World War II decades, the huge demand for low-qualified workers in the construction and mass production industries meant that countries were also able to absorb the masses of workers being shed from agriculture. The current equivalents – a large surplus of first-time job seekers combined with an excess stock of laid-off industrial workers – pose a particular problem if labour demand is limited to qualified personnel. (The problem of an excessive stock is especially acute in countries like Italy and, especially, Spain, where rural depopulation and de-industrialisation overlap.) The existence of a large number of easy-entry "lousy" jobs in low-level services is positive to the extent that they provide stop-gaps between school (or redundancy) and a career – a first foot inside the labour market for youth, returning women, or immigrants.[1]

We therefore return to the equality/jobs dilemma in a double sense. In order to generate mass employment opportunities, wages in low-level services should go down, but at the same time, to what extent can it be ensured that a low-wage strategy will not result in long-term or permanent entrapment in very poor jobs?[2] Addressing that question calls for examination of comparative trends of exclusion in both static and dynamic terms.

The emerging risk structure

The prevailing trends in inequality are reasonably familiar. Over the 1980s, the "Anglo" countries, led by the United States and the United Kingdom, have experienced a sharp rise in wage and household income inequalities, and poverty rates. While aggregate unemployment has fallen in the US and the UK, the dividends of a low-wage strategy are not unambiguously positive. Long-term unemployment remains high in Britain, and both Canada and Australia have high structural unemployment levels. In all cases, a significant price is being paid in terms of poverty and inequality. A worrying aspect of the new features of inequality/low-wage-employment/unemployment is that they hit young households disproportionately. On the other hand, Denmark and the Netherlands have succeeded in bringing unemployment down with no visible erosion of equality. In most other countries, inequalities have risen modestly (like Sweden), not at all, or have even declined (like Germany).

There is a strong cross-country correlation between earnings differentials and poverty rates (OECD, 1997a), but this correlation weakens in relation to post-social transfer household poverty rates. The "Anglo" countries generally exhibit a combination of worsening low-end wages with high household poverty. Most European countries have, through social transfers (as well as family absorption of unemployment), managed to contain household poverty despite worsening labour market conditions. Table 6.3 suggests that increasing wage inequalities do not necessarily diminish the relative job-disadvantage of weaker labour market groups, such as youth and low-skilled. In fact, despite more pervasive low pay, the United States has a pronounced unemployment bias towards youth and unskilled workers; vice versa, the low skilled do relatively well in Continental Europe, accounted for inter alia by employment protection practices.

The trend data in Table 6.4 tell a somewhat different story. Most countries have succeeded in lowering youth unemployment (with the notable exception of France and Sweden where overall unemployment has grown), but the low-skilled are clearly doing badly. Table 6.4 lends a measure of credence to the equality/jobs trade-off in the sense that unskilled unemployment grows more in high-wage, and

139|

Table 6.3. **Unemployment, low-wage employment, and poverty head-count indicators**

	Youth/adult unemployment ratio	Percentage of low-wage workers	Low-skilled/ all unemployment ratio	Poverty rate in young families
Australia	2.2	14	1.0	14
Canada	1.9	24	1.4	14
UK	2.1	21	1.4	25
US	2.8	26	2.1	27
Denmark	1.8	9	1.7	5
Sweden	2.2	5	0.9	3
Belgium	2.4	7	1.0	2
France	2.4	14	1.2	
Germany (Western)	1.0	13	1.7	7
Netherlands	2.0	14	1.2	10
Italy	3.7	12	1.1	

Note: Poverty is 50% of median equivalent income; low wage is less than ⅔ of median earnings.
Sources: OECD (1997a) and Luxembourg Income Study data files.

less in low-wage, countries.[3] That worsening labour market conditions affect young families in particular is evident from the rise in poverty rates, with the notable exception of the Nordic welfare states.

Thus, the relationship between wage inequality and unemployment is not straightforward: aggregate unemployment levels tend to be lower in the "de-regulated" economies, but at the price of more poverty. What complicates matters,

Table 6.4. **Trends in unemployment and poverty**

	Percentage change in youth unemployment, 1983-1994	Percentage change in low-skilled unemployment, 1980-94 (males)	Percentage change in poverty among young families
Australia	−9		+12
Canada	−16	+101	−2
UK	−18	+37	+80
US	−27	+24	+31
Denmark	−46	+90	−10
Sweden	+101	+220	−42
Belgium	−9		+4
France	+40	+150	+30
Germany	−25	+100	+120
Netherlands	−46		+31

Source: See Table 6.3.

however, is the question of who are the "losers". In Europe, the low skilled tend to be less disadvantaged than the young. But, as already noted, head-counts reveal little about marginalisation, exclusion and social cohesion. To what extent is there entrapment or cumulative under-privilege? There are two ways to examine this question: to identify the extent of systematic concentration of difficulties in households; to analyse flow or duration data. Both exercises suffer severe data limitation problems.

Beginning with duration and transitions, it can be expected that the longer the spells of unemployment or of low-paid employment, the more likely it is that people would find themselves in a downward spiral. Research shows that the probability of household poverty jumps sharply among the long-term unemployed. Poverty rates among the short-term unemployed in France, Germany and the United Kingdom were 17, 28, and 29%, respectively in 1994. Among those unemployed for longer than a year, the equivalent figures are 30, 48, and 64 (Nolan, Hauser and Zoyem, 2000).

Table 6.5 presents data on transition probabilities out of unemployment, poverty, and low pay for selected countries. There are three basic country patterns. In de-regulated, low-wage economies there is little entrapment in unemployment (except in the UK), but people are much more likely to be stuck in low-wage jobs and poverty. There is a relatively positive picture in continental Europe concerning entrapment in poverty but not for prolonged unemployment. The Nordic countries appear to have found a way to avoid the equality/jobs trade-off as they exhibit only modest rates of entrapment in either unemployment or poverty.[4]

Table 6.5. **Transitions and entrapment**

	Exit from unemployment (monthly outflows, 1993)	Average low-pay tenure (in years, 1986-91)	Exit from poverty (at t + 1)	Percentage poor continuously for three years or more
Canada	28		12	12
UK	9	3.8		
US	37	4.1	14	14
Denmark	21	1.8		
Sweden	18		37	
France	3	2.8	28	2
Germany	9	2.8	26	2
Italy	10	2.8		
Netherlands	6		44	1

Notes: Column 1 measures the percentage of unemployed no longer unemployed one month later. Column 3 shows the percentage who were poor in one year but left poverty the year after.
Sources: OECD (1997a), Duncan et al. (1993), and analysis on Danish registry-based panel data.

Different strategies thus produce different "B-class" clienteles. In continental Europe, unemployment is a likely avenue to long-term exclusion. It is very difficult to escape being poor/low-paid in America: the exit rates out of poverty are low and the chances of remaining in uninterrupted poverty in the United States are 5 times higher than in Europe (Burkhauser et al., 1995; Burkhauser and Poupore 1993).[5] For a large proportion of Americans, low-paid jobs are not stop-gaps but rather a state of permanency. Among the low-paid in 1986, only 38% managed to escape by 1991 (compared with 50-60% in Europe).[6]

Information on inter-generational transmission is even scarcer. Stratification research (Erikson and Goldthorpe, 1992; Shavit and Blossfeld, 1993) shows little change over time in the correlation between father and offspring social status (educational and occupational attainment). Even more surprising, perhaps, the correlation is also essentially similar across all countries. This picture is additionally confirmed in recent literacy studies (OECD, 1997b, Tables 3.8a, b, and c). Parents education level is in all countries powerfully associated with the measured cognitive competences of their offspring.

Moreover, British and American research indicates that inter-generational transmission of poverty is strong. Atkinson's (1975) follow-up of Rowntree families estimates that children of poor parents were 2.6 times as likely to be poor as other children. Corcoran (1995) shows that the children of poor American families have fewer years of schooling, earn at least one-third less, and are three times as likely also to end up poor. In contrast, Swedish data (Erikson and Aaberg, 1991) suggest that the link between parental and offspring poverty risks has weakened substantially In Swedish welfare policies, with the combination of promoting education and training and family income guarantees, it seems to make a decisive difference. Even with high aggregate unemployment, Denmark and Sweden have managed to minimise long-term unemployment, heavy youth exclusion, and entrapment in poverty.

Exclusion and social integration

Marginalisation is likely to harden when social deprivation accumulates within households. If low pay or unemployment "bundles" in couples, families or communities, individuals are more likely to become stuck in these situations as social networks weaken. Concentrated deprivation is likely to nurture and harden the sense of social failure. Thus, the meaning of unemployment depends critically on the setting in which it is experienced.

In a study for the European Community, we examined the relationship between unemployment, incomes and household situation among young, 20-30-year-old unemployed (Bison and Esping-Andersen, 1998). Poverty risks were low in Scandinavia, mainly because of generous welfare state support. But, they were also low in Mediterranean Europe, chiefly because almost all (91% in Italy) the unemployed continue to live with their parents. In Southern Europe, almost none of the unemployed live in a household without a principal earner. Where either the welfare state or the family is strong, in other words, there is little relation between being unemployed and being in poverty. This is not the case in countries where neither obtains, such as France and, especially, Britain. The log-odds ratio of being poor in France is 1.6 times that for Denmark; in Britain, it is 2.5 times. We also found that the unemployment/household-income nexus has a powerful effect on family formation. In family-oriented Italy, virtually no unemployed youth have formed families; in Denmark, more than 40% of unemployed youth already have children.

The tendency for unemployment to "bundle" in households also varies considerably across countries. Unemployed adult males are more likely to find themselves in a household with no other employed person in the United States (45%) and Austria (54%) than in Belgium (29%) or in the Nordic countries (around 35%). Cumulative unemployment within households implies not only declining human capital, but also the erosion of social capital. This may very well be a major source of entrapment and the inter-generational transmission of disadvantage. Indeed, it may be one of the mainsprings of the post-industrial proletariat.

Conclusions

The trends surveyed in this chapter suggest a difficult future of rising inequality and polarisation. It remains, however, difficult to predict who will be the main "losers", and the extent to which this will be permanent exclusion. Lack of education and skills is a growing handicap, certainly as far as providing a hedge against entrapment. But this conclusion is complicated by other variables. The low skilled are not everywhere the principal "B-team", and especially in Southern Europe their position is arguably stronger than youth or female first-job seekers. Might this be because jobs in Italy or Spain are less skills-driven than elsewhere? To a degree, perhaps.

Other factors no doubt play a part. One is the very strong employment protection enjoyed by the "insiders" who have jobs, whether low skilled or not. Another relates to the incentives of firms to hire young and female employees, even if, by and large, they boast superior educational attainment. Completed secondary school, or even a university education, does not translate into job skills. Where employers' training costs are high *and* where the public education system provides weak passages into the labour market, there a low-skill equilibrium might well become established. This is exacerbated by excessive stock (especially in Spain, Toharia, 1997), the strong protection of insiders, and possibly by strong family ties. The young unemployed in depressed Southern European regions, like

143|

the Mezzogiorno or Extramadura, are disinclined to move north because their reservation wage is equal to the value of living rent-free and in relative comfort at home.

The skill-employment nexus can be expressed in terms of relative prices. The over-representation of youth among the unemployed has declined in most countries – in recent years, the relative cost of training to employers has been lowered by public subsidy schemes (as in Italy where approximately 50-60% of all youth hires are in subsidised training contracts). An alternative is to lower relative wages: the de-regulation strategy. This boosts household demand for services and thus, indirectly, jobs, but it is unlikely to resolve problems of skill deficits unless public education already provides sufficient educational achievement across the board. This suggests that the de-regulation strategy can be potentially favourable only where the mass of "lousy" jobs are strictly stopgap rather than a source of entrapment. The latter is a real risk in the United States.

Finally, relative prices have an effect also on the long-term trend to the "tertiarisation" of jobs, especially for labour-intensive social and personal services. A "Baumol-type" cost problem can be countered through subsidies, whether direct public employment or consumer subsidies, but this may be offset by on-going changes in family behaviour. Hence, it cannot be assumed that low-skilled jobs will disappear, but it is reasonable to assume that such jobs will become traps unless those who occupy them at different times, are given access to mobility. For this to happen clearly means having access to skills. (Even unqualified service jobs often require a minimum of social skills, a factor probably favouring women and middle-class recruits, and telling against unemployed manual males.)

For policy makers, then, some of the trends usually interpreted as negative may contain an important positive side. A large reservoir of "lousy" jobs may well be one way of addressing the medium-range problem of what to do while waiting for a long-term education and training strategy to come to fruition.

Notes

1. Even regulated, high-wage economies in Europe are developing alternative "stop-gap" employment outlets, such as temporary contracts, black market, and self-employment. Whether or not "stop-gap" positions become chronic is another matter. Data for Spain paint a pessimistic picture, since less than 15% of fixed-term contracts eventually become permanent (Bentolila and Dolado, 1994).

2. The simple correlation between change in the skill-earnings gap and employment flows of low-skilled workers into personal services is $r = .495$. Regressing unskilled employment change in personal services on changes in the earnings gap yields an R-squared $= .245$ with an elasticity of $.079$ ($t = 2.29$). Thus, a 10-percentage-point rise in earnings differentials should raise the probability of unskilled employment in low-end services by 4.5 percentage points.

3. Logistic regressions for European countries indicate that low-educated men are dramatically more likely to be unemployed. The odds-ratio is 2.04 for Denmark, 3.44 for the Netherlands, 1.8 for Belgium, 2.7 for France, 3.4 for the UK, and 1.8 for Spain. The pattern is fairly similar for women. However, in some countries (Sweden, Italy, and Portugal), the less educated are no more likely to be unemployed than others.

4. Data on the employment situation of youth one year after completing school suggest a very similar pattern: between two-thirds and three-quarters have found employment in the UK, the US, Denmark, and Germany, while in Italy only 30% (53% in the Netherlands, 58% in Belgium and France).

5. Stevens (1995) shows that poor American whites who were poor in any given year have a 30% chance of remaining poor in 5 out of the next 10 years; for blacks, the chance jumps to 50%.

6. In a comparative study of occupational mobility among the unskilled, we found that entrapment in unskilled jobs was very strong in Germany, significant in the United States and the UK, but rather less so in Scandinavia. Our explanation for such international differences centres on systems of education and adult training. Thus, Germany's accent on vocational training leads to high overall qualification levels, but for those without the opportunities for mobility are *de facto* foreclosed. In contrast, Denmark and Sweden's accent on continuous education provides a "second chance" (Esping-Andersen, 1993; Esping-Andersen, Rohwer and Sorensen, 1994).

Chapter 7
21st Century Transitions: Opportunities, Risks and Strategies for Governments and Schools

by

Riel Miller
OECD Secretariat*

Introduction

Major socio-economic transitions are surges of change when, from one generation to the next, the work that people do, where they live and what they expect, are no longer the same. Is the world entering such a transition period? Will daily life by the third decade of the 21st century seem radically different for large parts of the world's population when compared with the last decades of the 20th century?

On all counts, the striking answer to this question is "yes". According to the findings of the OECD International Futures Programme (IFP) conference series on 21st Century Transitions the seeds of change are in place (OECD, 1998, 1999*b*, 2000*c*, 2001). However, turning these seeds of change into the socio-economic reality of the 21st century poses a dual challenge. First, creating the conditions that nurture far reaching transformation requires a wide range of distinct yet interdependent changes. Second, as the IFP's analysis underscores, a concerted effort will be required to bring the unfolding reality of 21st century transitions into line with people's ideas of what is desirable. In both areas governments have a strategic role to play in putting the pieces of the puzzle together.

This chapter has three parts. First, it offers a succinct overview of some of the key results of the conference series by sketching the nature of the opportunities and risks that might arise should 21st century transitions prevail. Second, it indicates the kinds of policies needed in order to nurture change on this scale and to stimulate desired outcomes. Finally, as a specific example of mapping strategic directions

---

* The OECD International Futures Programme. This is under the direct auspices of the Secretary-General, identifies and evaluates newly emerging issues, promotes strategic thinking, tests new ideas, and stimulates dialogue between government, business and research on long-term policy-relevant topics.

for government policies, it examines the relationship between compulsory schooling and 21st century transitions in advanced OECD countries.

The opportunities and risks of 21st century transitions

Opportunities

Technology: 21st century transitions have the potential to usher in pervasive technological advances on a par with those of previous periods like the steam engine, electricity and the automobile. Information technology could advance to the point where the result is seamless, global knowledge-sharing, be it about buyers, sellers, communities of interest, or culture. Some confidently expect computers using a range of sensory input and output devices, all-pervasive network connectivity, massive databases, and so-called "intelligent agent" software, to be deployed in ways that transform when, where and how people work, play and so forth.

Biotechnology could provide powerful new tools both for fighting diseases in all parts of the world and for reducing the ecological footprint of many industries including agriculture and food processing. Developing technologies for new materials and design for sectors like construction, manufacturing, and transportation could dramatically improve a range of efficiencies as well as the usefulness of many types of products – from buildings and vehicles to clothing and utensils.

Economy: A confluence of economic changes could spark a sustained period of above-average productivity growth to power 21st century transitions worldwide. Three broad developments open up tremendous potential for advancing overall well-being. First, the shift to a knowledge-intensive economy could boost productivity by transforming the organisation and methods of production and consumption. The particularly important dimension of this shift for advanced OECD countries is the prospect that the distinction between supply and demand sides of the economy will begin to blur. This would occur as consumers enter much more directly and actively into the initial part of the production process before the output is actually created.

Second, much deeper global integration could induce a virtuous circle of investment and growth as knowledge, capital, and trade flow freely. Here the evolution of planet-wide networks plays a crucial part in helping people co-operate and compete, experiment and learn. Third, and perhaps most challenging, a transformation in humanity's relationship to the environment could give rise to an investment boom in more ecological products and ways of living as well as more efficient energy and transportation infrastructures. Such an environmental agenda could dovetail quite effectively with the macro- and micro-level changes involved in moving towards a globally integrated knowledge economy and society.

Society: Growing diversity in the social fabric could well be one of the hallmarks of 21st century transitions. This trend is likely to be pushed along by changes in demographic structure, shifting income distributions, migration, and the erosion of traditional cultural reference points. Certain trends can already be identified as evidence of such social change, where heterogeneity of social structures match diversity in the economic, technological and educational spheres. A multitude of consumer, leisure and cultural choices are now available on a scale that would have been unimaginable even only fifty years ago.

The transition can be expected to induce major alterations – across the globe and starting from a wide range of departure points – in two of the key determinants of self-identity: social status (income, age, profession, etc.) and authority structures (nation, family, religion, etc.). Greater differentiation might in turn open up opportunities for diversity to fuel the creativity needed to make the most of new technologies, economic change, and social transformation.

Governance: Old forms of governance, in both the public and private sectors, are becoming increasingly ineffective. 21st century transitions are likely to involve new forms of governance that break decisively with two of the primary attributes of today's governance systems. These are the fixed, often permanent allocations of power embedded in the structures and constitutions of many organisations, and the tendency to vest initiative primarily in the hands of those in hierarchically senior positions. New departures in governance are, in turn, likely to be fundamental both for revitalising democracy and for reaping the positive potential of technological, economic and social change.

These changes will call for major advances in the practical skills and rules used in daily life by organisations and individuals, whether operating alone or in concert, locally or globally. The challenge for policy, in both the public and private sectors, is to ensure that people will have the capacity to exercise their liberty and to manage the constraints.

Risks

Technology: Leaps in the capacity and diffusion of new technologies always come with the risks of transition difficulties, misuse, and harmful unintended consequences. Some worry about the capacity, technologically and socially, to continue advancing and inventing new tools, products, and organisational forms for everyday work and home life. Others worry that the on-going transition costs may be too high, or that the risks to cherished traditions (including privacy) or the threats to environmental sustainability will – singly or together – be too great to bear.

Three specific dangers stand out. First, people worry about losing control of tomorrow's "intelligent" machines and genetically engineered life forms. Second, there are fears that radically new tools and products will exacerbate the schisms between haves and have-nots, risk-takers and risk-avoiders. Third, there is real concern that the benefits of technological advances will fail to materialise because the

149]

economic and social changes that shape and diffuse positive technical development will not occur.

Economy: Long booms depend on a constellation of factors coming together. If one or two of the pieces, like deeper global integration or progress in controlling ecological costs, fail to materialise, then the long-boom could turn into an extended period of stagnation or decline. Without above-average productivity gains to encourage technological, economic and social dynamism, there is a high risk that 21st century transitions will not take place. This, in turn, heightens the risk that there will not be adequate resources to address pressing socio-economic needs or to find the effective "win-win" solutions for destructive conflicts.

Constraints such as limited access to easy-to-use "appropriate technology" and out-dated methods for creating, assessing and valorising human capital threaten to slow change or render it too shallow. If advances towards the intangible economy's radically new organisational patterns of production, consumption and human settlement remain modest, it will also be harder to find ways to provide the compensation needed to overcome people's fear of both unfamiliar technology and the prospect of disruption to existing economic and social structures. Similarly, the rapid and much fuller integration of markets required for a long boom is unlikely to be politically feasible without mechanisms for compensating losers and guaranteeing minimum standards.

Society: A number of major risks arise in the context of increasing social diversity. There comes a point at which positive difference and diversity becomes negative inequality and segregation. There are thus risks of unacceptable inequality especially in the distribution of income, wealth and health. Similar concerns arise about too many individuals having access to only very low absolute levels of resources, as well as issues to do with personal security and human rights.

Three specific risks can be singled out. One is that changes on the scale provoked by 21st century transitions are highly likely to exacerbate old, while provoking new, social conflicts. A second is that people and institutions will not acquire the capacities needed to turn greater diversity into a source of creative solutions to tomorrow's challenges. Third, there is a risk that the backlashes sparked by greater diversity will triumph, imposing the uniformity espoused by, for instance intolerant forms of nationalism or religious fundamentalism. Without diversity as a wellspring for the everyday creativity and inventiveness upon which dynamism depends, there seems little chance of reaping the benefits of 21st century transitions.

Governance: The governance risks facing 21st century transitions would arise especially as institutional inertia and resistance by entrenched interests generate considerable conflict and potentially stifle efforts to transform old methods and invent new ones. Transition periods often give rise to deep-seated differences in the perception of risk and insecurity. Typically, those who are not actively creating he new rules and power structures tend to perceive major changes as driven by external and dangerous forces, which can in turn lead to the backlash from diversity and democracy mentioned above.

All of this would increase the risk that society-wide decision-making capacities – ranging from individuals and households to enterprises and legislatures – could end up being inadequate to the governance challenges entailed by desirable 21st century transitions.

Government policies for encouraging desirable 21st century transitions

Plausibility is not the same as inevitability nor is it desirability. Nurturing the seeds of 21st century transitions, reaping the benefits, and minimising the risks will call for strong policy leadership by governments at all levels across the world. A strategic path for facilitating transitions needs to take advantage of the interdependence and potential for synergy across technological, economic, social, and governance changes. The specific policies can be grouped into one of three categories: first, those policies that represent a continuation of existing approaches, second, policies of significant reform to facilitate fundamental change, and third, initiatives that break entirely new ground.

Continuity: There are a number of key policy areas where continuity with existing approaches will be important. Macroeconomic balances will need to be maintained to guard against inflation and excessive public deficits; so will improvements in the functioning of product, labour and capital markets need to continue through policies that promote the greater transparency and competition that structural adjustment requires. The scope of government regulation, taxation and spending will continue to be a matter of continual review, with approaches and methods refined. Similarly, international guidelines and frameworks will as now be the subject of continuing scrutiny and action, dealing with such issues as corruption, corporate governance, consumer protection, financial transparency, and the monitoring of global threats to health and security. Existing agreements that foster worldwide integration will need to be implemented and extended. These include multi-lateral treaties on trade and investment as well as other cornerstones of globalisation such as the 1948 Universal Declaration of Human Rights and the more recent Kyoto Protocol on greenhouse gases.

Reform: There will be other policy areas calling for considerable re-thinking of the methods and programmes currently in place, such as in social and educational services. Established government programmes were designed for the industrial era when the majority of people experienced similar life-patterns – starting with initial schooling, then steady employment, and lastly retirement at the same fixed age. New approaches to lifelong learning will need to embrace a much wider range of sources for acquiring knowledge and incentive systems for encouraging people to

151

learn on a continuous basis. Social support systems will need to encourage risk-taking and experimentation without creating dependency and dead-ends. In general, there will need to be a shift away from the direct provision of mass, uniform public sector services to much more diversified, decentralised and demand-driven approaches.

Breakthroughs: Entirely new points of departure will be required in order significantly to improve the capacity of all segments of society, including enterprises and local communities, to break with the rigid, hierarchical methods of the past. There will need to be new ways of doing things that stress personal accountability, internal motivation, and uniqueness. Policy breakthroughs will also be needed in order to address adequately the tensions arising from the asymmetry between, on the one hand, the relatively rapid spread of global markets and, on the other, the slow development in essential legal, institutional and cultural infrastructure.

Specific areas for breakthrough include the development of appropriate rules and institutions at national and global levels for ensuring privacy, granting ownership to intangible property, open knowledge sharing, reaping network externalities, and setting a wide range of new technical, economic and social standards. Establishing legitimate and effective global approaches to decision making and implementation will have important implications for addressing planet-wide challenges such as climate change, maintaining competitive markets and finding ways for the winners from global change to compensate the losers.

The implications of 21st century transitions for schools in OECD countries

Universal compulsory schooling, the basic education system of most countries, provides a useful example of what it might mean to pursue policies aimed at encouraging 21st century transitions. Born in and bred to the requirements and practices of the industrial era, schools of the 21st century may be situated in a very different context. For instance, the full shift to a highly integrated global knowledge economy and society seems likely to entail significant revisions in the goals, role, and methods of schools, certainly for the advanced OECD countries.

Three figures illustrate how the broad socio-economic context for schools might change. Figure 7.1 depicts how the transition to a learning society, that some detect in existing trends, might mean to move away from the mass-era ways of forging identity and making decisions. For much of the 20th century, people tended to belong to large, clearly defined groupings with fairly clear moral, political and behavioural codes. National, class and religious identities were clearly articulated and widely shared, in good measure because of schools' influence.

In the 21st century, socialisation is likely to remain one of the main goals for compulsory schooling. The emergence of a learning society, however, suggests significant changes in the context, and hence the content, of socialisation. The new goal is to equip children for a world where their sense of identity is derived from a diverse set

Figure 7.1. **Changing goals – A new context for socialisation**

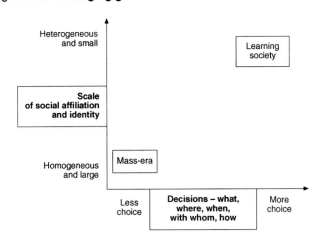

of specific rather than general communities, and facing a vast range of active, self-generated, rather than passive, choices. This is radically different from the mass era, which put a premium on norms of national allegiance, common culture and obedience to hierarchical discipline.

A learning society also implies a major break with mass-era schools as the main recognised source of what people know. In most OECD countries during the 20th century, a certificate or diploma indicating completion of compulsory schooling was a sufficiently precise way of indicating a person's basic competences, both behavioural and cognitive. A learning society demands a major change in this role (see Figure 7.2).

This is for two main reasons. First, in a context where all learning must be developed and used regardless of the nature of its acquisition, there needs to be formal recognition of all sources of "education". This applies to the lessons learned on the street and shop floor or the experiences of failure or success in a start-up enterprise, as well as what was learned in the traditional academic halls. Second, it will be essential in a learning economy to take advantage of people's precise competences in order to create a supply-side network capable of responding to active consumers. These consumers want to co-produce products that meet their personal desires instead of passively choosing from what is on offer.

In this context, the role of schools as both source and signaller of learning, the officially-sanctioned institution at the centre of Figure 7.2, is not just inadequate; indeed, such a monopoly is inimical to the recognition and use of all the learning taking place in society. The existing educational establishment is faced with substantial conflicts of interest when it comes to recognising learning that was neither

153|

Figure 7.2. **Changing role – Where people learn and how what they know is made transparent**

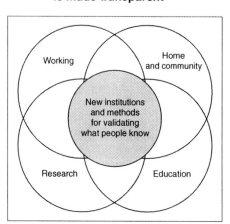

acquired within its walls nor corresponds to its *a priori* method for specifying certifi cation. New institutions and methods for validating what people know, without a vested interest in any specific form of learning or type of credential, would be more effective in creating the transparency, trust, and incentives that are needed for a learning economy and society.

Finally, Figure 7.3 suggests why traditional teaching methods may no longer be consistent with the goals and roles of schools in the 21st century learning society.

Figure 7.3. **Changing methods – Toward learning to learn and learning by doing**

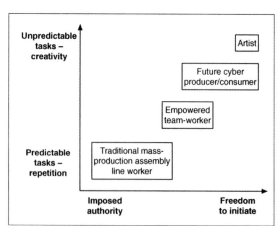

Without entering in detail into how people learn – a research area that is only now beginning to attract funding commensurate with its importance – there is a clear sense that the teaching methods of the traditional classroom were not designed with tomorrow's cyber producer/consumer in mind. Book, rote, and "chalk and talk" learning certainly have a place, but much less when the key is learning to learn to enable people to thrive in a creative, diverse, and changing networked world. The even older method of "learning by doing", if theory and practice can be satisfactorily combined, may turn out to be more appropriate to the 21st century. For schools, this could mean a wrenching change away from the efficient but passive classrooms of the industrial era to new modes of engaging the minds of students of all ages.

Conclusion

Pursuing this strategic path implies an important convergence of government policy goals towards the encouragement of liberty, diversity, and responsibility – a broadly conceived agenda for 21st century transitions. Convergence of the general policy goals will also be needed if the public sphere is to attain the requisite degrees of transparency, accountability and integrity. The specific policy frameworks and particular methods of implementation, however, will certainly vary widely throughout the world. The starting points for change are highly diverse and, crucially, aspirations differ. Combining the plausible with the desirable is perhaps the biggest challenge posed by 21st century transitions.

Chapter 8

The Driving Forces for Schooling Tomorrow: Insights from Studies in Four Countries

by

Hans F. van Aalst[1]
Netherlands and Consultant to OECD/CERI

Introduction

This chapter examines four studies from different countries and continents conducted at the end of the 20th century looking at major societal trends or "driving forces" identified as influencing schooling for the 21st century. Each was conducted as part of a major initiative looking to ensure that schooling is more strategically informed about major long-term developments; hence, they have a focus squarely on education, rather than on social or economic change *per se*. They provide a valuable insight into what education analysts and policy advisers from different countries have identified as the key forces to impact on education over at least the next couple of decades. These are not only forces "external" to schooling as the studies have, in differing degrees, also surveyed major trends within education itself.

With this long-term focus, the studies have addressed fundamental developments and issues more than is often possible in the relatively short cycles of political life – a great deal of attention, for instance, is given across the studies to values and ethical choices. The studies vary in the extent to which they arrive, through their consideration of driving forces, at the identification of clear future directions for schools to take. All support the view, however, that attention to driving forces can make a valuable contribution to the making of educational policies, though it remains an open question as to far they do in fact shape contemporary decisions.

The countries from which these studies have been chosen – Canada (Ontario), Germany (North-Rhine-Westphalia), Japan, and the Netherlands – while necessarily selective, provide insights from different continents and cultures. The paper is based on those reports that were available at the time of writing (end 1997/

early 1998). Of course, much has happened since then, both in terms of comple
tion and follow-up of the studies reviewed and in terms of new studies bein
launched. Parallel studies in other countries might equally have been included
The exercise could not be to compile an up-to-date review of education future
studies across OECD countries. Rather, it was to select some major initiative
launched before OECD/CERI began its own work on "Schooling for Tomorrow" each
with a strong long-term future perspective. Attention is given particularly to the
key driving forces identified as impacting on schools, their perceived educationa
implications and the methodological issues that arise about how these might help
to inform the policy process. Which aspects of these studies have been emphasised
in this chapter is also necessarily selective.[2]

Canada (Ontario): "For the Love of Learning"

The "For the Love of Learning" study was a public inquiry undertaken
between 1993 and 1994 to report on the key themes of shared vision, programme
aims and organisation, accountability and governance for schools in Ontario. It was
undertaken by a commission of five members (Ontario Royal Commission on
Learning, 1994). They worked with a staff and support, took extensive soundings
held hearings, and commissioned background papers. Their remit was defined b
the need to set new directions in education and to ensure that Ontario youth are
prepared for the challenges of the 21st century, in support of government commit
ments to economic renewal and social justice. The commission was concerned
about how to effect appropriate accountability and openness, while raising stan
dards and introducing relevant curriculum contents, improved retention, and better
links to work and higher education.

Driving forces

Changing economy and welfare: The service sector in Ontario has grown signifi
cantly, much of it in part-time work. The greatest potential for further growth i
either in well-paying professional occupations requiring relatively few people with
high levels of education, at one end of the spectrum, or in poorly paid service
occupations employing large numbers of people and calling for low levels of edu
cation, at the other. There has been a disturbing decline in the economic well
being of families headed by people under the age of 35, with growing numbers o
school-age children impoverished: "of all the economic problems that affect the
school system, none has a greater impact than poverty".

Families, values and society: Yet also, many more children live in two-income fam
ilies even than a couple of decades ago. The needs of today's working parents are
pushing schools to expand their role, either alone or in partnership with commu
nity groups. Families are getting smaller as the fertility rate declines. At the same

time, immigration has increased so that families are more likely to come from other countries and cultures. At the beginning of the 1990s, almost 40% of those living in Metropolitan Toronto were born outside Canada. The physical and ethnic diversity of young people challenges former certainties, as do the extensive changes taking place in the structure of the family itself.

In post-industrial society, consensus about moral values and education's proper role in this domain becomes frayed. At the same time, there is a greater sense of uncertainty and relativity. Many supposedly common values no longer enjoy clear support, and their key bases – especially religion and the family – tend to be devalued. Uncertainty is exacerbated by the sheer quantity of new information: "when the amount of new information doubles every 20 minutes or two years, or whatever, the criteria for being a literate or knowledgeable citizen are not self-evident".

Young people: School can be likened to a part-time job, with other parts of the lives of young people being as or more influential. Far more young people hold jobs, and work longer hours at them, than before. More express anxiety about their future job prospects than even a few years before. Youth culture has a variety and complexity that few adults fully grasp.

Young people as such may not have changed, but the world in which they operate has and their lives are more complicated today than in the past. The deadly threat of AIDS hangs over active sexuality, in addition to the traditional fears of unwanted pregnancies. Many young people are confronted with an array of problems generally beyond their control (poverty, racism, drugs, violent foreign conflicts, etc.). Unprecedented numbers of children have serious problems in their home lives.

The challenge of reforming schools

There is no serious evidence that schools are failing young people any more than before. Ontario schools are judged to be doing a reasonable, but not outstanding, job, and they need to improve to meet the challenges that now confront them. There is widespread unease, however, that schools have become kingdoms unto themselves, inadequately reporting their achievements to parents or to the world at large. More remains to be done for those whom the education system treats unfairly. Girls still confront obstacles that boys largely miss. Black, Portuguese, and Hispanic students have disproportionate difficulties, while the rural and remote smaller communities do not get their fair share of education funds.

The need for profound changes in the learning system is primarily because society has changed so dramatically in recent times – technologically, socially, economically, demographically. Schools cannot keep up, carry impossible burdens, and are ill equipped to deal with the future. At the same time, attempts to reform the

159|

system carry on apace, yet often little seems to change. It is very difficult to change massive, complicated and complex systems with strong vested interests.

There are powerful players in the education system. Some of these are obvious while equally powerful others are less familiar. The commission encountered an unexpected lack of consensus on nearly every aspect of education: people disagree about what constitute the major problems and about possible solutions. Too many continue to see panaceas in terms of their own particular approach. Too many attempts at reform ignore the role of teachers; insufficient attention is paid to the inequalities that are caused by social and family background in determining a child's school success; too few players in the system demonstrate the flexibility needed for real change to occur.

Despite the limits of reform, the commission took an optimistic view about the possibility as well as desirability for change. All players must be committed to a process of radical change if it has a real chance of success. This requires tapping into the common hopes and desires that run deep beneath the surface of the apparently conflicting positions, to reconcile the best ideas and interests of all stakeholders without ignoring the interests of any of them.

Aims and recommendations

Schools cannot do everything: On the contrary, they must concentrate mainly on what they are better equipped to do than the rest of society, and leave certain tasks to others who are in a position to tackle them. First and foremost, their purpose must be to ensure for all students – whatever their future jobs or careers – high levels of "literacy", building on basic reading, writing, and problem-solving skills, as well as good and deepening understanding across a variety of subject areas as schooling progresses. Various curriculum recommendations are made, including a strong plea for the improvement of mathematics and science teaching.

All parts of the learning system need to be assessed more frequently and usefully: Both students and teachers, so that individual teaching and learning, as well as the system as a whole, can be continuously improved. Hence the commission recommended the systematic monitoring of progress, while warning against reductionist oversimplification of the testing process. In addition, every student should also have a teacher who acts as personal tutor over a long-term period and a Cumulative Educational Plan is proposed with schools maintaining contact with students until 18 years of age. More information needs to be made available to parents and the public about what is taught and learned.

Schools must be part of a new, co-ordinated focus on socialisation: They should help prepare students to become responsible citizens and facilitate their move from adolescence to adulthood, schooling to employment. Every school must promote the development of basic moral values, such as a sense of caring and compassion respect for the human person and anti-racism, a commitment to peace, honesty, and justice. There is support for the value of smaller schools, and of smaller units within schools.

Home and school: Learning begins at birth with children's first teachers – their parents. Especially for children without parents, or without families who involve themselves in their children's education, the importance of early childhood programmes can scarcely be overstated. After this period, and throughout schooling, parents must be welcomed and given advice about how to support their children's learning. There is need for increased knowledge and communication in both directions between home and school, and the community role is also critical.

A major theme of the report is the need for *clarified roles and responsibilities*: Greater authority for the ministry, more influence for students and teachers in how schools are run, more precise responsibilities for boards, and a greater role for principals, parents, and the community. It suggests the need for an equal basis of per-pupil funding, supplemented by additional resources for some school boards on equity grounds.

Key intervention strategies

Even major reforms in these areas of education are unlikely to go far enough in turning around the entire system. Four key intervention strategies are suggested as "engines of transformation". First, it suggests a *new alliance between the school and its community*. Specific directions include making schools the physical centres of networks of many local organisations; creating school-community councils; enhanced co-ordination between the many ministry and social service agencies; differentiated staffing in schools; and the use of community experts in teaching.

Second, a strong priority is given to *early childhood education*, partly based on the research evidence on its effectiveness in combating disadvantage. Full-time schooling should be available if desired for every child from age 3; more systematic and effective attention to early literacy in grades 1 and 2; a standard test of basic literacy for every pupil at the end of grade 3.

The third "engine of transformation" is the *professionalism and continuing development of teachers*. No serious improvements can take place without the enthusiastic involvement of teachers. On-going professional learning, both formal and informal, must become a normal, integral part of teaching careers and should thus be made mandatory. The commission also proposed the regular mandatory evaluation of teachers' performance, as well as the establishment of a new professional body overseeing entry, practice and teacher education programmes.

The use of computers and related technology: Students and teachers would be more receptive to the entire learning process if that were more organised around ICT. The new technologies have the potential to offer qualitative change in the nature of learning. They permit a greater individualisation of the teaching process and can be used for assessing student's performance. ICT can also be exploited in support of teacher networks and to give parents access to information about their children's schooling. Thus, an adequate supply of hardware and software should be ensured to every school, with quality educational software geared to and based on Canadian realities and culture.

Germany (North-Rhine-Westphalia): "The future of education, schools of the future"

This study was initiated at the request of the Premier of North-Rhine-Westphalia to engage a public debate on the future of schooling and to underline education's priority politically in a time of enormous change (Denkschrift der Bildungskommission, North-Rhine-Westphalia, 1995). The main work was conducted by a committee of 22 experts from North-Rhine-Westphalia, and elsewhere in Germany and in Europe. It was carried out between 1992 and 1995, and involved different sub-groups and a series of reports. The group was given scope to develop the issues it felt important in addressing fundamental questions. What changes, cultural developments and value-orientations are needed by education in the future? What are the consequences of international developments for education? Intercultural contacts? The environment? What do young people need to help build social democracy in a responsible and open way?

Driving forces

Changes in society, demography and the world of the young

The key changes in society identified by this initiative focused on lifestyles and the increasingly pluralistic forms of social interactions; changes in values; new technologies and media; environmental issues; migration and demographic changes.

Despite increasing pluralism, the foundations of multiculturalism are still uncertain in some parts of the society. World development challenges call for new forms of internationalism. Changing gender roles demand new orientations. Demographic changes are also important: children are becoming a smaller part of the population, the size of working-age cohorts will also fall in decades to come while numbers of older people continue to grow. Families are getting smaller and taking more diverse forms.

There are growing tensions. As the importance of social action grows so the room to exercise such action seems to shrink. High levels of affection within families accompany growing rates of family break-up. The cultures in evidence in families, peer groups and schools seem at odds with the cultures of business, work and politics.

Relations between children and adults have changed, and are now often based on negotiation. The influence of the family, the school and other pedagogical institutions on the orientations of youngsters appears to have lessened. Peer groups are important for self-image from an increasingly younger age. While providing social bonds, there is also a strong competition between different peer group pressures. Children are losing their spaces for play and action, especially in cities; they organise their own, often isolated, activities. The media exercise a strong influence on the socialisation of children, with both negative and positive implications.

Economic change renders the "market value" of school qualifications less certain and conventional career patterns increasingly break down. Despite this, young people still attach a high priority to school attainment and qualifications in their thinking about the future. Whether professionally or in other senses, the transition from youth to adulthood is less clear. Sexual activity begins earlier, family and career formation later, so that young people live in the two worlds of youth and adulthood for longer. There are difficulties with orientation, insecurity and psychological unease, calling for the more accomplished exercise of self-management. The disparities between children in their capacity to manage these tensions are growing.

Changes in work and business

The restructuring of the economy from "old" industries towards "new" ones, such as the media, environmental technology and fashion, is longstanding and continues apace. The growth of services is a very strong trend and this is where new employment is found. More important even than the shifts between sectors are the changes within sectors and firms. The desired characteristics include flexible specialisation, high quality, rapid reaction to market changes, reliable delivery and service, innovation and marketing. New technologies will be part of most if not all work. Fluency in the use of technologies will be as basic as reading, writing and calculus. Future problems will lie less with the operation of new technologies, however, than in understanding, navigating and managing highly complex application systems.

Positions corresponding to longstanding job-descriptions are disappearing, and will be replaced by flexible combinations of people with different skills. Communications with clients and suppliers become increasingly important. Established boundaries between the self-employed and employed blur; tele-work and diverse forms of "time on work" grow. Part-time working will increase, but as it is currently concentrated in lower qualification areas that carry greater risks of social security and employment, altogether insecurity increases.

163|

There will be plentiful chances for the well qualified but not all can be assured high salaries. Alongside, the risk is clear of a growing group of the less qualified, constantly vulnerable to unemployment. While an increase of the general level of qualifications is desirable, this should not mean that those with lower qualifications face quasi-permanent exclusion.

Over the next two or three decades, the numbers of working people will remain approximately constant, assuming the continuing entry of women and immigrants into the labour force. Even with optimistic economic growth rates, the unemployment rate is expected to remain high. Lack of vocational qualifications will remain powerfully correlated with unemployment.

Jobs and vocations will change several times during the lifetime. Against around 50 000 hours of professional work stand around 75 000 hours of non-vocational work (home keeping, voluntary work, etc). The relatively weak trend to better integrate the two in terms of payment and social security will continue. There is some evidence of a trend for people to identify increasingly with their work, as their source of creativity and motivation.

Aims and recommendations

The purposes of education and lifelong learning

One of the most important goals of education is to promote in individuals the capacity to judge and act in a socially responsible way. Involvement in decision-making and the assumption of responsibility should thus be characteristic of the daily practice of schools. Individuals must be able to participate in the changes in work and business and to innovate. General education has tended not to connect early enough with working life. Nor have entrepreneurship and the development of work-relevant competences been accorded sufficient priority. At the same time the future lives of current students will for most include at least some time outside a paid job.

In fact, the competences for modern work practices overlap substantially with those needed in other spheres of life: capacity to learn; concentration; logical-analytical thinking; ability to handle complexity; organisational, communication and teamwork competence; problem-solving skills. Students should understand that continuous learning is now integral to all aspects of life and develop the motivation for this. Initial education should concentrate on a robust base of knowledge characterised by highly integrated subject content, with an emphasis on key qualifications, and competence to learn and work. Schools should provide experience with "learning on demand" and "distance learning".

Lifelong learning is not just a feature of the world of work but is at the core of the democratisation of education. Each should develop his/her own learning plan.

At least in upper secondary education and beyond, comparable qualifications should be able to be gained in different settings. Good information is critical in order to access a wider array of learning settings, and the role of "coaches" and "brokers" could usefully be much further developed. The media offer diverse possibilities for differentiated and creative learning – for work, schooling, and for private purposes. "Information overload" means that schools need to sharpen the abilities to judge, value, and use information.

School reform, accountability, autonomy

So far, educational reform has not fundamentally changed what goes on in schools. Only latterly has it become clear the extent of the social change that impacts strongly on schooling, meaning that tinkering with traditional models of education and schools does not promise success. There is increasing tension between these models and the challenges schools are confronting on a daily basis. The tradition of explicit, closed principles, systems and planning should be replaced by approaches that allow for local development in orientations and policy design and development. As change is needed at all levels and as this is a step-wise process, rather than the implementation of a clear-cut model, it must take time.

How schools are organised makes a considerable difference to the education children receive. There is, however, no consensus on a one-best organisational structure, hence organisation should be decided at the level of the (regional) community. Society demands increasingly flexible, locally-sensitive arrangements, a demand reinforced by recognition of the value of business management concepts such as corporate identity, lean production, flexible teams, learning organisations, etc. State regulation should be minimal, and concentrate on basic aims and structures, financial and legal framing conditions, and the quality of outcomes. An intelligent system of quality assurance is needed, with both internal and external evaluation. The inspectorate should be reorganised around the central purpose of quality improvement.

The individual school is seen as the focus of educational policies. It should be an independent, autonomous unit, and promote social responsibility in its learners (students, but also teachers and other staff). Schools should have the major responsibility for planning, evaluation, development and accountability. Autonomy means not only a reassessment of the school/system relationships, but of those with local stakeholders as well.

Life inside schools and the curriculum

The school should be a learning institution, for both teachers and students – "a place to learn and live". The transfer of knowledge and the development of

165|

© OECD 2001

identity and social experiences should be more closely aligned. Social learning should be fostered, as should applications in relation to biographic, historical and environmental experiences. The basic competence of learning to learn can only be gained through concrete and meaningful exercises.

General and vocational education should be equally valued, and subjects and integrated learning should both have a full place in the school curriculum. These should be ordered around four key elements: i) "Dimensions", reflecting basic perspectives from which individuals experience the world; ii) "Key problems": questions and conflicts that students encounter in daily life; iii) "Key skills": self-managed learning, flexibility, communication competence and team-work, creative thinking, etc.; iv) "Cultural competences" (Kulturtechniken): forms of work, reading and writing, accessing information, understanding different disciplines and the complex connections of knowledge with concrete situations. Time for learning and time in schools are scarce, and schools and students must exercise control over how learning time is organised. Not more than 60% of time should be devoted to the core curriculum.

Schools should play a more prominent part in helping children to operate in a diversity of social settings, and learning and living should more closely connect. A sense of social and educational stability within the school is important for children's healthy development. There should be a clear sensitivity to gender issues. Health education should be part of school life, and schools should be active in combating violence, racism and drug abuse, even though they cannot be expected to solve these problems.

Japan: "The model for Japanese education in the perspective of the 21st century"

This section reports an initiative set up through ministerial request to the Japanese Central Council for Education, and conducted between 1995 and 1996 (Central Council for Education, 1996). The Council is an advisory body on strategies for education reforms. The initiative was conducted through a complex process of sub-committee work, consultation and discussion. The spur to the initiative was the great changes being experienced by Japanese society – internationalisation, the information revolution, advances in science and technology, the ageing society, economic restructuring. The questions are then about the responsiveness of existing educational arrangements to this change and the aims for schools in the future. In particular, there is need to reflect on the place of creativity and personal growth, recognising the fundamental importance of the development of each individual child. There are also urgent contemporary issues to address, such as excessive competitiveness in the examination system, bullying, and school refusal.

Driving forces and implications for schooling

Children's lives in Japan

Children today live in an atmosphere of material affluence and convenience, but leading very busy lives with lack of "room to grow". A significant amount of time is taken up by school life and by study at home or in *juku* (private "cramming" classes). There is a marked increase in the amount of time spent in virtual experiences. This leaves insufficient time for direct or natural living experience and precious little for household tasks. The age when independence is attained is being delayed. Physically, there has been a noticeable improvement over the years in children's agility, but a general decline in other areas – the ability to react quickly, muscular strength, endurance. With the rapid decline of the birth rate, young people in Japan are living in an increasingly ageing society.

There is a worrying lack of social experiences, and the ability of children to form relationships is weakening. Bullying and refusal to attend school are increasing, with public concern over dramatic cases involving suicide, violence, etc. One cause of these problems is seen to be inadequate consideration of individuality and mutual differences as Japan is a "society bound by homogeneity". There are thus major problems of ethics and values to be confronted. At the same time, there is somewhat contrasting evidence: children have a positive international attitude; they express a strong desire to contribute to society through participatory activities; a large number still reports school life to be enjoyable, though with a tendency for this to decrease at the higher schooling levels.

The curriculum implications are that there should be less subject matter to cover, while giving young people "room to grow". The core curriculum should be focused only on fundamentals: Japanese language, Japanese culture and respect for foreign cultures, foreign languages, logical and scientific thinking, significance of family and social life, sensitivity toward art, consideration for the needs of others. School activities should be diversified, with a larger place for the non-academic. There should be easing of the excessive emphasis on entrance examinations. The five-day school week should be implemented, and a set period of time should be put aside for integrated studies, either in- or out-of-school. Credits at the upper secondary level should be available for achievements in out-of-school activities.

The home, community, and society

The educational role of the home has weakened. This is closely connected with the widespread adoption of a company-centred life-style and a range of spreading use of convenient private services. Leisure has tended to be neglected in Japan. People experience a constant feeling of being spurred on by something, often ill defined. It is in this context that many search for different values and

167|

self-realisation, such as room to grow and a rich sense of humanity. There i
also a decline in the educational power of communities, with urbanisation, rura
de-population, and the loosening of solidarity in local communities. Given tha
these major trends are closely connected with the life-styles and the very struc
ture of modern society, they will not be easy to reverse nor new frameworks t
construct.

In addressing these issues, the Council proposed that family and communit
involvement in school activities and management should be encouraged, an
facilities made more accessible to the public. Learning opportunities in the hom
and the active involvement of fathers in home-based education should also b
encouraged. Activities for children in the local community need to be promote
– playgrounds, events, tours, sports, volunteer activities, experiences with nature
Similarly, the "fourth sector" – purpose-oriented organisations and circles linkin
people with common interests – needs to be supported.

Science, technology and the information society

The era of being able to build on the scientific and technological achieve
ments developed by Western nations is now past, and a high priority must be fo
scientific and technological creativity. Simply supplying good quality products wi
not be sufficient. To address this need, the love of science should be actively pro
moted in schools. Expensive high-performance equipment that individual school
cannot afford should become accessible through being pooled. More emphasis i
needed on the links between science and other subjects, and on discovery an
creation. This is another reason why the curriculum should not be fully loaded.

A range of areas is suggested for the "informatisation" of education: schoo
ICT facilities and equipment, teacher training, R&D in educational software, IC
"literacy" and individual competence to generate, select and use information. A
"new form of school" should be explored, attuned to the information- and commu
nications-oriented society. The electronic networking of schools and of educa
tional information should be greatly developed.

The information-intensive society is reaching a new stage with global commu
nications networks. Global two-way exchange of information comprising a fusion o
text, images and sound becomes possible. This will bring about wholesale
changes in the future society and the economy, but again their form is unclear
Already, it is clear that the economic structure needs to be reformed, and the
established patterns of lifetime employment and seniority-based promotion are
being radically shaken. The development of science and technology is likely to
continue to accelerate, and with that comes uncertainty: "We fear a growing
unease on the side of the people as science and technology becomes more

sophisticated. More detailed and more specialised, they will also become more difficult for them to understand".

Global and environmental issues

Economic, social and cultural exchanges and a gradual deepening of international interdependence (in energy, global environment, population, and armed conflicts) will develop further and grow in complexity, leading sometimes to tension and competition. Promoting international understanding is thus a major priority for schools, including through exchange activities and communities using the Internet, and through listening and speaking in foreign languages. There will be increasingly strong pressure for Japan to contribute to the solution of global environmental and energy problems which question modern mass life-styles.

Education in the future – stability and change

However society changes, schooling must still attend to certain universals that do not change. It should foster in children a rich sense of humanity, a spirit that prizes justice and equity, the power of self-control, co-operation, consideration for others, respect for human rights and a love of nature. The term "zest for living" (ikiruchikara) was chosen to describe such qualities, that are fundamental to life in a period of turbulent change. Children need to learn and appreciate their own language, history, traditions and culture.

Education also has a duty to respond flexibly to change, with the courage to grasp accurately and speedily the implications of those such as internationalisation and the information-intensive society. Knowledge becomes obsolete at an increasing rate, making lifelong learning essential. The future cannot be accurately forecast and remains obscure, so that the ability to make judgements on the basis of circumstances at any given time becomes increasingly important. With the development of multi-media and the information-rich society, there is a stronger demand for creativity in ways of using knowledge and information.

The Netherlands: "Futures for basic educational policies"

This initiative took place in 1996, initiated at ministerial level, to facilitate a societal dialogue and develop visions for future-oriented educational policies (In't Veld, de Bruijn and Lips, 1996). While there is intense activity in the Netherlands to generate options for the improvement of education in the short- and medium-term, the scale and rapidity of change compel greater attention to be given to the longer term. Extensive changes can be expected in the ways of communicating, working, learning and living, changes that education should accommodate. Conventionally, this process of accommodation is delayed: as there are often great difficulties experienced in coming to terms with recent historical changes (such as growing ethnic diversity), such hesitation to confront the future is perhaps unsur prising. In its deliberations, important on-going educational trends and societal influences on education – "driving forces" – were identified, as well as "bows of tensions" (competing values). Combinations of the driving forces and values led to six types of future school and three scenarios – "compositions" – being constructed.

Key educational trends and driving forces

Among the changes taking place in education, some of the more important are:

- *Changes in content*: Purely vocational qualifications are tending to disap pear; there is a shift from knowledge to skills and competences (social and communication skills, learning to learn, verbal competence in different languages).

- *Role of parents*: Parents expect more tasks to be performed by schools, and they become increasingly the "clients" and "consumers" of educational ser vices; traditional lines of demarcation and segregation by religion are replaced by social and cultural segregation.

- *Working methods in education*: Fewer children will attend special schools; the focus of equity policies is shifting increasingly from groups to individuals and organised as projects; the use of new technologies is still marginal rather than fundamental.

- *The role and position of teachers*: The teacher labour market is problematic; with increasing differentiation comes also hierarchy; professionalism itself is a problem, compared with, say, the health sector; the shift, especially in upper secondary education, from subject-matter specialist to learning coach has a detrimental effect on status and salaries.

- *Administration and finance*: The process of decentralisation continues and a new intermediate layer is created; in areas of risk, the influence of munici palities grows; more attention is focused on education's "output" and "value-added"; schools are increasingly gaining revenue from diverse sources.

More broadly, for the future people will have to function in a wide variety of contexts, placing a particular premium on competence in communication. ICT will lead to major changes, but their direction and form are hard to predict or antici pate, generating further uncertainty. The variety of life styles is expected to increase, so leading to greater alternatives to the family. Children will thus grow up in situations increasingly different from each other. Differences and inequali ties will become better accepted and accommodated. At the same time, many cit izens will no longer be able to keep abreast of rapid societal developments and in this sense "drop out".

Increasingly, questions will be asked about meaning, values and norms: what they are and what the basis that they provide for action, as well how diverse values can be accommodated and promoted. The trend towards greater individualisation is expected to continue, but in tandem more than hitherto with the search for new forms of social connectedness. Increasing emphasis will be expected to be placed on local issues, fuelled by globalisation and by the felt need for security and autonomy. There will also be greater awareness of the importance of emotion and affection in human relations.

Competing values ("bows of tensions"), futures, scenarios

Competing values were organised into sets, described as "bows of tensions", that were seen as critical to the ways that schooling and policy will be played out. They are fundamental to different possible futures. [While the dimensions within each cluster are presented below as contrasts ("versus") they should more correctly be understood as a series of continuums.]

- *Values and pluralism*: Individual development vs. education for social cohesion; strong beliefs in specific norms and values vs. tolerance, relativity; uniform set of norms vs. plurality; strong identification with dominant culture vs. detachment.

- *The influence of technology*: Brokering vs. connoisseur-ship; words vs. images; virtual vs. real schools and teachers.

- *Responsibilities and financing*: Centralisation vs. decentralisation; collective vs. private responsibility; collective vs. private financing; financing by supply vs. by demand.

- *Broad or focused mission*: Schools as centres of learning vs. as youth institutions; focus on learning within vs. outside schools; internal professionalism vs. external support systems; limited vs. flexible opening times.

- *The curriculum*: Knowledge vs. skills; cognitive development vs. the whole person; broad vs. core curriculum; broad vs. specific standards.

- *Methods*: Focus on content vs. on students; fixed groupings vs. individual arrangements; homogeneous vs. heterogeneous grouping; special vs. integrated; rational/technical vs. emotional/relational; fixed vs. flexible selection; compulsory education organised on the basis of age vs. developmental level.

- *The school and its environment*: Parents as supporters vs. as consumers; intervention vs. non-intervention in families; schools as autonomous vs. in networks/ partnerships; focus on relations with the public vs. private domains.

171|

- *The role of the teacher*: Monopolist *vs.* broker; educationist *vs.* subject-matter specialist; focus on formal curriculum (product) *vs.* focus on hidden curriculum (process).

- *Effectiveness and methods of change*: Nature *vs.* nurture; focus on capability to shape society (proactive) *vs.* schools follow changes in society (reactive); universal changes *vs.* differentiated application sensitive to context (*e.g.* urban/non urban).

- *Values and educational philosophy*: Non-selective *vs.* selective; education systems as "closed" *vs.* more mixed with further systems; uniformity *vs.* diversity; strong *vs.* weak responses to equity.

Policies are always future-oriented in some sense, but education pays insufficient attention to the driving forces, whether to reinforce them or, as in some cases (*e.g.* the increasing risk of dropping out), to compensate for them. Driving forces work directly on education, but also through educational policies that are open to societal influence. Different values are critical, and as there is no consensus about values there are multiple possible futures. Variety in school systems is perceived as likely to increase, contradicting the formal uniformity that so underpins much educational policy. This contradiction may lead to unproductive outcomes – growing inequalities, overloaded administration, ineffective school choice. But, variety should be positively developed, with the basis of differences made explicit.

Scenarios help to understand possible futures in a more systematic, informed way. Different images of schools of the future can be constructed, giving different weights to the driving forces. This initiative came up with six types of future schools: *i)* "The differentiated school"; *ii)* "The achievement school"; *iii)* "The school of practice"; *iv)* "The school as a place to learn"; *v)* "The school as home"; *vi)* "The multiform school". Three scenarios or "compositions" were also constructed, incorporating not only characteristics of schools, but also of policies and administration: *i)* strong systems based on the uniqueness of each child; partnership/balanced diversity involving parents and schools; *iii)* uniform, coherent provision and system.

Reflections on the driving forces and their implications

Emerging and problematic themes

The inherent uncertainty of the future, exacerbated through rapid change, is both itself a major driving force in its own right and makes forecasting impossible. All studies also agree on the importance of uncertainty: the Japanese refers to "a period of turbulence and violent change, in which the way forward is obscure"; the Canadian report of an "uncertain and intimidating future".

Knowledge is perceived as uncertain and changeable, not definite and permanent. The sheer quantity of new information is bewildering and destabilising. The criteria for being a literate citizen are not self-evident. Rapid economic change puts a question mark against the marketability of school qualifications as well as the content and skills learned in schools. As science and technology become more sophisticated and specialised, they also become more difficult for people to understand. Many young people are conscious of the environmental and health crises to which few solutions seem at hand and which add to the sense of uncertainty. A dominant perception of uncertainty, however, may simply lead to reactionary or nihilistic responses; more fruitful would be to recognise new patterns of producing, mediating and using knowledge and search for the appropriate ways of learning (OECD, 2000b; Gibbons et al., 1994).

The changes in knowledge and its role in the economy described in the studies do not add up to a clear picture. There is discussion of "new literacies" (especially in the Canadian study). Both the German and the Japanese studies suggest that children should learn more in situations and from people outside schools, which is also attractive and motivating for many children. Learning such literacies may, however, be difficult to organise effectively in most school settings given that they involve both codified and tacit knowledge. Given the attachment of schools to the powerful value of enlightenment of the individual through understanding the world "as it is", then practical, entrepreneurial and technological know-how may not integrate easily with the conventional school repertoire.

A further general plea that derives from the growing skill needs in the economy is for investments and participation to lead to ever-higher levels of education. There is a tension involved in balancing the pursuit of commonality and shared competence, on the one hand, and diversity and individuality, on the other. The different studies confront this tension with somewhat different emphases, often rather generally. "Higher levels for all" strategies are ambitious in some ways but "safe" in others: without proven alternatives at hand it is natural to seek to invest further in what seems already to work. Yet, ever-higher levels of schooling, as well as being expensive, run up against the law of diminishing returns. Dropping out at the lower end may be the corollary of rising educational levels at the higher one. Policies for "leaner" forms of learning may actually prove more effective, but they have to first be shown to work.

The new social circumstances of children are emphasised in the studies. The general impression given is of major problems. Daily routines and pressures may obscure just how far educational policy and schools are engaged in the desperate search for solutions. One idea is for local networks to be responsible for tackling the problems that children may have, in close co-operation with parents. The Ontario study is clear that the task of teachers is first and foremost the (intellectual) development of the new literacies, while it is the responsibility of local networks, including schools, to create the *conditions* for children to be able to learn. The Japanese study also emphasises the important role of local community. The German study attaches greater importance to the school as a place to live and to develop personal and social identity, though local networks are also mentioned.

What is less clear is how the responsibilities between the different partners can be defined in practice so that there is reduced pressure on teachers to enable them to concentrate on teaching/learning. The structuring of teachers' daily work allows little interaction with the outside world, while pressures from society to deal with other issues force interaction forward, bringing teachers into cognitive conflicts (see the German study in particular). This leads many teachers to adopt survival strategies, leaving little time and energy for more structural innovation. Yet, all four studies stress that structural reform is needed and with traditional reform no longer adequate. One question is thus of how to manage this conflict. Do "intervention strategies" (Ontario) or school autonomy (North Rhine-Westphalia) provide the answer? What room is left for system-level change or is now the relevant unit that of networks of different sorts? And, how will networks respond to such factors as the variety of social circumstances and relationships, declining permanence in institutions, and the emotional needs of children and adolescents?

The media are widely seen to exercise a strong influence on children, with ICT bringing great changes. But as the direction and form of those changes are mostly unpredictable, they are difficult to anticipate or react to. There is positive recognition in the studies that ICT can further qualitative change in the nature of student learning, with the new media addressing new capacities in young people. Yet, the new cognitive qualities that may be developed remain imprecisely developed, as do the conditions that would empower them. At the moment, they seem to be mainly developed by chance, often outside schools, with new industries providing parallel examples of informal learning. Such cases certainly deserve closer attention.

It is widely recognised that the hidden curriculum in schools exercises a considerable influence on children, and this is put forward explicitly (North-Rhine-Westphalia) as justification for their autonomy. On this argument, it is only if a school is a living, learning and democratic organisation, fostering both individual development and social responsibility, can it seriously prepare children for the new society. Whether schools are actually permitted to do this is another question.

Schools as we know them have grown as part of an industrial society that has recently undergone radical change. People acquired security from certain key structures – the nation state, schools, labour organisations, "welfare state" provisions for social protection – which are less certain or secure in the emerging "risk-society" (Beck, 1986). Some people are stimulated and creative in such an environment, many others cannot cope. Highly creative and rewarding learning systems, perhaps outside schools, may run alongside very unadventurous institutions. Extremes are thus possible, whether in relation to people or to learning. Greater balance may well be needed between these.

Driving forces in the "toolbox" of policy-making and innovation

All four studies report that education does not pay enough attention to driving forces. But they also agree that schools are overloaded and under intense pressures from society. Trends only tend to be acted on once their consequences are already felt, so that recognition that action is needed may well be too late. All the studies comment on the fact that educational systems change very slowly, a problematic reality but also sometimes desirable, suggesting yet more tension. The timely identification of driving forces is thus critical to their value. To this end, futures studies certainly have a place to gauge the strength and significance of different trends.

The studies all agree on the fact of uncertainty. Despite this, the Ontario and Japanese studies seem confident in their recommendations, in contrast with the Dutch study. The latter instead argues for the merits of alternative scenarios or "compositions", permitting the elaboration of a repertoire of options with which to respond to unexpected changes in society. The justification for this line is that otherwise the risk is of being too slow to act or else of taking counterproductive measures. The North-Rhine-Westphalia study takes another position: dealing with the unforeseeable is best done by schools, whose sensitivity to trends will often be more acute than that of central bodies.

Will such an "internal" focus prove to be compatible with the need to interact with its wider environment if driving forces are to be translated into school policy? People drawn from outside education will need to be consulted. An interactive process of matching trends with specific educational measures requires the imaginative dialogue between those within education and key stakeholders in the trends: identification of those who "carry" a trend is important as is establishing channels of informed communication. There is thus an important role both for those from outside education and futures experts. It may also be valuable that concrete alternatives to the existing educational arrangements be developed, nourished and monitored as seedbeds of educational innovation. Such approaches may, however, sit uneasily with the perspective of "systemic reform". The links between identified driving forces and local experience should also be developed.

There are possible limitations and drawbacks to confront with driving forces methodologies. They might suffer an in-built conservatism: they do not deliver visions and goals, and perceptions about the strength of societal trends and their

175|

potential impact on education are influenced by current, often implicit, perceptions and values (including possibly those of the main authors). A range of inputs
and expertise may thus be needed to ensure balance, often drawn from outside
education. The use of these methods for policy-making should be complemented
by others that are sensitive to weak signals about change. Experience in sectors
outside education with dealing with unpredictability suggests that imagination
and early communication at an early stage about possible futures may be much
more useful than planning models (*e.g.* Minzberg, 1994; van de Heijden, 1996).
Instead of asking the "what?" and "how?" questions, the "what if?" questions may
be the really pertinent ones.

Notes

1. This chapter is based on papers prepared by Hans van Aalst for a joint Netherlands/
   OECD seminar on Schooling for Tomorrow held in Scheveningen in April 1998.
   Between 1995 and 1998, he was a consultant with OECD/CERI working on schooling and
   knowledge issues. The selection of texts in this chapter, and the views expressed, are
   those of the author rather than of the national authorities concerned.

2. In relying exclusively on written reports, the coverage is also biased towards the more
   firmly agreed and confirmed trends. Often, the relevant knowledge is instead in heads
   and "communities of practice" than in written documents.

Chapter 9

Attitudes and Expectations in Relation to Schools: Swedish Findings and Some International Comparisons

by

Sten Söderberg
National Agency for Education (Skolverket), Sweden

Introduction

The main focus of this chapter is on public opinion and the attitudes of parents towards schools and education, with some consideration as well of the opinions of teachers and pupils. While studies of these matters in an international context are relatively scarce, the findings generated can illuminate important issues relating to schooling for tomorrow.[1] It should be stressed that the evidence reviewed is taken mainly from one country and from earlier in the 1990s; they should thus be interpreted with some caution. The findings are based mainly on the national attitude surveys carried out by the National Agency for Education in Sweden.[2] The surveys simultaneously address nationally representative samples of the main stake-holders: *pupils/students* (from the age of 13 and upwards), *parents, teachers* as well as *the general public*. They aim to capture opinions along four broad dimensions – "faith", "quality", "participation" and "change" (see Söderberg and Löfbom, 1998). Most of the findings are taken from the 1997 surveys of the general public and parents in Sweden, with some additional information from the similar 1993/1994 enquiry (hereafter referred to as 1993), other Swedish studies, and from the OECD/INES Network D study carried out in 1994 on attitudes and expectations (OECD, 1995).[3]

The 1990s were characterised by dramatic changes in the educational system in Sweden, and the findings need to be interpreted against this background. The strong government control that was previously exercised in virtually every field was replaced by a goal-oriented system extending considerable local control. The responsibility to meet the national objectives decided by the Parliament (*Riksdag*) now lies with the local authorities (municipalities). An important feature of this decentralisation is that the state grants to the municipalities are no longer earmarked for education or other special purposes. Since 1990, the teachers and other school staff have been employed by the municipalities.

These changes have been coupled with other substantial reforms, including the reformulation of national curricula, a re-designed three-year upper secondary cycle, and new goal-oriented marking and national testing systems. Another important reform has been the "opening up" of the system to allow for more school choice, including strengthening the private sector – an initiative of a conservative government in the early 1990s and left largely intact since. The proportion of pupils attending private compulsory-level schools has increased from around 1% to over 3% over this period, still not a high percentage by international standards but the change has been widely felt in the educational system and in debate. Important also to note was the economic recession that characterised especially the first half of the 1990s in Sweden which brought extensive cutbacks for schools and their staff as in other sectors such as health and child care. With their newly extended decentralised powers, the municipalities were widely perceived as being the culprits for the cuts.

Public opinion towards schools and education

Faith in schools

The faith that people have in the good performance of the major public institutions is a basic indicator of support for different aspects of the welfare society. Through various sources, it is possible to trace such patterns of support throughout the 1990s. From 1991 to 1994, there was an increase in the public "faith" in schools, health care and the police – the so-called "social sphere" – followed since then by a decline. The decline between 1994 and 1997 is probably an effect of the severe cutbacks in welfare institutions. By 1997, the proportion having a great deal or a fair amount of faith in schools was 37%, while a quarter of the public indicated little or very little faith (see Figure 9.1). At these levels, schools were in approximately the same position as taxation authorities and banks. "Faith" in schools was lower than in health care and the police – following a common pattern in Sweden – but higher compared with the church, the press, and especially politicians whether national or local. Other sources (Holmberg and Weibull, 1997) reveal that faith in schools is also higher than it is towards the judicial system. Thus, the relative and increasing distrust in schools is not unique to them but applies to a number of important sectors in society, and especially to politics.

The findings support the common-sense observation that the position in which an institution is held is heavily influenced by concrete experiences of its services. Teachers exhibited more faith in schools than do parents who in turn were higher than the general public, although it should be noted that a fifth of parents and as many as 12% of teachers indicated little or very little faith in how well schools perform their tasks.

Figure 9.1. **Faith in schools**

Percentage having very much or quite a lot of faith in the way that different institutions in society perform their tasks: general public, parents and teachers, 1997

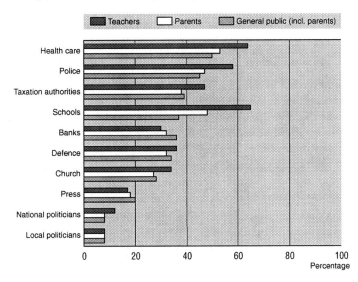

Goal attainment

How do people look upon the objectives of schools and their capacity to achieve their objectives? Certain of the national objectives are regarded as essential by the general public, the most important being to impart sound knowledge and skills, provide education of equal value, and support pupils with special needs, regarded in 1997 as essential by over 60% of the respondents (see Figure 9.2). Several other national objectives were also regarded as essential by a majority of the Swedish public. Overall, this suggests that there is a broad consensus about the content of the national curriculum and its objectives. The objective receiving the lowest priority was that referring to preparation by schools for higher education, regarded as essential by only one third of the public, well down on the 45% regarding it as essential that schools educate for the labour market.

Evidence from the OECD 1994 survey suggests that the level of support for the main school objectives is similar in other countries. In relation to knowledge and skills, the average percentage in across the OECD survey agreeing with how "essential" or "very important" was a range of the subjects taught in schools stood very similar to the Swedish levels. The lowest average percentage agreeing with the high importance of the subjects was found in Denmark (56%), the highest in

179|

Figure 9.2. **How well do schools achieve their objectives?**

Percentage of the general public thinking that the objectives are essential, and percentage thinking that schools succeed very well or quite well in achieving their objectives, 1997

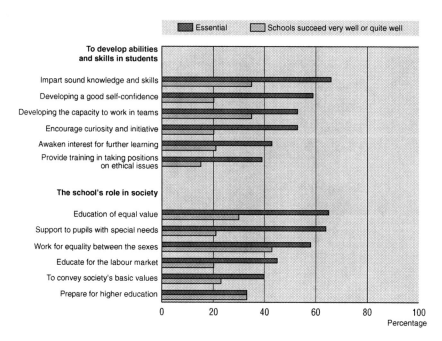

Portugal (75%) (OECD, 1995, Table C.21). In relation to the role of the school in providing support to students, the cross-country average for people thinking that it is essential or very important for schools to prioritise help with learning difficulties was very high at nearly 90%, and the variation between countries quite small. Sweden with 88% was very close to the international mean in this regard (*op. cit.*, Table C.26).

In Sweden, what is particularly striking are the very large gaps that exist between the importance that people attach to the different national objectives and how well schools are perceived to fulfil them. While two thirds regarded it as essential for schools to impart sound knowledge and skills, only a third (35%) believed that they succeed well or very well in doing so. The biggest such gap was in relation to the duty of schools to support pupils with special needs. The task on which schools were seen to perform best was in working towards equality between the sexes; where they are thought to be worst is in preparing young people to grasp and take positions on ethical issues. These (mis)matches clearly represent an area on which it would be interesting to have more international comparative data.

One of the findings that attracted most attention in the Swedish media was that the general public, parents, and teachers had a much lower view of the school system's capacity to carry out its duties in 1997 than they had had three years previously. Far fewer considered that schools succeed in imparting a good level of knowledge and skills or in providing support to pupils with special needs (see Annex, Table A.1). In 1993, about half of the general public believed that schools succeeded well in imparting knowledge and skills; three years later this had reduced to only a third. A similar pattern of increasing distrust is thus apparent as found for faith in schools.

It thus seems that Swedish people both support their educational system in terms of its objectives and their importance, and yet are critical of how well it performs. In international comparisons, the OECD 1994 survey showed that the confidence in how well schools achieve their objectives in developing important qualities in students (such as self-confidence, being a good citizen or able to live among people from different backgrounds), varies considerably between countries. The proportion of the Swedish general public which was very or fairly confident in the capacity of schools to do so was considerably lower (around 40%) than in most other participating countries. The mean across all the countries participating was 53.4% (OECD, 1995, Table C.23).[4] A possible explanation is that a high level of education tends to foster critical minds, but this would not entirely explain the differences. For example, in Denmark or France, countries that also have enjoyed a long and well-developed educational tradition, confidence in the capacity of schools to develop important qualities was clearly higher than in Sweden. It stood at nearly 70% in Denmark – the highest among the participating countries – and at 62% in France. Apart from anything else, it suggests that levels of public confidence do not always reflect actual differences in performance.

Schools yesterday and today

Another approach to understanding public opinion is through asking people to make comparisons with the school they themselves attended. In 1997, three out of ten in the general public, and four out of ten parents, maintained that schools today are better than the school they attended (see Annex, Figure A.1). These are somewhat lower figures than in 1993, as might be expected given declining faith in schools between those dates. On the other hand, they are considerably better than in 1987, a period characterized by a good supply of resources to schools in Sweden, while then the IEA/SIMS results indicated relatively weak performances (giving rise to considerable debate on educational effectiveness). The contrast with similar comparisons carried out in 1969 is particularly striking. The end of the sixties was the period of great educational reforms and expansion. Then, almost all parents thought that the school of 1969 was better than the one they had attended earlier.

181

The general conclusion might thus be that a rise in educational level leads to more critical thinking about, and higher demands on, the educational system. It is possible that a well-functioning school system in a paradoxical sense contributes to weakening its own position. Further supporting evidence might be found in the fact that upper secondary students in programmes preparing for further studies were far more critical of the quality of teaching and relations to teachers, in both the 1993 and 1997 pupil surveys, than students in vocational programmes.

Attitudes to teachers

Attitudes towards teachers have also been studied. The general public was asked to agree or disagree with a number of statements taken from the educational debate, for instance, concerning teachers as an "exposed" group, or as a group with many privileges, or as having too little experience other than in education. Far more Swedes in 1997 (62%) regarded teachers as an exposed rather than an over-privileged professional group (17%) (see Annex, Table A.2). The general attitude is more supportive than critical, a tendency reinforced between 1993 and 1997. At the same time, a majority (55%) felt that teachers have too little experience of working life outside school, which is not necessarily criticism as many teachers share the same view. In the 1997 teacher survey, around 40% of teachers felt that they lacked knowledge about working life outside school. This was especially evident among teachers in basic compulsory school, if less among those at the upper secondary level.

The view of the teaching profession as "exposed" also indicates a lack of status, which is a serious problem in relation to meeting mounting recruitment needs. In a comparative context, the OECD 1994 survey showed that less than half of Swedes (48%) thought that secondary teachers are very or fairly respected (OECD 1995, Table C.25), a figure well below the overall mean for participating countries at 57.6%. The variation in perceived respect for teachers between participating countries was less than might have been expected, with the exceptions of Spain (which had the lowest percentage –32%) and Sweden, on the one hand, and Austria on the other, which had the highest proportion (74%).

Attitudes to change

As mentioned at the outset, the 1990s was a period of dramatic change in the Swedish educational system. In 1997, around four in ten parents, and over half of teachers, agreed with the proposition that there were too many new things changes in schools (see Annex, Figure A.2). Regardless of position in the educational system, whether as pupil, teacher or parent, this proportion increased substantially between 1993 and 1997. Considerably fewer parents and teachers (around 20%) thought that schools are secluded and insufficiently influenced by the world outside, which remained fairly constant between 1993 and 1997 though this might still seem a relatively high figure. Even so, in times of major societal transformations, it is noteworthy that it has been far more common to see schools (and teachers) as over-exposed rather than under-exposed to change.

To conclude, in Sweden by 1997 growing distrust and criticism of schools was apparent, perhaps to a more widespread degree than in many other OECD countries. While a matter for concern, this distrust is hardly justified on the basis of international comparisons of actual performance. It is at least partly a reflection of cutbacks in economic resources. And, other aspects of the survey findings portray improvements not deterioration. For instance, no more students were dissatisfied with school in 1997 than they had been three years previously, and indeed they tended to be happier with the quality of teaching and relations with teachers (see Annex, Table A.3). Contradictory directions of change raise a number of questions. What are the relationships between a rise in educational level (and quality) and the demands on the educational system itself? To what extent is criticism of 'the system" a reflection or not of criticisms of local schooling? Does the media tend to focus on problems rather than progress in schools, and to what effect? Some of these issues will be illuminated subsequently in this chapter.

Parental views

Satisfaction with the system and with local provision

Many parents are clearly critical of schools and how they operate. But this criticism is far more explicit in terms of the "system" rather than the local school. This becomes clear in comparing how parents look at two objectives, both regarded as essential by over 70% of parents: knowledge transmission and support to pupils. Twice as many parents (78%) were satisfied with what their own child is taught at school, than with how Swedish schools in general succeed in imparting sound knowledge and skills (40%) (see Annex, Table A.4). Similarly, twice as many parents (41%) were satisfied with the possibilities to get extra support for their child if needed, than with how Swedish schools succeed in providing such support. There are thus gaps, not only between what is regarded as essential and how schools are seen to perform, but also between how schools generally are perceived to perform and the operation of the local school. There is thus a need to complement or substantiate "public opinion" on schools, with evidence relating to more closely experienced educational realities.

Although parents are more satisfied with the local school, this does not mean that the general level of satisfaction can be regarded as high. In the 1997 survey, parents were asked to judge the quality of the school attended by their child in terms of a number of criteria. Parents are clearly more satisfied with the education provided – both contents and teaching methods – than with the prevailing conditions, such as

183|

school environment, class size and possibilities for extra support (see Annex Figure A.3). While eight out of ten parents found that educational content is good c very good, almost one out of three parents expressed dissatisfaction with class siz and support.

Desired and perceived influence, and the demand for choice

When parents are asked about their desire to participate in decision-making a similar pattern emerges. A majority of them in the 1997 survey (between 86% an 54% depending on the question) wanted to participate "very much" or "quite a lot" i decisions regarding possibilities for extra support, class size, norms and rules, an school environment. Considerably fewer felt the desire to influence decisions o actual educational matters – content, work procedures, or choice of textbooks an teaching aids (see Annex, Figure A.4). What is more striking, however, is that two ou of three parents (70%) expressed a strong interest in choice of school, and almost ha (47%) expressed a similar interest to influence the choice of teachers for their child.

The desire of parents for influence is not, of course, unique to Sweden. In th OECD 1994 survey, the public were asked to judge the importance for schools t keep parents well informed and involved. The cross-country mean agreeing tha this was "essential" or "very important" stood at a high 82%, with Sweden close t the mean, with no country reporting a lower percentage than 72%. The variation that were apparent, however, might indicate some interesting cultural difference in attitudes to parental involvement. Two of the other Scandinavian countries, fo instance, reported lower figures at slightly less than three-quarters (Finland Denmark), while the country with the highest support for parental involvemen was the USA, with the very elevated percentage of 95% (OECD, 1995, Table C.26) Again, this is an area where more comparative data would be of great interest.

From the Swedish findings, there are significant gaps between desired an perceived influence, in line with findings from other national studies on influenc and participation. A much-discussed study in the national debate on educatio and participation was that conducted by the first Swedish Government Commis sion on Power Distribution (SOU, 1990, p. 44). It found that schooling is the secto in society where the perceived scope to exercise influence is the smallest, a judged by the groups of citizens most concerned (in this case, the parents o school-age children). Other groups of directly concerned citizens were sampled fo the comparison sectors, which were working life, health care, child-care, accommo dation and consumption of goods.

Exercising choice of school is the form of influence most open to parents. Four i ten of them found that they "very much" or "quite a lot" had the possibility to choos a school. This compares with the much lower 23% feeling able to influence the possi bilities of getting extra support, 15% the school environment, or 7% the class size. A seen, these are all issues to which parents attach importance (see Annex, Figure A.4). These findings relate to Hirschman's distinction between "exit", "voice" and "loyalty" (Hirschman, 1970), terms which characterise different ways of handling change and exercising influence.[5] Many parents can certainly be seen as loyal, but when it comes to making a difference to their child's schooling, more regard "exit" as an effective and feasible option compared with the exercise of "voice". Another way to express this is in the distinction between the "consumer role" – being able to choose what one wants to use – and the "user role" – being able to influence what one uses (see Annex, Table A.5) (see also Lindblad and Pérez Prieto, 1998). In this regard, the findings reported in Table A.5 are not very encouraging. The perceptions of parents as users weakened between 1993 and 1997 and their position as consumers did not improve, and this despite the so-called "choice reform" implemented over this period.

Reasons for choice

The national attitude surveys did not specifically study the reasons parents give when exercising choice over a school for their child. In a Swedish study from 1992/1993, when the "choice reform" was relatively fresh, a representative sample of parents were asked about the most important factors to take into account in choosing a school for their child (Skolverket, 1993a). Quality issues weigh much more than either proximity or "profile". Quality issues, referring to both the quality of education and the social climate, were stressed by almost all parents (around 95%), with geographical proximity and access to friends from the neighbourhood mentioned by around three-quarters. Educational or content "profile", such as Montessori, music or language, was stressed by only a little over one third of all parents (36%), while religious profile was a priority for only 7% – a relatively low figure which may well be higher in certain other countries.

Another Swedish study addressed a representative sample of parents who had made an active change of school. Again, quality issues were found to be more important than either proximity or profile (Skolverket, 1996). In this study, it was possible in addition to distinguish parents who had chosen a private school from those who had opted for another municipal school. For parents who had chosen a private school, profile became a relatively more important factor, while for those choosing another municipal school, geographical closeness was accorded relatively greater importance. It is not clear how stable is this pattern. It may be that the growing range of "profiled" schools in Sweden during the 1990s may have increased their relative interest that would not be shown by the earlier studies.

Unequal opportunities to choose and exercise influence

The 1992/1993 study referred to above showed that parents living in big cities and those with the highest level of education most support the choice option, know best what the possible choices are, and have the greatest interest in actually choosing a school. Only a third (32%) of parents with basic compulsory education knew the range of schools among which choices could be made, compared with nearly two-thirds (62%) of those with an academic education. The educational back ground of parents not only influences the choice factor, but also the other means of influencing daily life in schools. In the 1997 survey, parents were asked both if they were prepared to make efforts to change things in school, and if they actually had tried to change or influence something. While a large majority of all parents (83%) were pre pared to make a personal effort to change something in school, this was especially true for parents with an academic education (90%) compared with those with compul sory basic education only (70%) (see Annex, Figure A.5). It was also twice as common that the "educated" parents had actually tried to influence something in school (60% of parents with an academic education, compared to 32% of parents with the basic level). Only a quarter of parents with an academic education agreed that there is "No need for change" as a reason for not trying to exercise influence, compared with almost half of the parents with only the compulsory attainment level.

Once again, there is evidence that a rise in educational level leads to increased demands on the educational system itself. There is a correlation between education and self-confidence: over 60% of parents with a basic compulsory education felt that they "don't know how" to influence or that "others are more competent" to do so, compared with around 40% of parents with an academic education.

Attitudes to the private sector and cohesion

The interest in choice and private solutions should also be understood in relation to more deeply embedded values concerning the objectives of schools There is a stable consensus among Swedish parents on the cohesive functions of schools, with widespread agreement that classes should be mixed, bringing together pupils from different social and cultural backgrounds (see Annex, Table A.6). Four-fifths of parents agreed on this, both in 1993 and 1997. Over half the general public thought that choice of schools would widen rifts in society; at the same time, 43% were supportive of more private schools. It is reasonable to conclude that belief in the school as a "public good" is still stronger in Sweden than for seeing it as a "private good". Attitudes to choice and to private education alternatives represent a contro versial political issue, as discussed later. Nevertheless, the elevated numbers of par ents who support choice and more private schools can be seen as an indication of changing values and of the greater demands being made on schools.

Parents as conservative or radical

The attitudes and demands of parents are pressures for change but in which directions? Parents, pupils and teachers were asked how they looked upon a number of possible changes in schools, all derived from the educational debate. While the three groups expressed strong support for such matters as greater openness, more co-ordination of teaching across subject borders, and more independent work for pupils, parents were somewhat less supportive, especially compared with teachers (see Annex, Figure A.6). On the other hand, parents were clearly supportive of more tests and more homework: over 40% of parents thought that these were good directions for school change.

Another issue in the educational debate is the appropriate grade/age for awarding marks in basic compulsory school. In Sweden, these are currently awarded for the first time in grade 8 when pupils are approximately age 14, this having been done at an earlier age in previous schools systems. In 1997, over 60% of parents were supportive of marks at an earlier age – a considerably higher proportion than found among either teachers or pupils (see Annex, Figure A.7). Such findings indicate that many parents are in favour of schools being similar to those they had attended, and this to a greater extent than for teachers.

Some might interpret an emphasis on homework and discipline as an expression of a more "conservative" attitude. Whether or not this is appropriate terminology, such an emphasis is even more evident in several countries than in Sweden. In the OECD 1994 survey, a little under half of the Swedish public judged regular homework to be essential or very important – well below the OECD average (57.5%). In certain other countries, the emphasis on homework was markedly higher, most notably in the USA (78%) and in Finland (71%), and in others is markedly less (in Denmark and Spain, according to these data, it stood at less than 40%) (OECD, 1995, Table C.26). "Discipline" is another term that can be linked to a conservative attitude to schooling and as much as a high average, 77% of the public in OECD countries in the 1994 survey affirmed that maintaining discipline is essential or very important for schools. While the Swedish public shared this view (79%), the emphasis was higher still in certain countries like the USA (93%), Finland (91%), and the UK (90%), while significantly lower again in Denmark (56%) and Spain (60%) (*ibid.*).

While the terminology "conservative", "radical" or "progressive" can be loaded, findings such as these support the view that, to the extent that the views of parents exercise an influence on schools, this may be to conserve rather than to change. There also appear to be some important cross-national cultural differences in this regard.

The media and other influences shaping opinions on schools

The evidence shows that personal experiences, whether of their own schooling or that of their child's, are the single most influential set of factors shaping opinions on schools. Whether parents or not, about two thirds of the general public in 1993 attached a major importance to their personal experiences of schools (see Annex, Table A.7). Around half considered themselves influenced by contacts at work with children and young people. What is written or said in the media, and by politicians especially, seems to be of considerably less important. Perhaps surprisingly, national media are seen as more important than local media in shaping opinions on schools. A third (35%) of the general public in 1993 agreed that they are influenced by national media on schooling matters compared with 27% by local media, figures that are still well down on personal experiences. Nevertheless, the role of the media, especially at the national level, should not be underestimated every third person, according to our findings, agreed that the media are very or quite important in shaping their views on schools. This proportion might even be seen as high, considering that only a fifth of the public express any positive degree of faith in the press at all (see Figure 9.1).

Thus, the media do have a responsibility in how they treat school issues. A Swedish study connected to the first survey in 1993 (Skolverket, 1993b), investigated this to stress two conclusions. First, the media tend to focus on the negative and the sudden, rather than the positive and the continuous. In the study, 43% of the analyzed features were judged as negative, 21% as positive and 36% as neutral. Secondly, the media have a responsibility in deciding who gets a "voice" and thus enjoy other ways to influence public opinion. In the study's analysis, teacher unions were frequent "voices" in the media as were party politicians; on the other hand, researchers and parents were seldom seen or heard.

Consensus and conflict in the politics of schooling

Schooling is by tradition a highly political issue, as the 1997 survey confirms. Respondents were asked about their political sympathies, which proves to be an important variable in explaining differences in attitude to schools. The differences were bigger in the judgments made of how well the system performs, than in what are regarded as important objectives for schools (see Annex, Table A.8).[6] While some patterns emerge regarding priority objectives – e.g. Social Democrats tend to lay somewhat greater stress on education for the labour market, Moderates on society's basic values – the general picture is of a high degree of general consensus on aims. In judging system performance, however, the former are clearly the more positive. This conclusion holds whether the judgements concern how well schools succeed in imparting sound knowledge and skills, or in educating for the labour market or whether today's schools are better than those attended by the respondents.

There are also clear differences in how people with different political viewpoints look at the issue of private schools and choice. While around three out of four supporting the Social Democrats or the Left Party thought that greater school choice leads to widening societal rifts, this applied to only a third of the Moderates' supporters. It is striking, however, that more of the Left Party group (45%) favoured more private schools than those who sympathize with the Social Democrats (33%), indicating a desire for alternatives and diversity which cuts across traditional political lines.

Schools, working life and the labour market

While the rhetoric of employers' demands often finds expression in the national educational debate, there is little systematic or empirical evidence on how employers and the social partners actually look upon schools. These are difficult issues to handle methodologically, as has been found by national research studies and in the work of Network D in the OECD/INES programme. Because of these difficulties, no systematic or representative employer surveys have been conducted on these matters and the Swedish national attitude surveys do not provide much additional clarification. However, findings from the general public survey do offer some indications on the importance attached to "opening up" schools towards the labour market. The objective of educating for the labour market might be seen as an expression of the demand for greater school openness and relevance to society, while the objective about conveying core societal values might instead be an indicator of the demand for schools to be more detached and focus on stable and eternal values. In the 1997 survey, the labour market objective was seen as, if anything, more important ("essential" by 45%) by the general public than the value-conveying objective (40%) (see Figure 9.2).

Relatedly, more regular contact with activities outside school – such as study visits and links with enterprises – was the single most desired change for schools, as expressed not only by parents but even more so by pupils and teachers (around 90%) (see Annex, Figure A.6). Similarly, there was an almost equally overwhelming acceptance among all three groups of the need for more effective use of information communication technology (ICT) in schools. Evidence from the 1994 OECD survey indicates that the interest in ICT use in schools may be even greater in other countries (though the time lapse since the survey was conducted suggests caution given the rapid changes in this field). In the 1994 survey, 63% of the Swedish public stressed the importance of ICT as a school subject, a relatively high figure compared to certain other subjects like technology/technical studies, the arts, and physical education, but down on the cross-country mean of 71.5%. Those most in favour of ICT as a school subject were the public in the USA (86%) and in Austria (79%) (OECD, 1995, Table C.21).

The desire for greater openness is also reflected in finding mentioned earlier that 55% of the Swedish general public in 1997 thought that teachers have too little experience of working life outside school, a view shared by as many as 40% of teachers. The openness issue is thus one where there is a relatively strong consensus in Sweden.

189

Inter-generational issues and taxpayer attitudes towards schools

The 1997 survey results suggest that there is a fair degree of consensus across the generations on the value of, and objectives for, schools, especially among age groups up to 64. The oldest group, aged 65 to 74 years, seemed to attach relatively less importance to most of schools' objectives than the rest of the population. They also gave less overt support to certain school subjects like science, civics, English and physical education, but this did not hold for Swedish and Mathematics. (The general pattern of lower support among pensioners might nevertheless be something of an artefact, for they tended to use the categories "very important" or "rather important" more, and "essential" less, than the other age groups.)

In judgments of how well schools succeed in reaching their objectives, the general pattern is that the younger tend to be more positive. Across the different key objectives for schools to achieve, the youngest age group with the most recent experience of schools was the most positive, and the oldest age group the least positive (see Annex, Table A.9). Again, the data should be interpreted with care. The proportion of older people (aged 65-74) who felt that they "don't know" was markedly higher than in the other age groups. It could simply be that the oldest age group, with their own schooling far behind them, are less involved in issues connected with schools and schooling. More analysis would be needed to ascertain how far the age differences on the positive/negative dimension are firmly held or else reflect a sense of ignorance about school developments.

How far might the revealed age differences in attitudes suggest problems relating to willingness to fund schools adequately? How far is there cross-generational solidarity? In the 1993 survey, a question was asked concerning whether more or fewer economic resources should be allocated to the different tax-funded activities that contribute to the welfare society. The main finding is a pattern of wanting "more of everything" – about two thirds of the respondents felt that schools, health care, and care of the elderly should each have more resources (see Annex, Table A.10). The only sectors where more than 10% felt that costs should be reduced were social welfare services (17%), culture (21%) and defence (44%). The latter finding could be interpreted as support for the cutbacks in defence costs which have since been implemented in Sweden, while a cut in spending on culture would not have much effect on overall spending – though probably a substantial one on cultural activities themselves. The overall pattern of support for public spending thus does not offer much guidance to decision-makers in terms of priorities. But, this is itself a finding of importance – another piece of evidence of the consensus that exists on the support felt for schools, schooling, and other public institutions among many taxpayers.

There are nevertheless some differences in priorities between the generations, and between parents with children in school and others. Up to the age of 64 he different age groups are equally inclined to allocate more economic resources o both schools and to the care of the elderly (about two thirds). After age 64, only a little over one in four supported the allocation of more resources to schools 28%) while over three-quarters wanted more to be spent on care of the elderly 78%) (see Annex, Table A.11). Similarly, parents with school children (who domiate in the age group 26-45) were clearly in front in their support of more esources going to schools compared with "non-parents". Of greater significance, erhaps, is that the willingness to allocate more resources to child care drops rapdly after age 45, just at the time that it has come to be regarded as the first key itage in lifelong learning and citizenship education strategies in many OECD countries. (At the same time, no significant inter-generational differences were ound in the willingness to allocate resources to health care, which has an obvious elevance to all citizens.) These findings in all, then, indicate a need in ageing oopulations for stress to be placed on intergenerational solidarity and support for nvestments in services essential for children.

The position of different socio-cultural groups and the aims and operation of schools

Certain differences between socio-cultural groups have already been discussed in this chapter. A main finding is that a higher level of education is associated with a more critical attitude, including among parents with different educational backgrounds. Similarly, inter-generational differences have already been touched on. This section considers instead issues of ethnicity and urban/ ural background among parents.

An increasing number of immigrant parents, to the extent they have differing attitudes, expectations and demands, may well exercise an influence on the practice of the schools of tomorrow. A general finding from the 1997 parent survey indicates that immigrant parents are more satisfied with schools' performance, as evealed both in judgments about how well schools achieve their objectives at the evel of the system as a whole, and in relation to the local school. This includes more positive assessments of parents' perceived possibilities to influence decisions and school policies. These and other related differences exist, even when account is taken of differences in educational level. To some extent, there are differing rames of reference and/or levels of demand in play compared with Swedish-born oarents.

Immigrant parents, on the other hand, tended to be less satisfied with aspects of the social climate in their local school, relating to "peace and quiet", he sense of security, and victimization. They are distinctive in relation to the curiculum, being more eager to influence what is taught in lessons and the choice of extbooks, and laying greater stress than Swedish-born parents on certain school subjects: foreign languages other than English, and religion. There are no clear differences in attitudes to choice, "a school for all", private schools, etc., although immigrant parents are somewhat more interested in actually choosing a school (75% compared with to 69% of Swedish-born parents) and slightly more, proportionally, have actually done so.

The findings show few major or systematic differences between parents living in rural areas and in city/suburban areas, but there are some. Parents in rural areas, for example, were more satisfied with those aspects of schooling that are normally connected with small schools such as class sizes and the provision of support. These parents also attached greater importance to the objective of schools to educate for the labour market. They stressed the school subject physical education to a greater degree. The most obvious differences, however, concern both attitudes and experiences relating to choice. Approximately four-fifths of parents in city/suburban areas found it important to be able to choose a school, compared with 62% of rural parents. About half (48%) of parents in city/suburban areas thought that they actually had a choice, compared with under a quarter (23%) of rural parents. There were similar differences in attitudes to private schools and the effects of choice. These findings illustrate that choice of school is, at least in Sweden, still an urban phenomenon. It should also be noted that there is a correlation between geographical residence location and educational level, which might explain some of these differences given that higher educational level is related to the interest in, and opportunity for, choice.

Conclusions

In terms of shedding light on future scenarios for schools, the general impression given by the findings from the Swedish 1993 and 1997 national attitude surveys is that there is a good deal of support for the status quo. Despite the criticisms of how well the educational system succeeds in achieving its objectives, this criticism is more overt in relation to general, "public opinion", level than to local provision. Public opinion findings about schools and schooling should thus be qualified by opinions based on experienced educational realities. Generally teachers and schools are regarded as over- rather than under-exposed to change and the attitude to teachers is supportive rather than critical. But this also signals an increasing lack of status in the teaching profession, which is worrying for future recruitment. There is a broad and stable consensus among Swedish parents on the importance of schools for social cohesion, though education remains an area of political discord, especially in judgments about whether schools succeed or fail in their tasks. The findings further suggest that many parents tend to be in favour of a school that is more like the one they attended themselves. Increasing demands from parents might therefore be a force contributing to the status quo. Evidence rom the OECD 1994 survey indicates that this may be even more so in countries other than Sweden.

Support for the status quo, however, is not unqualified. The pressures on schools are tending to increase – rising educational levels lead to more critical attitudes and to higher demands being made on the educational system itself. It is possible even to suggest that a well-functioning school system thus contributes to its own weakening. And, although parents seem to be more satisfied with the local school than with the "system", this does not mean that the general level of satisfaction among parents in all respects can be regarded as high.

From the findings, parents' desire to influence schools is evident, in Sweden and in other countries. Furthermore, the Swedish findings clearly indicate that there is a significant gap between desired and perceived influence in relation to many aspects of schooling. Choice of school is the means of influence most available to parents. The demand for choice and diversity revealed by the surveys is only to be expected so long as schools do not find other ways of meeting demands. The high proportions of parents supporting choice and more private schools are an indication of changing values and demanding expectations. Hence, "market" and "pseudo-market" elements in schooling have grown in importance and will challenge, more or less strongly, elements of the status quo. This conclusion is supported by the data indicating that desire for alternatives and diversity cuts across traditional political demarcations.

There are other indications of demand for change. One is the relatively clear consensus – both among different stake-holders and the public in several OECD countries – on the need for schools to be more open to working life, surrounding society, and to new technology. Support for modernization and opening schools to post-industrial labour markets increasingly dominated by services and technological innovation is definitely a factor for change. So is the changing composition of the parental body: increasing numbers of immigrant parents may not only stimulate action through their differing levels of demand but also through their desire to exercise a stronger influence on the school curriculum.

If collected systematically and interpreted with discrimination, survey data on public opinion and parental demand can make a significant contribution to the understanding of the changing conditions of schools. Data from pupil and teacher surveys, which have been referred to less in this, might be even more useful, as experiences of daily life in school exercise a very powerful influence on the opinions on education held by the different stakeholders. And, as the pupils of today are the parents and the teachers of tomorrow, their experience of schools will have a lasting impact on their future priorities as citizens, parents, and teachers.

Notes

1. International studies on students' attitudes to school are relatively more common often in the context of international student assessments; recent examples are OECD PISA, IEA/Civics, and the WHO work on "Health Behaviour in School-Aged Children", a of which include attitudinal items.

2. The surveys, which are conducted every third year and so far have been carried ou three times – 1993/94, 1997 and 2000 – constitute one of several tools used in the eva uation and follow-up work of the agency.

3. The earlier OECD study focused on public opinion relating to schools and education i twelve OECD countries: Austria, Belgium (Flemish community), Denmark, Finland France, Netherlands, Portugal, Spain, Sweden, Switzerland, United Kingdom and US/ Substantial parts of the third Swedish surveys of the general public and parents hav been conducted as a comparative study of the five Nordic countries (Sweden, Denmark Norway, Finland and Iceland) – the so-called Nordic Attitudes Study – as an initiativ from the Nordic Ministerial Council. The results have been available since Spring 2001

4. Due to translation problems with the confidence scale, the percentages for Swede had to be re-calculated. This did not disturb the general comparative pattern in th indicator regarding important qualities.

5. "Voice" indicates trying to change things by taking issue (raising your voice), whil "exit" means seeking change by choosing something else, such as another politica party or employer or school. Staying "loyal" and not trying to change things at all i another option.

6. In the table, only those who sympathize with the three biggest political parties in th country are shown: The Left Party, the Social Democrats (Labour) and the Moderat Party (Conservatives). Insufficient numbers support the other political parties to yiel adequate statistical precision.

Annex to Chapter 9

Figure A.1. **Percentage of parents and of the general public thinking that today's school is better/neither better or worse/nor worse than the school they attended themselves**

Comparisons between 1969, 1987, 1993 and 1997

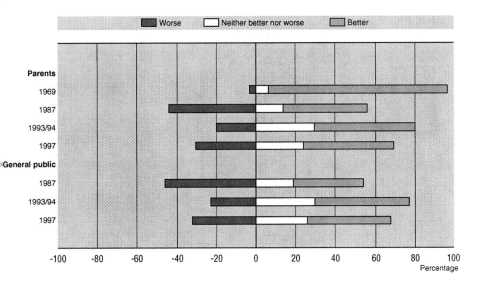

Figure A.2. **Percentage of pupils, parents, and teachers who agree that there are too many new things and too big changes in schools**

Comparison between 1993 and 1997

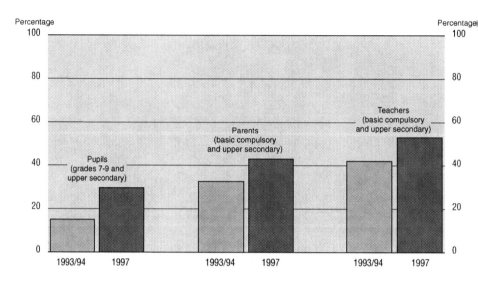

Figure A.3. **Parents' view of their child's school in different areas, 1997**

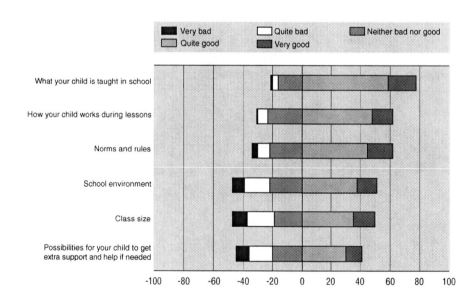

Figure A.4. **How much do parents want to participate in decision-making in school, and how much do they think that they actually are able to participate in decision-making? 1997**

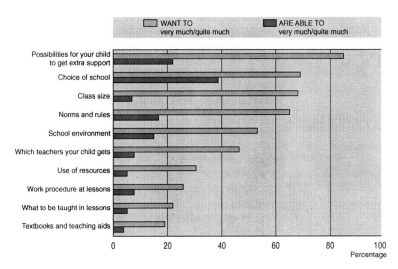

Figure A.5. **How prepared are parents to influence school and their views on reasons for not trying to influence**

Parents with a compulsory basic education (max. 9 years), compared to parents with an academic education, 1997

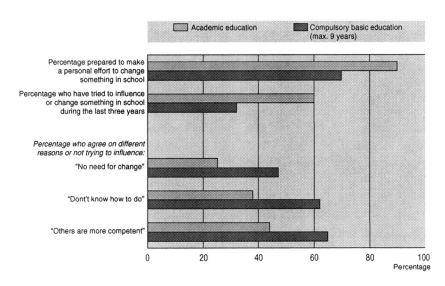

Figure A.6. **Percentage of pupils, parents and teachers who think that the following proposals on how work in schools should be changed, are very good or quite good**

Compulsory basic school, grades 7-9, and upper secondary school, 1997

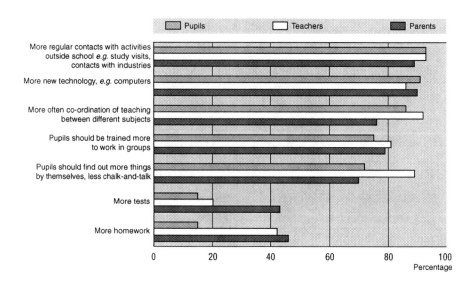

Figure A.7. **Should pupils get marks earlier in basic compulsory school?**

Views of pupils, parents and teachers, 1997

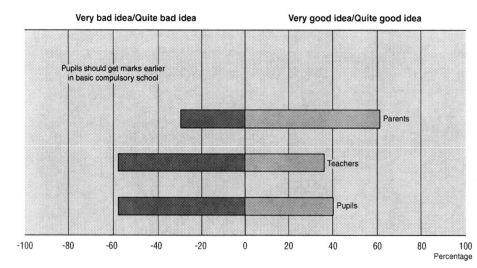

Table A.1. **Proportions (%) of the public, parents and teachers considering that schools succeed (to a large or fair extent) to meet different objectives, 1993 and 1997**

	General public		Parents		Teachers	
	1993	1997	1993	1997	1993	1997
Developing competences						
Impart sound knowledge and skills	48	35	52	40	72	54
Encourage curiosity and initiative	31	20	37	31	43	34
Provide training in taking positions on ethical issues	26	15	28	19	36	30
The school's role in society						
Education of equal value	35	30	39	36	54	34
Support to pupils with special needs	34	21	37	25	34	17
Convey society's basic values	28	23	32	27	51	42

Table A.2. **General public attitudes towards teachers, 1993 and 1997**

Percentage of the general public agreeing with:	1993	1997
"Teachers are an exposed group"	58	62
"Teachers have too many privileges"	25	17
"Teachers should have more experience from working life outside school"	59	55

Table A.3. **Pupils' views of their teachers, 1993 and 1997**

Percentage of pupils who consider that all or most teachers:	1993	1997
Have sufficient knowledge of their subjects	–	83
Are committed to their subjects	73	77
Teach well	58	67
Care about what pupils think	55	60
Can be trusted and turned to in confidence	43	48
Make use of what students learn in their leisure time in school work	–	23

Table A.4. **Parental views on school performance – Swedish schools in general and school which own child attends**

Percentages, 1997

		Very or quite well/good	Neither well/good nor bad	Quite or very bad
Child's school	What your child is taught in school	78	16	5
Swedish schools	Impart sound knowledge and skills	40	41	17
Child's school	Possibilities for child to get extra support/ help if needed	41	20	15
Swedish schools	Support to pupils with special needs	20	28	43

Table A.5. **Parents as "consumers" (want to) and "users" (feel able to): views in relation to choice of school and to influencing the possibilities for their own child to get extra support, 1993 and 1997**

Percentage of parents who very much or quite a lot:	1993	1997
Choice of school		
– Want to influence	70	70
– Feel that they are able to influence	40	41
Possibilities to get extra support for their child if needed		
– Want to influence	90	86
– Feel that they are able to influence	32	23

Table A.6. **Parental attitudes towards "a school for all" and private schools, 1997**

Percentage agreeing with the following statements

"School classes should be mixed, with pupils from different social and cultural background"	80
"More private schools is a good thing"	43
"Choice of school will lead to widening rifts in society"	53

Table A.7. **Factors influencing opinions on schools: percentage of the general public, parents and "non-parents" assessing factors to be very or quite important in forming their opinions on schools, 1993**

	General public	Parents	"Non-parents"
Experience of own child's school attendance	71	87	42
Experience of own time in school	63	61	66
Contacts at work with children or young people	50	54	45
Discussions with relatives and friends	33	32	35
National media (TV, radio and press)	35	32	39
Local media (TV, radio and press)	27	26	33
Statements from politicians	15	14	15

Table A.8. **Opinions on schools among people of different political sympathies (the Left Party, the Social Democratic Party and the Moderate Party)**
General Public Survey, 1997

	Political sympathy		
	Left Party	Social Democratic Party	Moderate Party
Essential/very important for schools to...			
– Impart sound knowledge and skills	89	92	97
– Educate for the labour market	77	84	77
– Convey society's basic values	77	70	81
Schools succeed very well/quite well in....			
– Imparting sound knowledge and skills	36	43	32
– Educating for the labour market	28	33	13
– Conveying society's basic values	25	22	16
Today's school is better than the school I attended myself"	34	55	31
Attitudes to public good/private good			
– School classes should be mixed, with pupils from different social and cultural background	85	84	70
– More private schools is a good thing	45	33	68
– Choice of school will lead to widening rifts in society	75	71	32

Table A.9. **The views of age groups on schools' success in meeting certain objectives**
Percentage thinking that schools succeed well or very well, or who don't know (DK), 1997

	Age group			
How well do schools succeed in giving...?	18-25	26-45	46-64	65-74
Knowledge and skills (very well/quite well)	44	32	33	25
Knowledge and skills (DK)	5	4	8	16
Education of equal value (very well/quite well)	37	30	25	22
Education of equal value (DK)	5	7	8	24
Giving support (very well/quite well)	30	21	16	14
Giving support (DK)	7	9	7	16

Table A.10. **Percentage of the general public wanting more or fewer resources allocated to different tax-funded activities, 1993**

Percentages wanting to maintain constant resource levels are not presented

	More resources	Fewer resources
Schools	68	1
Health care	70	2
Care of the elderly	69	1
Police	57	2
Environmental conservation	54	3
Child care	45	6
Higher education	35	3
Social welfare services	26	17
Culture	18	21
Defence	9	44

Table A.11. **The views of age groups, parents, and those with no school children on the allocation of economic resources to childcare, school, and care of the elderly**

Percentages thinking that these activities should have more economic resources, 1993

Age group/parental status	More economic resources should be allocated to:		
	Child care	Schools	Care of the elderly
18-25	60	66	62
26-45	55	77	70
45-64	32	64	66
65-74	30	28	78
Parents	46	76	68
"Non-parents"	45	54	70

A New Century and the Challenges it Brings for Young People: How Might Schools Support Youth in the Future?

by

Kerry J. Kennedy[1]
University of Canberra, Australia

Introduction

Young people across all societies attract attention from the older generation because of their behaviour, their likes and dislikes, and their general attitudes to life. The more they depart from what is seen to be mainstream, the more attention they attract. It has always been thus. Plato is often cited for his unfavourable attitude to a certain type of young man:

> "So he lives his life day by day, indulging each appetite as it makes itself felt. One day he is drinking heavily and listening to the flute; on the next he is dieting and drinks only water. Then he tries some exercise only to lapse into idleness and lethargy. Sometimes he seems to want to be a philosopher. More frequently, he goes in for politics, rising to say whatever comes into his head. His life lacks all discipline and order, yet he calls it a life of pleasure, freedom and happiness and is resolved to say the course" (*The Republic*, Book VIII, 561-d).

Less familiar perhaps are the parallel criticisms made of those who were to become the front line for the United States and her allies during World War II. Mortimer Adler outlined the views attributed to commencement speakers on the eve of the war as follows:

> "They all recognised a danger sign in the disaffection of youth, its distrust of any cause which spoke the language of principles. They argued against what they called the prevalent materialism, the single-minded self-interest of the college graduate's aim – to take care of himself and let the rest go hang, to get ahead in the world by beating his neighbour." (Adler, 1940)

203|

The post-World War II Baby Boomers, the generation "Xers" born in the 1960 and 1970s, and the current millennial generation, have all come in for their share of criticism. Youth rebellion, or at least adult perceptions of that rebellion, has perennial quality about it. Any proper appreciation of this must take account of the conditions or contexts that generate the actions and reactions. Plato, for example, was particularly critical of "democratic" youth because of the views that he had formed on the dangers of democracy in Ancient Greece. The pre-World War I commencement orators referred to by Adler were alert to a new, foreboding political context in a society that just two decades earlier had been "made safe" for democracy. Contexts reveal the conditions in which young people find themselves at any particular time. The reactions of young people should be understood as a two-sided process – a reaction to particular conditions or contexts and as an active attempt to re-form those contexts in the light of aspirations and values.

An issue for educators today and tomorrow, therefore, is how should the conditions in which young people live be understood and with what significance should they be attributed. The relevant contexts include the economy and the labour market, and education and training, together with the different transition between them. Within these broad contexts are conditions embedded in the social environment of young people that also exercise specific influences on them. They are in fact subject to multiple sets of influences, some of which are external to their control and others of which reflect more personal predilections. If the attitudes of young people, including various forms of rebelliousness, reflect structural conditions in the economy and society, it is more sensible to focus policy thinking on these rather than on the behaviours they produce. Such an approach cannot help but be linked to the role of schools and schooling as major contextual influences on young people.

Contexts and conditions of the youth landscape

Education, training and the labour market

Education and training are profoundly significant characteristics affecting young people. On turning 15 years of age, a young person can expect to spend, on average in OECD countries, another six years in education – a sharp average increase of 1.5 years since 1985. Graduates from tertiary studies are likely to earn substantially more than those from upper secondary education. There are thus considerable incentives to attain higher and higher levels of education. Where young people quit education after the lower secondary cycle, their earning potential tends to be "between 60-90% of those individuals who have completed upper secondary education" (OECD, 2000a, p. 295; see also pp. 289-294). While income is not the sole measure of a rewarding life, the point here is that education and income will remain strongly linked in the future. Without high levels of educa tion, young people will suffer severe constraints on the various life options available to them.

Access to and continuation in education and training are thus key issues for young people. Now, continuation to upper secondary studies has become the norm and enrolment rates across OECD countries at age 17 stand at over 80% (OECD, 2000a, p. 129). The significance of this figure can be appreciated when it is recalled that "in 1945 some 80% of the 14-year olds in Western Europe left school and joined the workforce" (Coleman and Husén, 1985, p. 21).

There are at least two major sets of issues for young people to highlight. The first is the real concern relating to the young people who do not continue in education and training. Worrying numbers are still early school leavers (up to 20% of teenagers in 1997), are neither in education, training nor a job (9% of the 16-19 age group in 1997), or leave with low level educational qualifications (25% of the 25-29 age group in 1997; OECD, 1999a, pp. 10-12). This not a new nor transitory situation. Coleman and Husén referred to similar figures and concluded, along with others in the 1970s and 1980s, that a "new educational underclass" had emerged, who were missing out on the increased access and opportunities brought with better education and training. It is not too much to argue that this "underclass" is now a permanent feature of the youth landscape. Policy initiatives addressing this underclass have abounded over recent decades (see e.g. OECD, 1985); unfortunately, the latest statistics only seem to confirm the structural nature of the problem.

The second set of issues, more or less closely related to the first, has to do with the nature of schooling in the 21st century. In around half a century, the provision of a full secondary education has moved from catering for an elite to mass provision. What should be expected of schools that are currently retaining students for longer and longer periods of time? What changes in structures, curriculum, pedagogy and teaching are needed to cater for a changing school population and new aims for education? Within these far-reaching questions what is clear is that a secondary education still geared for an elite is not what is needed as the context has changed dramatically. The pathways from mass secondary education are multiple, the school population is diverse, labour market requirements are shifting. Change rather than stability is the order of the day. Schools and schooling will remain structural features of the youth landscape but in future they will not serve young people well if they remain mirror images of institutions as they were in the past. (Further discussion of schooling implications follows below.)

It might be assumed from the foregoing that the possession of higher levels of education is a sufficient condition for formal labour market entry. Are the 80% or so of young people who stay on for upper secondary education in OECD countries automatically guaranteed a job? Any answer to this question cannot be based on traditional thinking and concepts about the transition from school to work nor assume that full-time permanent employment will be available in the future. What can be said is that education is a necessary but not sufficient condition for labour market entry. It provides the basis for further education and training and, if oriented in the right way, can provide skills and competences that will enhance a student's employability. The lack of a direct link between the possession of qualifications and employment is, of course, problematic for young people. It adds to the uncertainty that is already characteristic of adolescence and raises serious issues about the relevance of the final years of schooling.

Transitions from school to work are taking place later than was the case in the past: the transition is now likely to take place between the ages of 18 and 22 (OECD, 2000a, p. 12). In 1997, the unweighted OECD average for 18-year-olds in education and training but not employed was 56.3% while a further 18.3% were both employed and in education and training. 14.3% were in employment but not in education and training. For 22-year-olds, the corresponding figures were 25.4% in education and training but not employed, 11.1% in both, and 46.2% in employment but not in education and training. This has led one commentator to observe that "the 'young' are older than they were several decades ago" (Freeman, 1999, p. 92). This prolongation of the period of youth also means a delay in their independence, their "rites of passage" into adulthood, and their ability to contribute to society as active citizens. The economic indicators point to a deep structural issue for young people – their "coming of age" in a new economic environment.

There are other implications for this delayed "coming of age". In the broader social policy context, there is the issue of who should assume responsibility for young people who lack financial independence but who need to be engaged in education and training or active job seeking. Is this yet another parental responsibility? If so, how do young people in their early twenties deal with an extended period of dependence and how do parents manage an essentially "adult" family? How do young people in these contexts develop personal relationships outside the family when they are still dependent on their parents? Do the same social mores apply to adult dependent offspring as to young adolescent children? These are all issues centred around people's private lives but they also have ramifications for public policy. This is particularly so in those households where finances cannot be stretched to continue to provide for adult children, when the prolongation of youth may well generate further disadvantage.

Making the transition into employment is thus problematic for many young people: overall across OECD countries, "teenage and young adult unemployment rates are in double digit figures and were higher in 1997 than they were in 1979" (OECD, 2000a, p. 14). The transition from school to work for those with lowest attainment is especially problematic. One study comparing youth unemployment in France, Germany and the United States showed that young people with less than upper secondary education, experienced high levels of unemployment over a five-year period after initial education. In the case of Germany and the United States, those with both upper secondary and tertiary education also experienced significant levels of unemployment (OECD, 1999a, p. 80). As for the duration of unemployment (two years or more), the same study showed that this was clearly concentrated among the educational underclass. Higher levels of education may thus tend to shield young people from lengthy periods of unemployment, while for those with low levels of education, many are caught in a cycle that is difficult to halt without intervention. Either way, unemployment is a structural feature of the youth landscape with the potential to affect all.

Transition issues concern employment not just unemployment – the nature of work available to young people and their consequent remuneration. Young people do hold part-time jobs but no more than the population in general (OECD, 2000a, pp. 285-286). More will hold temporary jobs or contracts, however, relative to the rest of the population. Related are the levels of expected remuneration. Despite their increased educational attainments over the past two decades, there has over the same period of time been a "decline or stagnation in the relative earnings of young people" (OECD, 1999a, p. 16). However, this may change over time, at least initially the rewards may not match the effort required for successful entry into the labour market.

Thus, while the overall picture is neither rosy nor unrelentingly gloomy, prospects are not spread equally. For many young people, longer periods of time spent in education will pay off with a job and, possibly a career, but not without considerable effort and perhaps some experience of unemployment, temporary employment and/or low wages. For the educational underclass, on the other hand, jobs will be scarce and periods of unemployment will be lengthy. The transition to employment may never be made without further education and training. Yet, further education and training is only a necessary but not sufficient condition for embarking on a successful life course. Even those who attain well will need to be resilient and entrepreneurial.

Social conditions influencing young people

While the social conditions influencing young people are often difficult to grasp with precision, there is a body of evidence about today's youth landscape. The extent to which young people appear to be disengaged from traditional political processes has been well documented. Halstead, writing in The Atlantic Monthly about the so-called "generation Xers" has observed that:

> "A wide sampling of surveys indicates that Xers are less politically or civically engaged, exhibit less social trust or confidence in government, have a weaker allegiance to their country or to either political party, and are more materialistic than their predecessors." (Halstead, 1999, p. 2)

These observations are supported by other international evidence. Hahn (1998) investigated students' political values and understandings in Denmark, Germany, the Netherlands, the United Kingdom, and the United States.[2] Students were asked to report on their levels of political trust, experiences and interest, their confidence and views on political efficacy and their future civic participation. The researcher's own words are unambiguous: "the questionnaire responses are quite dismal (...) the depth of students' political cynicism (...) is troubling" (p. 31). Results on the political efficacy and confidence scales were slightly more positive than on that of trust. Nevertheless, UK working class students, for instance, do not feel nearly as effective as those from private schools, suggesting a more pervasive problem of perceptions of powerlessness in democratic societies. Democracy is in principle for all citizens, including the young, yet their commitment to it may well be limited when its benefits are not obvious. As school-to-work and life transitions become more hazardous and complex, young people experience greater uncertainty and this may well be reflected in growing political cynicism.

The uncertainty affecting youth is also reflected in the evidence relating to youth suicide (though data in this area, particularly cross-nationally, are fraught with problems of definition and validity). In some countries, the trend is upward. For example, in Australia suicide among 15-24 year-olds rose from 11 to 17 deaths per 100 000 persons in the cohort between 1978 and 1998, and accounted for 25% of all deaths in this age group (Department of Health and Aged Care, 1999; see also Department of Health and Aged Care, undated, pp. 1-4). The incidence of male suicide in this group was more than four times higher than for females. A comparative study of suicide among 15-24 year-olds found a similar increase in suicides over time in Finland, and by 1995, there were 22.8 deaths per 100 000 (Fahnrich, 1998, pp. 13-14). When these figures are broken down by gender, they show 36.6 for males and 8.4 for females, a similar ratio to Australia. In Germany, also studied by Fahnrich, there has actually been a decline in recent times. In 1995, the overall youth suicide rate was lower than Finland's at 8.8 but the gender difference is still clear with a male-to-female ratio of around 3 to 1. It was higher still at 5 to 1 in the United States, while the overall youth suicide rate in 1997 was slightly higher at 9.5 per 100 000 (National Institute of Mental Health, 1999, p. 1). In New Zealand, the youth suicide rate increased sharply from 12.6 to 29.9 per 100 000 of the population over the 1985-1996 period, with 39.9 for males and 14.3 for females (New Zealand Health Information Service, 1997, p. 2). The existence of a universal trend towards increased youth suicide is questionable, as in some countries (e.g. Germany, Japan, and Switzerland) the youth suicide rate has actually decreased over the past decade. These cases notwithstanding, the data reviewed give serious grounds for concern for many countries.

What accounts for these data? Some researchers, consistent with the classic sociological tradition represented by Durkheim (1951), have linked structural changes in the economy and society to the increasing incidence of youth suicide (Hassan, 1990; Taylor, 1990). There are also psychological factors that appear to predispose young people to suicide such that sociological explanations alone are insufficient. Fahnrich (1998) refers to the interaction of risk factors that might contribute to or trigger suicidal behaviour, focusing particularly on depression, substance abuse and anti-social behaviour, and the breakdown of social relationships involving family and peers. These factors are similar to those identified by Hassan (1990): the general disillusionment of youth in a post-modern world, substance abuse and violence, breakdown in family relationships and mental health issues. How these factors interact for different individuals remains largely unknown; that they interact with often tragic results for some is only too well known. Hassan places emphasis on community responsibility, particularly to create conditions that will allow at least some suicidal youth to begin their lives afresh and with a sense of purpose. The policy message is the need to focus efforts on creating conditions that will assist, rather than exacerbate, the plight of suicidal young people.

The issue of suicide highlights other social conditions that are often present, if not pervasively, in the youth landscape. These include drug and alcohol abuse, changing family structures and relationships, increased violence both at school and in society as a whole, and juvenile crime. There are different national contexts shaping the nature and prevalence of these conditions but wherever they exist, they can affect a broad range of young people. What is more, they tend particularly to affect those young people who already suffer some form of disadvantage, excluding them further from general social resources and opportunities. Lack of parental resources, of educational qualifications, of supportive social networks, and of access to labour markets can all lead to dysfunctional social behaviour. Multiple forms of disadvantage reproduce social exclusion for many young people. Suicide may be among the most tragic outcomes, but there are many other dysfunctional processes from which young people may well have difficulty in extricating themselves. In most places, for instance, young people overtly break the law when they experiment with drugs and this can be "a first step in a spiral leading to more serious offences" (Council of Europe, 1998, pp. 17-18). They need to learn how to negotiate different social conditions in ways that have positive outcomes, but some will find this easier than others.

Learning to negotiate complex environments will be a key skill for young people in the future. Not all environments are externally imposed, and young people freely enter into some of them (as with so-called "youth cultures"). The latter often reflect young people's attempts to express their individuality and independence. There has been extensive theorising about the extent to which there are youth subcultures around single features such as music (Weinstein, 1994; Dotter, 1994; Kruse, 1993) or whether these are simply one aspect of the multiple ways in which young people learn to express themselves (McCracken, 1997). Whichever way it

209|

should be understood, a key point is that young people are more than capable of developing their own forms of cultural expression. In this way they are able to exert agency over the world and begin to shape it in ways that are consistent with their own emerging values. Young people thus live in the tension whereby they can be active creators of cultural standards and norms while at the same time subject to the pressures and processes of the mainstream.

Nowhere is this tension better illustrated than in the development over the past decade of the "dance party" or "rave party" as perhaps the most distinctive expression of youth culture (and the subject of recent academic attention; see Thornton, 1995; Valentine *et al.*, 1998). The "rave party" represents a move from the narrow confines of the disco to much more open spaces with many more people to listen and dance to "techno" music and its many derivatives. For some, it represents the creation of a new community of the young where PLUR (peace, love, unity and respect) reigns in a TAZ (Temporary Autonomous Zone in which "separate, self-governing events take place between the cracks of society's fabric" (*The Spirit of Raving*, undated). For others, it is a danger zone for young people – of prevalent drug-taking seen as normal activity. Whichever the viewpoint, rave parties are an international phenomena with avid, sometimes cult, following. The main point is that young people will develop, or at least strongly endorse, their own forms of cultural expression irrespective of adults' attitudes. Policy should be informed by an understanding of these forms of cultural expression, not so much in a moral-behavioural sense, but as a means of addressing what young people themselves appear to be searching for in a turbulent environment.

Characteristics of the youth landscape

If a "bird's eye view" were possible of the conditions of young people in the new century, what would it reveal? The following draws together schematically the issues that have been raised in the first section of the chapter, in the form of five characteristics defining the key features of the young person's future environment.

The features indicate the uncertainties faced by young people. Schools of the future will have to take them on board if they are to serve a positive and constructive role. Linear notions of smooth progression from one phase of life to another are no longer adequate. There is no formula for making easy transitions nor a single set of processes that will guarantee success, though in general young people will need to be better-educated, and more resourceful, flexible, independent and entrepreneurial in charting their life course. This will be easier for some to achieve than others, especially those young people who are already burdened with educational and/or socio-economic disadvantage. Schools will only be one, but an

1. Later transitions to work and adulthood	Young people spend more time in education and training thus lengthening the period of dependence on parents and delaying their entry to the labour market.
2. The conditionality of education and training	Education and training are necessary but not sufficient for success in the future. Qualifications will not guarantee a smooth life course but without them, that course will be highly problematic.
3. The unpredictability of labour markets	Smooth transitions into the labour market cannot be expected and unemployment may feature in the lives of all citizens at some time. Getting a "foothold" in the labour market will be essential but may well be problematic.
4. The turbulence of the social environment	The potential for dysfunctional behaviour will be ever present, especially for those without qualifications and who suffer other forms of disadvantage. But for all young people, there will be risks to be negotiated. Basic institutions such as the family are undergoing rapid change that will impact on many young people.
5. The agency of young people	It is clear that while young people will have much to contend with in the future they also have the potential to create their own forms of cultural expression. This can be a positive feature of youth development, but it also has the potential to be negative and even destructive.

important, factor, that can positively contribute to their lives. How might they be reconfigured to do so?

Schools for tomorrow

A basic distinction to draw as starting point is between the aims of reconfiguring the processes of schooling and reformulating the basic functions of schools in society. The term "social anchor" has been coined to describe the function of schools in the market-oriented societies of the new century (Kennedy, 1999). In a fast moving, global and technology-driven society, schools must play an important role in providing stability for young people. This indeed remains their basic function in society. It does not imply that schools should remain as they are today or were yesterday. They must address the real needs of young people, recognising

211|

the main features of the youth landscape and designing learning opportunities and organisational structures around these.

Such schools will need to be characterised by attributes such as:

- Flexibility of structures and learning opportunities.
- Relevance of learning experiences.
- Explicit standards for expected student learning.
- Incentives for lifelong learning.
- Engaging teaching.
- Nurturing environments.
- Participatory culture.

These attributes will better cater for student populations growing up in an unpredictable social and economic environment. By providing a supportive and flexible environment that focuses on the changing needs of students, schools can be places of both stability and challenge for students. To attain these ends, four strategies are outlined in this section: *i*) the deregulation of the school curriculum; *ii*) the development of new community partnerships for schools; *iii*) the adoption of new forms of school organisation, including new approaches to the teaching profession itself; *iv*) the development of new pedagogies that recognise active learning as central to student development.

The deregulation of the school curriculum

The school curriculum is one of the few areas of school policy that has not been subject to deregulation in recent times. The opposite has been the case in many places. In Australia, England and Wales, New Zealand, and the United States, there have been concerted initiatives by national governments to ensure greater uniformity and consistency in the school curriculum. A study by Kennedy and Mills (1996) showed considerable similarities in curriculum provision across national jurisdictions. The reasons are not difficult to locate. The curriculum of schools represents a significant policy instrument affecting cultural formation, social cohesion and economic development. Its main function has been to prepare a skilled workforce committed to the nation and its objectives. High attainment in terms of school curricula has been a critical pathway for social mobility so that powerful support for the curriculum comes from influential parents as well as from politicians and policy makers. It is thus a courageous government that will make radical changes to the school curriculum.

A key characteristic of current curriculum provision is its static nature, with change tending to take place only at the margins. Despite important shifts in school populations, the nature of work, and social conditions affecting young people he curriculum remains largely intact. This is as true in comprehensive as in dual systems. The basic assumption appears to be that one set of experiences is good or all students and groups of students.

This approach to curriculum will not serve students well in the future. New approaches need to be developed that are student-focused so that exactly the kind of flexibility required of students themselves will also be found in curriculum provision. In the secondary years, students will need to be able to move easily between at least four broad areas of study:

- Social and cultural studies (history/geography/civics).
- Literacy, numeracy and scientific studies.
- Vocational studies.
- Community learning studies (service learning and community oriented projects).

These headings simply indicate the broad contours and require considerable expansion to be operational. The school and classroom should not be the only sites of learning by students. There should be an easy movement in and out of school and learning acknowledged wherever it takes place. Students should not be tied to age/grade placement. They should be able to accumulate credit in relation to defined outcomes at times and in ways that suit their own particular contexts.

If students are to be flexible on graduation, they need flexible learning arrangements that build independence, decision-making skills, creativity, and a commitment to learning itself. Ironically, such an approach calls for more rather han less monitoring of student outcomes. Progress against expectations and goals would need to be assessed on a regular basis. A deregulated curriculum does not surrender responsibility: instead, it enables students to make choices and requires schools to know their students in more profound and meaningful ways. Such an approach would lay the foundations for lifelong learning. It would acknowledge that young people need to be prepared for a world in which their own initiative and ideas will play a fundamental part in determining their life chances.

New community partnerships for schools

If the school curriculum is to be deregulated, schools will need better and more extensive relationships with their communities. If students are to spend more time in the community, undertaking vocational studies and community projects and service, then close links need to be developed between the school and its immediate environment. Schools cannot continue to be like monasteries – he self-proclaimed learning centres of the industrial age. They must welcome

213|

community members onto their sites and open themselves up to genuine local involvement. There are numerous examples of successful practice that can show what is possible, and the literature on schools as sites for the delivery of integrated community services is growing (Dryfoos, 1992; Fredericks, 1994). The growth and spread of ICT offers the opportunity for schools to become community centres for Internet services, especially for disadvantaged groups. For schools to be focal points for lifelong learning under community governance is natural given the nature and location of capital investment in school infrastructure. In a sense this is to reinforce a longstanding role of schools as integral elements of their communities.

Schools in the future, then, should be both in and of the community, enabling students to pass with ease back and forth in their learning journeys. They should not be seen as "sacred sites" where arcane and irrelevant knowledge is dispensed during the hours when students are prevented from engaging in more exciting activities. They should be the arbiters and facilitators of skills and knowledge that equip young people for life. Rather than forsaking the traditional cultural role of the school, this would be to enhance it in line with the new realities and conditions for young people. Schools should be where young people can grow and be nurtured, not so as to understand a world that has already passed them by but to be enabled to construct a world of their choosing for increasingly turbulent times.

New approaches to school organisation and the teaching profession

The above changes would all call for new organisational structures for schools. If they are to act as the hub of community-based learning they cannot be managed as hierarchical, single purpose, passive structures, accountable primarily to state bureaucracies and unconnected with the real world that their students live in. Management must be more outward-looking and governance more community-focused than it often is today, with strategic directions informed by contributing to the learning society.

Teachers in these schools will continue to nurture students but they should not be the only facilitators of student learning. There should be greater reliance placed on community resources to provide teaching and learning experiences for students. The teaching profession needs to broaden its base to admit others to play ancillary but important roles. There are very rich resources for learning in communities – other professionals, artists, gardeners, business owners and so forth – all of whom have the potential to help prepare young people for the future. Schools in the future must be structured in such a way as to facilitate this broad community participation. It is not an exaggeration to refer to "a new social partnership" for schools and their communities.

At the same time, teachers will have a fundamental role in ensuring the much-needed stability or "anchoring" referred to above. Their part is critical in curriculum construction and the monitoring of student learning. They will guide young people into different experiences that meet their needs and aspirations, providing pastoral care and counselling. In all, the demands will be greater but so should the rewards as well.

New pedagogies with active learning at their core

How students learn is as critical as what or where they learn or who teaches them. The engagement of students in learning and their lifelong commitment to continue doing so must be key objectives for the future. The Internet both facilitates learning directly and offers a model or metaphor to help re-think learning as a more active and engaging process.

The Internet will undoubtedly play an increasingly important role in the lives of young people. It is unconceivable that it will not play a central role in schools and the community as a learning tool in the future. Young people tend to adapt easily to it and schools may be the only locations where equal access can be guaranteed. Computers need to be ubiquitous throughout schools and the community as do the staff to provide technical support. Software for real learning – not just drill, recitation and response – needs to be widely available. Students must be able to move easily back and forth between programmes, the Internet and more traditional learning resources as part of their daily work, work that is done creatively, independently, and at the students' own pace.

It is in this sense that the Internet offers a metaphor for pedagogy. It is open, accessible and full of potential. It permits access to information but leaves individuals to decide what is important. It facilitates communication across national and cultural barriers. It provides the conditions under which learning can take place but it does not construct it in any particular way. These need to be the characteristics of pedagogy in the future if students are to be really engaged and become committed to lifelong learning.

Conclusion

For schools to provide the "social anchor" for young people in the future cannot be achieved by reproducing the educational conditions of the past. Rather, they must take seriously the conditions that currently influence young people, acknowledging the turbulent and unpredictable lives they face. Schools do need to be reconfigured so that the life chances of the young will be enhanced. To achieve this represents a considerable challenge for policy-makers as the extent of the changes being suggested is considerable. Yet they are not necessarily greater in scale than other changes on the current public policy agenda. Schools

215|

were originally created in their current form to serve an industrial society and must inevitably change to meet the new challenges and directions pursued by governments themselves. Little purpose is served by pretending that the curriculum, school structures and personnel, and teaching methods that served the industrial state will well serve the knowledge society. Young people face fundamentally new challenges in the personal, social and economic dimensions of their lives. They need schools that fully recognise those challenges.

Notes

1. This chapter was completed during a study visit with OECD/CERI in Paris in Summer 2000.
2. A recent study using the same instruments has recently been completed using an Australian sample: Mellor, S. (1998), *"What's the Point?": Political Attitudes of Victorian Year 11 Students*, Research Monograph No. 53, Australian Council for Educational Research (ACER), Melbourne. The study confirmed Hahn's results.

Chapter 11

Schools for an Emerging New World[1]

by

Alain Michel
Inspecteur général de l'Éducation nationale, France

Introduction

"The most acute problem for people of our time is the tension between the global and local, and how it is expressed. In our modern democracies, we might have the impression that leaders think globally and citizens locally. This route would lead to the withering away of democratic debate, and to difficulties of engaging in dialogue among ourselves, even in political circles. How can a dynamic dialectic be established between the global and local? This must still be defined."

The aim of this paper is to consider this dialectic, as posed by Jacques Delors before the French Commission for UNESCO in 1997 (Brunsvick and Danzin, 1998), in its ramifications for schooling.

The virtual global village and a new regionalism and localism

Recent developments in our societies have seen the emergence of a planetary village, resulting from prodigious technological strides in communications, and a renaissance of regionalisms and local action. Viewed from another angle, globalisation, because of the risk it brings of soulless standardisation, can lead to fragmentation and a reduced sense of belonging to a wider community. The excesses of unbridled markets, in which prices and the market are more important than social and cultural relationships, are being met with a reaction of narrow nationalism, regionalism and parochialism. These threaten peace and raise the spectre of resurgent racism and intolerance. This is a first dimension of the tension between the global and the local. It is an important one in considering the aims of schools because, by educating citizens to be aware of these risks, they can shape the future of our societies.

Another dimension is the new relationship between time and space that glo balisation implies. It can thus be regarded as heralding a new civilisation. Instan network communications, the juxtaposition of the virtual with tangible reality, an the acceleration of scientific and technological change, are pushing towards th predominance of immediacy to the detriment of an appreciation of the longer term; to zapping and surfing rather than the search for knowledge. The bywords o this short-termism are "mobility" and "flexibility". We are meant to put faith in th heuristic and self-regulation rather than societal visions; rapid reaction, not for ward planning. Operating in virtual and ephemeral spaces erodes individuals' cul tural reference points while fostering new forms of mobility and meta geographical wandering.

All this provides new challenges for institutions, including nation-states, an also schools and other learning settings. As Paul Valéry once said of the age of th cathedral: "the time when time did not count has passed". We are contestants in race that requires us rapidly to adjust in neo-Darwinian fashion to our changin competitive environment. The result is the worship of flexibility and reaction an the questioning of established traditions: planning, Taylorist and Fordist model of organisation, and the endeavour to manage economic and social chang through centralised decision-making. Globalisation and its spirit of competitio require finance on a massive scale and yet decentralised management – anothe example of the global/local dialectic. Public administrations are deemed anachro nistic for being centralised and bureaucratic, for salvation now lies in decentralisa tion and the exercise of autonomy by players on the ground. Such infatuation wit modernity, as an end in itself without any societal vision, is sustained by contem porary managerial discourse. This has invaded the private sector, and increasingl public services too including schools, and serves further to legitimise this seem ingly inexorable if perilous process.

The process has led some, such as Le Goff, to denounce this as a new form o clandestine persuasion, a "gentle barbarity" (1999). In his view, worthwhile ambitions – autonomy, transparency, participation, shared projects – come at th cost of alienation, stress, and the denigration of culture and history. Such a assessment may seem harsh, but the issues are real ones. Managerial discourse i education, which has accompanied the development of a scholastic consumerisn by parents and students (Ballion, 1982), has also been criticised by Johsua (1999 for reducing consideration of major societal issues simply to those of appropriat management instruments.

And yet, it is difficult to deny the value of new approaches to enhance effec tiveness and transparency in education systems and the autonomy of practitio ners in ways that reflect local circumstances and foster innovation. Local actio and the revitalisation of citizen participation may be indispensable in forgin social infrastructure now that the welfare state is in crisis. Echoing de Tocquevill

t may help to redefine the foundations of democracy in a world of growing complexity, one in which individuals come increasingly to claim the right to be different. He pioneered the subsidiarity principle for apportioning responsibilities
across the different levels of decision-making – a principle now adopted by the
European Union, as well as its member States in ways shaped by their different
histories. More globally, as pointed out in UNESCO's 21st Century Dialogues
(September 1998), the on-going third industrial and global revolutions have not
led to the establishment of a new social contract (Mayor and Bindé, 1999).

New expectations for schooling

We have sketched the context in which new and often contradictory expectations have become manifest *vis-à-vis* schools, reflecting an awareness of the far-
reaching transformations of our so-called post-modern societies (Michel, 1996a). A
first set of transformations is the acceleration of technological change, especially
in communication. This has a number of major consequences for the missions of
schools, which now should:

1. Prepare students from an early age to accept change and the continuous
   questioning of what once was taken for granted in everyday life. This is not
   straight-forward as all of us need some constants to fall back on.

2. Cope with the accelerated obsolescence of knowledge and skills, implying
   lifelong learning for all and the continuous professional renewal of teachers
   and trainers.

3. Prepare students to question the results of change – rather than regard it
   as an end in itself – and to review science and technology critically in terms
   of their ethical and practical implications for the future. Rabelais's warning
   from the 16th century has never been more apposite: "Knowledge without
   conscience is but the ruin of the soul".

4. Integrate communication technologies effectively into schools. It is not sufficient just to invest in more computers, educational software and CD-
   ROMs, or Internet connections, to enhance learning. This is for reasons of
   equity as well as effectiveness: if schools remain aloof from these technologies, children from needy backgrounds will be at still more of a disadvantage compared with the more affluent families who are ICT-equipped.

The second fundamental transformation concerns globalisation. World-wide
economic competition has a number of major consequences for education. To
begin with, competition in knowledge-based societies hinges on productivity differentials that themselves reflect differences in human capital. Competition from
countries with low labour costs compels the rich countries to move certain activities offshore and create jobs using advanced qualifications in high value-added
sectors. Educational "malthusianism" is thus impossible: an increasing general

219|

level of education has become an economic necessity. As a result, there has been massive educational growth in all European countries, posing new challenges relating to mass education at the secondary and higher levels and exposing the inadequacy of the further training available for adults. Economic and social objectives converge in this regard. Key messages about quality – that competitiveness depends on qualifications and competence at all levels and not just among managers – is entirely consistent with the equity objective of combating the two tier society in which individuals are excluded through lack of basic education and of functional literacy.

Globalisation calls for greater individual mobility, more flexibility, and the openness to work with partners having different cultures and codes. Communicating in the partner's language is increasingly useful. All this means that demands on education are growing and call for rethinking the current curriculum, which is still tailored to the earlier 20th century industrial society rather than the 21st century post-industrial, global world.

Despite the major growth of national education systems, a "process of creative destruction" as described by Schumpeter (1947) is leaving a growing proportion of excluded people behind, whole populations in the developing world as well as groups in developed countries. New social fractures have emerged, which are causing their own divisions in education, despite efforts to compensate for socio-cultural handicaps through policy approaches such as positive discrimination (AFAE, 1999). Many countries have witnessed rising youth unemployment and new forms of insecurity, poverty and exclusion. The situation is especially critical in big city suburbs, where a soulless urbanism exacerbates the sense of rejection by young people who have developed their own counterculture. This exclusion stems particularly from economic conditions, and from the erosion of established local support institutions and networks of solidarity, including the family.

Often, blame for this exclusion is laid at the door of schools, charged with failing in their educational and social duties. There is usually scant justification for these criticisms, as schools are often the only institution left in some areas as a last bastion against the breakdown of societal values. Yet, precisely because schools are seen as the last hope, criticisms tend to focus on them. This is especially difficult for teachers and other education workers when, in the most disadvantaged neighbourhoods, it is they who have engaged in collective hard work and innovation.

The new imperatives of effectiveness and equity

In a context of growing expectations and educational needs within limited budgets, school systems are hard-pressed to meet two major aims: boost their effectiveness and reduce social inequalities. Even if they might want to, the extent of change in the economic and social environment precludes schools from the option of simply continuing with the status quo. They must not only adapt but also lay the foundations for a future that respects a humanist understanding of social life and fundamental rights of the individual (Michel, 1994, 1996b). They must help to form critical, active citizens controlling, rather than being controlled by, technical progress, who can give meaning to individual and community life, uphold the planet's ecological sustainability, develop tolerance, and contribute to identifying genuine futures for society. The European Union may offer a favourable context to do this, given that it is a collective enterprise to build the future on principles and practices developed through genuine dialogue between different cultures yet which share fundamental reference values.

Acknowledging that schools must change does not mean that the direction, scale, pace or forms of that change are already clear. France, like its European partners, is confronting a range of fundamental issues in this regard that deserve the fullest possible democratic airing. Among these questions are:

- In a world of increasingly instability, including at the geo-political level, what are the most important missions for schools? There seems to be consensus around four of them:

  - the transmission of knowledge, specific and general;

  - the preparation for working life (not limited only to occupational training);

  - the development of personal skills and civic responsibility;

  - the promotion of equality of opportunity and equity.

The consensus is less clear, however, in judgements about the relative importance of these different goals and how they can be pursued simultaneously.

- In the light of effectiveness and equity objectives, how to manage the growing diversity of students resulting from both mass education and new forms of social division? How to achieve unity without uniformity? How to diversify learning tracks and methods without falling prey to segregation? How far and for how long in the school cycles should there be the same educational track for all? These questions raise issues relating to "common culture", core curriculum and a "survival kit" of knowledge and skills for the 21st century, as well as how to construct different educational pathways and the most appropriate forms of student guidance for making choices between them.

- How to enhance the quality of the curriculum, and of teachers whose work is increasingly complex? What is the new professionalism of teachers, and of others who work in education, implied by the changing demands of schooling and the best use of information and communication technologies?

221|

- How far should decentralisation and the autonomy of schools be developed in order to foster innovation and change? What should be the role of the state and what mechanisms used to steer change? How can the objectives of a specific school be reconciled with those at the local, regional, national and European levels, or even global-level objectives insofar as young people need to be prepared for international mobility and made aware of planetary issues?

These fundamental questions of steering change, and the optimal degree of decentralisation, are explored closely in this chapter, as they lie at the heart of tensions between the local and global. The relationship is also explored in the territoriality of education policy and the battle against inequalities through positive discrimination, as illustrated by the French policy of educational priority areas (*zones d'éducation prioritaire*, ZEPs).

Decentralisation and steering

Michel Crozier stated in 1979 that society cannot be changed by decree. Neither can schools. All countries have seen the limits of top-down reforms being reached, reforms that come and go as frequently as do ministers of education. Educational systems are complex and cannot be steered exclusively, or even mainly, from the top. Everywhere, initiatives are flourishing on the ground although these too are not enough because they tend to be specific to individual schools and not easily transferred elsewhere. Local initiatives need to be combined with those coming from further up.

We have elsewhere analysed the sources of complexity in education systems and the need to search for new forms of national direction that allow greater local latitude, while preserving national control and hence coherence throughout the system (Michel, 1993). This is possible when education is considered a public asset that creates intra- and inter-generational externalities, including social relationships, and not just a private asset of human capital generating income flows during a person's working life. Joutard and Thélot (1999) have also emphasised the need for equal opportunity to accompany the diversification of successful educational tracks and of approaches to teaching and learning. This means increased autonomy for schools, yet within a national framework to limit geographical and social inequalities.

Greater leeway should be granted to schools and local layers of government to help foster innovation, better meet students' needs and make for a closer fit between schools and their environment. But, with the complexity that accompanies greater local autonomy, and assuming the need to retain a certain minimum unity and stability, a crucial element of the system's management becomes the rapid, effective circulation of relevant information to all involved. This is to underscore he principle highlighted by Prigogine and Stengers (1979): a system's tolerable complexity – before excessive instability sets in – depends on the speed that information circulates between all of its elements. Effective information flow is thus an important component of steering a decentralised system.

A second component is forecasting and forward thinking (termed "prospective" in French), the latter being more qualitative and longer-term. Education calls for a long-term approach and cannot rely only on short-term management. Students must be prepared for a world that will have changed substantially by the time they leave school. In light of the inherent inertia in schools and systems, major changes and competences for 10-15 years' time need to be factored in.

A third component is well-developed tools for assessing the cognitive and non-cognitive development of students, schools, and innovations, as well as for evaluating policy outcomes and the state of systems and their staff. A new culture of evaluation has emerged in the French education system, but much remains to be done.

The fourth component tends to be neglected but it is crucial for steering change: strategic communication. At all decision-making levels, system orientations and objectives need to be explained. Strategic communication gives meaning to daily actions; better still, it should underpin genuine co-ordination among all relevant stakeholders, extending as far upstream as possible. Strategic communication also means prompting, encouraging, facilitating, accompanying, co-ordinating, disseminating and enhancing the value of innovations, especially through cross-fertilisation by networks. Communication has an even more fundamental dimension: awareness of, and becoming able to live with, change in learning organisations.

The education system as a learning organisation, change as a systemic process

In a rapidly changing, multicultural world, necessitating adaptability and local autonomy, change depends on all the different levels of decision-making. This places a particular premium on overall coherence and on consistency between key objectives shared across all the levels. Steering the system in this context needs to transcend a mechanistic approach to educational reform. Instead, change should be seen as a collective adventure in which the educational enterprise is continuously re-inventing itself, which process implies accepting a degree of uncertainty. An apt metaphor for such change is of a living being constantly interacting with its environment. As expressed by Edgar Morin, the education system should be viewed as "self-eco-organising", whereby a set of actors and bodies are linked through extensive interchange (Morin, 1990). Through interaction with its environment, the education system can react, evolve, learn, create, and be *self-organising*. Change is thus a systemic, continuous and sustainable process of adaptation,

223

and one reflecting the richness of local diversity. As national objectives must accommodate this source of diversity, the pace of change cannot be uniform.

The aim should not be the vain endeavour to attain a new equilibrium, in conditions of continual environmental turbulence. This turbulence renders meaningless the constant diagnoses of states of crisis and transition. As movement brings imbalance, then in a rapidly changing world all institutions, including schools, are always in some form of crisis or transition (Black and Michel, 1998). Instead, the search should be for the achievement of a dynamic stabilisation of forces that are out of balance.

Change as a systemic process also has to obey certain rules of consistency – between the global and local levels in moving beyond the tensions that are among the imbalances discussed above to be stabilised, as well as consistency in the directions taken by the system's innovations. Curriculum reform, for instance that does not address the evaluation of student learning (formative and summative), pedagogical methods, and initial and on-going teacher training, is thus likely to fail. A similar example is the introduction of computers and ICT into schools which will prove ineffective without corresponding organisational changes and initial and updated teacher learning.

Educational research emphasises the key role of the local level

Educational research has identified the need for "micro" analysis of how the educational system works to qualify macro-sociological findings, such as the the ory of reproduction crystallised three decades ago (Bourdieu and Passeron, 1970 Baudelot and Establet, 1971). French studies have shown that mass education has had little general impact on reducing social inequalities, which have merely moved up to higher levels with expansion (Michel, 1999), but research has also identified the role of the educational system itself in generating inequalities beyond any exogenous social determinism. In this, the local dimension is an important one (Duru-Bellat and Mingat, 1993).

French studies on the importance of the school effect (Dura-Bellat and Mingat, 1993; Dura-Bellat and Henriot-van Zanten, 1999; Cousin, 1993, 1996, 1998 agree with findings from English-speaking countries, Belgium, Spain and Portugal Special attention has been paid to lower secondary schools (collèges), because of their role in guiding students towards one of the three upper secondary tracks (general, technological or professional) in lycées, and, within the general, between the literary (L), economics and social science (ES) and scientific (S) programmes Despite official insistence that all these tracks and programmes enjoy equal standing as excellence takes diverse forms, hierarchies do in fact exist. There are major disparities among collège students' test results, based on evaluations at the start of the lycée, and in their attainments in national examinations in terms of graduation from the *collège*. There are also different patterns of evaluation, orientation and student profiles that have a major impact on educational careers and subsequent life-chances.

Such results argue for a clear focus on the local level, yet combined with caution about extending school autonomy too far. These disparities between the *collèges*, which also exist between *lycées*, can be used to argue for greater latitude being given to schools to operate competitively. The justification is that this will make them more accountable for their own performance and unable to claim that poor results are the result of bureaucratic constraints beyond their control. But, the risk is that this will merely accentuate a visible tendency towards "multi-speed" schools, whereby the best schools are the preserve of families rich in economic and/or cultural capital. The risk of widening the outcome gaps between schools is a real one. IEA international studies, including the Third International Mathematics and Science Study (TIMSS), have shown that whereas there is no correlation between level of student achievement and the extent of a country's decentralisation, the latter is associated with greater variance among students and schools. This spread has prompted countries such as the United Kingdom and the United States to strengthen their national curricula and standardised tests.

All countries are thus in search of the optimal level of decentralisation, as national authorities in the most decentralised seek tighter to reduce socio-geographic disparities and the most centralised, such as France, have devolved and decentralised for more than a decade. An OECD INES study on the locus of decision-making (conducted in 1993, repeated in 1998), also underlined the need to distinguish between school autonomy and decentralisation to the regional and/or local levels. For countries with the greatest degree of educational devolution are not those in which schools enjoy greatest autonomy – supervision from nearby is often more burdensome than supervision from afar. In light of this, should more power be given to schools or local authorities? But, deciding the desirable level of (de)centralisation, the powers to be kept or not by the state, or the best route for Europe-wide educational development cannot be resolved on purely technical grounds as the choice is above all political. It should be linked to an overall vision of society and of education within it.

How far to develop the territorial dimension in education policy?

France, as noted, has a long-standing tradition of centralisation in education. Political, economic and administrative centralism is an important dimension of what Braudel referred to as "the French identity". Colbertist, Jacobin, and later Napoleonic, traditions have left their profound stamp. The later 19th century Third Republic gave primary school teachers – the "black hussars of the Republic" – the task of integrating children from disparate provinces in which different languages

225|

were spoken (Alsace, Auvergne, Brittany, Languedoc, the Basque country, Provence, Savoy, etc.) or whose parents were immigrants. Integration was to come through the learning of French and civic and moral education, including love of nation and awareness of citizens' rights and obligations.

This French tradition of secular compulsory schooling aiming to unite people around a common language and set of values, has continued to this day. More traditional interpretations are now challenged by the multiculturalism and growing legitimacy of cultural and religious diversity, as well as by "political correctness" which have given rise to lively political debate. Such challenges and debates not withstanding, awareness of the importance of schools in maintaining national unity, and scepticism about either the "communitarian" or the North American "melting pot" models, have meant that a large majority still support the republican notion of integration, albeit to varying degrees (Ferréol et al., 1998; Schnapper 1994; Wievorka et al., 1997).

This political support has especially coloured the decentralisation and school autonomy debate, and it cuts across the traditional left vs. right political divide. The debate has been as much about the integrating role of schools as about the effectiveness or equity of the educational system. The French remain firmly attached to certain central prerogatives of the state. While the country has become decentralised and devolved increasingly since the 1980s, federalism is supported by only a small minority. The situation is thus quite distinct from that in Germany, Switzerland, the United Kingdom or Spain.

Nevertheless, social inequalities, insecurity and poverty, as well as the concentration of disadvantage in urban areas (especially big-city suburbs), prompted Minister of Education Savary in 1982 to embark on a major departure in education policy. It was innovative in at least two respects:

- For the first time, a public service applied a policy of positive discrimination. Certain categories of the population were favoured in resource allocation, rather than benefits decided individually in terms of economic or social parameters or educational merit.

- It was also the first time that geography was used as the criterion for allocating educational resources. This was an explicit acknowledgement of the importance of local context and was justified by the need for close co-operation between the different public services, families, social and economic partners and local authorities in combating school failure.

This signalled a break with the traditional republican principle of formal equality of all citizens in accessing public services, implementing positive discrimination and enshrining it in law. This important step has shaped the possibilities for *local* considerations to emerge in education policy-making, including a specific rural education policy linked to broader planning to maintain primary schools or create secondary schools with small enrolments in areas threatened by depopulation and decline. A report in the early 1990s by the General Planning Commission called for "educational land-use planning". Schools that serve only small numbers but that are vital in their areas inevitably pose problems of effectiveness and equity, some of which could be addressed by the suitable use of the internet and remote teaching. In the next section, however, the focus shifts from rural policy to that of *zones d'éducation prioritaire* (ZEPs), which contribute to managing the "dynamic dialectic" between the local and global levels.

From "education priority areas" to "education priority networks" (1982-1999)

Set up in 1982, the education priority areas (ZEPs) adopt a multi-faceted approach to combat school failure in geographical areas facing a variety of socio-cultural and economic handicaps. They aim both to improve academic achievement and combat social exclusion. This requires a comprehensive approach towards schools and their environment, hence the territorial dimension and the need for concerted action by educators and other administrative, economic and social players, aimed especially at families. The criteria for constituting ZEPs are both educational (proportions of students lagging behind, failing to advance to the next level, dropping out, and leaving with no qualifications) and demographic, social and economic (concentrations of low family income, foreign-born and minority populations, single-parent families, the unemployed, large family size).

Each ZEP, co-ordinated by a manager and advisor, is based on a strategic project setting out tangible, specific and measurable objectives, in turn derived from a close analysis of the local situation and of needs arising. Results are regularly assessed with objectives and procedures updated as necessary. An external audit every three years can prompt changes in how the boundaries of these areas are drawn and which schools are covered. The objective is to improve educational achievement through strengthened, diversified educational efforts focused on student needs. There is a strong focus on early schooling from the age of 2, differentiated pedagogical methods, extracurricular activities with community partners, academic support beyond the classroom, and health care and security. Teamwork, co-ordination across schools and ZEP projects, and tailored training for teachers and other school staff are all major factors making for success. Additional funding, staff bonuses, and career benefits can be gained in ZEPs. In 1998, there were 563 ZEPs in operation, involving 6 185 schools and nearly 1.2 million students (about 10% of total enrolments).

Despite the coherence of this policy approach, the periodic evaluations have shown only mixed results and hence they remain controversial. Some contend that the achievements made in narrowing the gap in test scores between ZEP students and the national average are relatively modest for the resources spent. Others argue that

227|

recent growing inequalities have led to greater concentrations of problems in ZEPs, further concentrated because of the drive to improve the match between ZEP boundaries and areas of greatest need. On the latter view, even a modest narrowing of the gap with national averages represents significant progress and, without ZEPs, would instead have widened.

An evaluation report has shown how some ZEPs work better than others (Moisan and Simon, 1997). Based on observations from many areas, they sought to identify the key factors of educational success. These were found to be consistent with the general findings of educational research, including the importance of addressing family attitudes towards education and the need to give priority to basic learning skills, including extracurricular activities to boost motivation. They also highlighted the key role of human resources and of evaluation and communication as mechanisms to help steer change.

Faced with the persistence of failure especially among the most disadvantaged students (as in other industrialised countries, see OECD, 1997c), the French government decided to organise a series of local forums followed by a national ZEP convention in Rouen in June 1998 (Assises nationales des ZEP, 1998). The conclusions that emerged from this round of discussions provided the basis to relaunch priority education. Inter alia, this was done by creating "education priority networks" (réseaux d'éducation prioritaire, or REPs) and defining "success contracts" based on ten priority guidelines (BOEN, 28 January 1999). The re-launch has been tied closely to urban planning policy, since a majority of ZEPs involve schools in such areas. REPs group schools together within narrowly drawn areas conducive to local influence, with most networks headed by a collège.

The REPs have helped to address geographical inequalities by integrating primary and lower secondary schools with special problems that were not before in ZEPs. This was needed because, as Charlot has emphasised (1999), they had gradually shifted from a "positive discrimination" to a "territorial differentiation" approach. Such differentiation is tantamount to creating and enshrining social inequalities and education ghettos. Certain schools can come to be stigmatised – shunned by middle-class families who would prefer to send their children to private schools than to those bearing the "ZEP" label. This only accentuates the handicap experienced by these schools – more targeted positive discrimination comes at the cost of increasing the ghetto effect, with all its attendant disadvantages in relation to effectiveness and social justice. Here again is a tension, even a contradiction, inherent in any policy based on sensitivity to the local environment and it suggests that there are limits to those policies that seek to reflect the territorial dimension.

Another perverse effect of territoriality and an expression of the tension have been analysed by Charlot (1994, 1999), Henriot-van Zanten (1990) and Johsua (1999)

The growing autonomy of schools, the use of contracts, and new partnerships are causing contradictions to emerge at the local level whose sources (and solutions) are national, even international, and which threaten the very break-up of the educational system. Some, like Derouet and Dutercq (1997) and Dutercq (1999), have explored the relationships between the local and global in education through analysis of *governance*. This is especially relevant to the French situation, where a majority is still attached to the "republican school" (*école républicaine*) as a means to integrate diverse communities and mix different social classes. But, this does not mean that an essentially 19th century concept can be maintained into the 21st century – new interpretations are needed that are adapted to the contemporary context.

Local community, the nation-state, and Europe

Altogether, schools are now faced with an imposing set of tasks and responsibilities. They should educate students to be informed citizens, ready to act locally as the community is the main theatre of genuine democracy through which the nation can, as Rosanvallon suggests (1995), rebuild itself. They should reinforce solidarity in the face of a welfare state in crisis. They must "think European" in helping to forge a new political entity giving greater stability and peace in a turbulent world.[2] They should foster a universal outlook, because global policy-making will be the only way to address the challenges being faced world-wide, especially the environmental challenges. Furthermore, schools must prepare students for careers of ever greater mobility, adaptability, and openness to other cultures, at the same time as providing a sense of belonging and identity, which means acting to preserve local or regional cultures in danger. In other words, schools must help provide people with roots in order to build deeper foundations, enabling them to be more open to others and to diversity. Tomorrow, people will have to be both the Narcissus and Goldmund depicted by Hermann Hesse – the "troubadour of knowledge" whose "mind resembles Harlequin's coat", as described by Michel Serres (1991).

In contemporary France, the state's role is to be strategic at the same time as modest in renouncing a number of its traditional prerogatives, caught as it is between the emerging regional voice, a stronger Europe, and globalisation. In the middle of these movements, what is the future of the "republican school" so dear to the heart of the nation? Can it survive? There is much more involved in answering this than mere national or patriotic sentiment. It is secular and has been fashioned as the crucible of universal values, symbolising liberty, equality and fraternity, and the defence of human and citizens' rights. There are very few, even among the most fervent europhiles, who want to abandon the national education system. Just as the French respond to globalisation by putting themselves in the vanguard for "cultural exception", so are they also inclined to advocate an "educational exception". In continuing to build Europe, France's European partners will have to make allowances for the deep French attachment to this "republican school" in arriving in the future at the "dynamic dialectic between local and global" advocated by Jacques Delors. This does not mean the rejection of international outreach by schools, whether through increased exchanges or through pursuit of equivalence, even convergence, of diplomas and education systems especially within Europe. The real fear is the disappearance of the "republican school" and its values in an increasingly market-dominated world.

Notes

1. This chapter, which is an abridged version of an article initially published in *Futurible* (No. 252, April 2000), derives from the work of the international conference on Schooling for Tomorrow ("L'École Horizon 2020: Séminaire international de prospective de l'éducation") held at the Futuroscope (Poitiers, France) in October 1999. The conference was co-organised by EPICE and Futuribles International, in association with OECD/CERI, the European Commission (DGXII), the Conseil Général du Département de la Vienne France, and the AFAE (Association française des administrateurs de l'éducation).

2. Surprisingly, Habermas (1998) does not refer to the crucial role of education in advocating this direction of development.

Chapter 12

Visions of Decision-makers and Educators for the Future of Schools – Reactions to the OECD Scenarios

by

Walo Hutmacher
University of Geneva

Introduction

This chapter looks at the probabilities and desirabilities of different futures as perceived by some influential voices in education. The scenarios developed through the CERI/OECD "Schooling for Tomorrow" programme have been constructed based on certain trends in industrialised societies and a number of key actors in the current debate on schools. None of the scenarios is expected to emerge in "pure" form in any country. They serve, however, to raise the important question: "What is the likelihood that changes in the future will follow one particular direction rather than another?" The approach of this chapter assumes that these probabilities are importantly shaped in turn by the relative desirability of the changes outlined by the scenarios in the social forces within and around education systems.

Views expressed on the likelihood and desirability of the different scenarios

The scenarios offer an excellent means for structuring a debate on the future direction and development of schools and education policy. They have already been used for this purpose, notably during two conferences involving leading education officials, heads, teachers, researchers and representatives of the business world and civil society. One of these conferences held in Rotterdam was international in its participation, the other in Switzerland (St-Gall) had a more regional focus. At both conferences, the participants became familiar with the scenarios and discussed their implications.[1] They then completed a short questionnaire evaluating the likelihood and desirability, on a 15-20 year time scale, of each scenario.[2]

In Rotterdam, around three-quarters completed the questionnaire, broken down as follows:

Decision-makers/officials	33
Researchers, consultants	20
Teachers, educators	14
Business	3
Students	3
Total	73

At the St-Gall conference, from around 150 participants, 100 completed the questionnaire, broken down as follows:

Decision-makers/officials	32
Teachers	25
School heads	23
Students	6
Business and trade unions	9
Other	5
Total	100

The Rotterdam Conference was a joint Netherlands/OECD event under the Schooling for Tomorrow programme. It was attended by approximately 100 delegates from 24 countries. Many participants were officials or policy-makers in their national education systems, experts, researchers, and a small number from the business community and students. St-Gall is a Swiss canton of 400 000 inhabitants situated to the east of Zurich, moving from an industrial to a knowledge economy. In August 2000, the education authorities organised a major conference on the future of their education system.

As these were only relatively small-scale surveys, only the main differences have been taken into account in comparing the results from the conferences. The participants were obviously not representative of the population as a whole, but their opinions are of interest because of their role in education, and their interest in education policy and the future of schools. They are well informed about these issues in general and have some, even considerable, influence in the education sector of their respective countries. Many leaders and experts are also former teachers who have been shaped by the dominant culture of schools and educational institutions. Though population, they are by no means statistically representative, these groups express the views of an informed and policy-sensitive section of the education community.

What are likely futures for schools?

Figures 12.1 and 12.2 show the distribution of replies according to how likely the participants assessed that each scenario would become reality.[3] In contrast

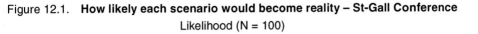

Figure 12.1. **How likely each scenario would become reality – St-Gall Conference**
Likelihood (N = 100)

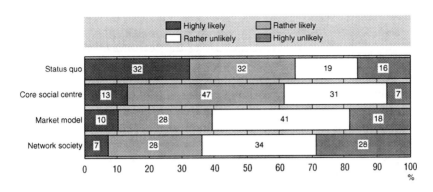

Figure 12.2. **How likely each scenario would become reality – Rotterdam Conference**
Likelihood (N = 73)

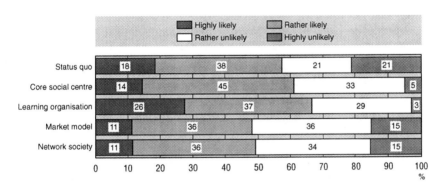

with an even spread of responses across the four options (highly or rather likely, rather or highly unlikely), the proportion of decisive replies – "highly likely", "highly unlikely" – is low and thus the share of "cautious" replies (rather likely or unlikely) is high. The non-commital, "on-the-fence" replies account for around 70% of responses for most of the scenarios. The inability to give decisive answers, whether affirmative or negative, underlines the sense of uncertainty many feel towards these issues. The one exception is the scenario "The status quo contin-ues". In this case, one in three in St-Gall found this "highly likely" (though only one in six in Rotterdam did so), and the levels judging this "highly unlikely" were also fairly low: one in five replied in Rotterdam and one in six in St-Gall.

Taking the decisive and cautious responses together, somewhat over half in Rotterdam (56%) thought that the status quo was likely to continue, rising to almost two-thirds in St-Gall. In other words, these informed, insightful players on the educational scene believe that 10-15 years is just not enough time to turn around institutional inertia and out-dated educational practices. Against this assessment of inertia, however, the highest proportions of affirmative replies (highly or rather likely) were given to the "re-schooling" scenarios: 63% for "Schools as focused learning organisations" in Rotterdam and 60% for "Schools as core social centres" at both conferences. Few considered these scenarios to be highly unlikely. Indeed, a quarter of the Rotterdam conference participants believed in the high likelihood of the "Schools as focused learning organisations" scenario. In contrast, only a third to a half of the respondents thought that the "de-schooling" scenarios were likely to occur, and these were considered to be "highly unlikely" futures by significant proportions.

What are desirable futures for schools?

Views about desirable futures are far more clear-cut, as Figures 12.3 and 12.4 illustrate. At both conferences, two-thirds of the respondents considered it undesirable for the "status quo" to continue, approximately half of these judging it highly undesirable – this from conference participants among whom nearly two in three believe that it will in all likelihood continue.

Just under half in Rotterdam and one-third in St-Gall thought the move towards the market model was likely, despite this being deemed undesirable by an overwhelming majority (three in four) of the conference participants. Over half rejected the market scenario as "highly undesirable" in Rotterdam, and a third did so in St-Gall.

Figure 12.3. **How desirable is each scenario – St-Gall Conference**
Desirability (N = 100)

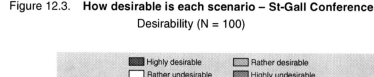

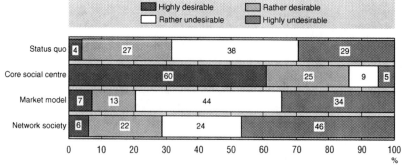

Figure 12.4. **How desirable is each scenario – Rotterdam Conference**
Desirability (N = 73)

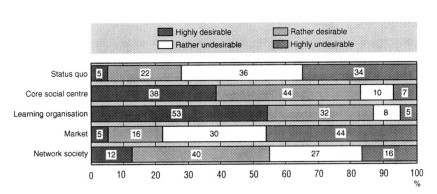

There was a division of opinion among the Rotterdam participants over the desirability of the "Technology and the network society" scenario: half were in favour, half against. This differs from the results in St-Gall, where only a little over a quarter (28%) judged this scenario to be desirable. A possible explanation is that the impact and potential of ICT were discussed at far greater length at the international Rotterdam conference than at the St-Gall event organised within a national and local context.

The most desirable scenarios for these respondents were undoubtedly those described as "re-schooling". In Rotterdam, they were supported by more than four out of five, with over half even believing the development of "Schools as focused learning organisations" to be highly desirable. Only one of these two scenarios was included in the St-Gall questionnaire and this was supported by 85% of respondents.

Taking account of the slightly different profiles of the participants at Rotterdam and St-Gall, there seems to be rather similar reactions to the OECD/CERI scenarios. Two similar soundings on the scenarios have been done, in smaller and more homogeneous groups and using the same questionnaires: one at a seminar for union representatives of primary and secondary teachers (SER) in French-speaking Switzerland (N=16), and the other at a conference for managers from the Swedish Education Agency, Skolverket (N=17). They produced broadly the same likelihood and desirability responses.

Summary and discussion of the results

Summary

The findings from all these exercises are summarised in Figure 12.5. It shows the positive responses on both likelihood and desirability (though the negative

235|

responses could equally have been used to show the same information), and the "highly" and "rather" replies have been combined. The events (Rotterdam St-Gall, etc.) have been distinguished by different shapes and the scenarios by different shades of grey.

Some general patterns emerge from this summary overview:

• While opinions on likelihood (vertical axis) range across approximately 25% to 75% depending on the group and the scenario, views on desirability (horizontal axis) cover the whole range, from 0% to 100%.

• Opinions on each scenario tend to be clustered together, showing the general similarity of views about both likely and desirable future development. These can be summed up as:

  – "Status quo": likely but undesirable;

  – "Core social centre": likely and desirable;

  – "Market model" : unlikely and undesirable.

Figure 12.5. **Comparisons of likelihood and desirability scores at different events**

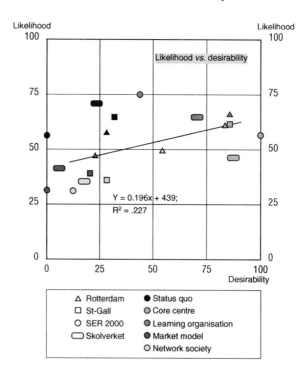

Source: Author.

- At the three events where participants were asked about the fifth "Focused learning organisation" scenario (that was not included at St-Gall), they were in general agreement about its likelihood as high, but less agreed about its desirability. As for the "Technology and the network society"[4] scenario, the Rotterdam participants are clearly distinct from the other three, particularly in terms of believing this to be more desirable.

- Views on likelihood and desirability tend to correlate: broadly speaking, the more desirable the scenario, the more likely it is thought to be, as indicated by the trend-line. A similar matching is also found in the individual responses. Respondents are therefore relatively optimistic, considering desirable options to be likely and undesirable ones unlikely. There are two exceptions. At each event, the "Status quo" is thought to be notably more likely than it is desirable, while the opposite applies to the "School as core centre" scenario, which is considered more desirable than likely.

Dividing each dimension broadly in half gives four alternatives in terms of which most respondents judge the future scenarios as either likely or unlikely while desirable or undesirable, summarising the patterns already discussed:

	Desirable	Undesirable
Likely	– Core social centre – Focused learning organisation	– The status quo continues
Unlikely		– The market model – Technology and the network society

The two "re-schooling" scenarios are considered by many to be both desirable and likely, while the "de-schooling" futures are usually considered both undesirable and unlikely. Only the "Status quo continues" scenario is judged by most of those canvassed to be undesirable but reasonably likely to occur.

Discussion

The scenarios represent snapshots of what schools and educational institutions might become over the course of just under a generation. While presented in a sober, relatively neutral tone, few remain indifferent to the actual options they represent. Apart from ideas about their varying plausibility, they tend to arouse feelings of enthusiasm or rejection, or both. The scenarios project a picture, reminiscent of the inkblots in a Rorschach test. In similar fashion, reactions to them are revealing of the beliefs, hopes, apprehensions, and fears of those whose views are

237|

canvassed. Such reactions transcend managerial and professional rationality; they reveal more profound aspects of imagination and aspiration. This is especially clear in reactions to the desirability of the scenarios, but it is also visible in the correlation between views on desirability and likelihood – what people want tends to influence their worldviews of how futures will unfold.

Positions tend to be clear-cut when it comes to what people want. The "Status quo" scenario, based on a dominant bureaucratic system, is rejected but there seems to be little enthusiasm either for models driven by market forces, or for the one characterised by a diffuse network structure and the prominence of information and communication technologies. Respondents do not want schools to remain as they are (though they may fear that they will, if only through inertia), yet neither do they support de-institutionalisation or privatisation.

There is thus a clear preference for the two "re-schooling" scenarios. This might be called a return to fundamentals. At around 80% support, they clearly represent the "dream" schooling scenarios for those questioned. What do these visions convey? Briefly put, schools would remain in the public sector, operating in a largely consensus-based environment where funding is guaranteed, but where central government and education departments would play a different role. In contrast with the situation at present, they would be able to provide everyone with better access to knowledge as a public good but confine themselves to setting educational goals for schools through strategic medium-term targets and a general frame of reference and guidance. While education would be increasingly individualised, schools would keep the key collective function of providing a place of social integration at the local level. The acquisition of knowledge and skills by all would be of central concern but socialisation – passing on the values of community, democracy and solidarity – would be just as important. Reducing the social inequalities of education would be permanent goals of systems and individual schools.

"Re-schooling" would create a greater focus on individual schools while redefining their *modus operandi* and their role in the local community. In this way, the dream futures that emerge appear to be close to the Carnoy analysis of work, the family and the state, also in Chapter 5 of this volume. He identifies the need to revitalise communities corresponding to particular geographical localities, where the places for children's development also spontaneously connect up adults and indeed where elementary and secondary schools are able to become the centres for social connections at the neighbourhood level. It is this role that is especially distinctive in the Carnoy and the "re-schooling" dream scenarios, implying significant change from the status quo. Schools would be at the same time more autonomous and accountable, more open and connected to their immediate environment and more overtly dedicated to it. They would embody a strong approach to local community infrastructure as institutions based on collective living and co-operative earning. While every school would be distinctive, they would be characterised by inclusive approaches to education and skill development for all students, and would re-organise themselves and reshape their procedures and practices to meet the ambitious goals they would be set. They would fully integrate ICTs and actively promote lifelong learning. In distinguishing between the two "re-schooling" scenarios, it would be useful to find out more about whether "schools as core social centres" is thought to be appropriate more for compulsory schooling, and "schools as focused learning organisations" for upper secondary and vocational institutions.

The similarities of likes and dislikes, despite the differences in participation and perspective, and in linguistic, institutional and political backgrounds, represented in these different events, should be underlined. Broadly similar attitudes to schools of the future were expressed at an international and a regional conference, a Swiss teaching union seminar, and a gathering of managers at the Swedish Education Evaluation Agency, some minor differences notwithstanding. This convergence suggests a shared culture and probably also similar interests in the stakes involved. Across different backgrounds and perspectives, the views reported here seem to express the attitudes of a particular group that could be called the informed and policy-interested section of the education community. While our samples are not representative in any statistical sense, these similarities across such different contexts suggest that other members of this informed and policy-interested community would reveal similar attitudes towards the scenarios if asked in still other events and settings.

Members of this community seem to agree with the need for change – they reject the "status quo" – but are sensitive to the problems that change would bring (and hence judge likely that the status quo will actually continue). They appear convinced that "re-schooling" represents the means to ensure the continuation of public sector schools meeting highly demanding quality standards. These findings are not entirely unexpected: the changes these respondents dream of would not reject traditional values, where schools are responsible for social integration, and their own interests are invested in the support of public education. Aspects of these scenarios are also in line with the management strategies pursued by many countries for a decade or so, with an emphasis on educational decentralisation, as illustrated by the four national forward-looking studies reviewed by van Aalst in Chapter 8. If there is a surprising element, it arises from the degree of consensus around a "renewed vision" for schools, especially among groups as different as educational administrators and teacher union representatives.

At these reported conferences and seminars, every feedback presentation on the questionnaire results elicited surprise; not so much at the findings *per se* but at the degree of consensus. To test the extent of this consensus, further exercises of this sort deserve to be repeated. The scenarios are admirably suited to stimulate a debate on schools of the future. Such surveys can reveal the extent of common visions and the discussion of these can then provide the basis for a more dispassionate debate on policy options than is often possible.

Nevertheless, there are limits to what can be extrapolated on the basis of these findings. They were generated within the relatively protected, non-committal setting of conferences or seminars. Without questioning the sincerity of the replies, there may well be gaps between what is said in such a context and what someone would be ready to do in practice. Supposing that these findings do accurately reflect the attitudes of the specific groups questioned, the latter represent only a fraction of the mass of those concerned by education and schooling. While they are of interest, as occupying influential positions in education systems with opinions that count in policy-making and change, they are still only a fraction, and indeed their aspirations may conflict with the interests and visions of other stakeholders.

Perspectives on the future

All this emphasises the value of the scenario method and indicates one avenue to explore when gauging the likelihood of a range of different scenarios for education systems. It is based on a simple assumption – that developments deemed likely and/or desirable have more chance of happening than those that most people think are unlikely to occur or are undesirable. This assumption remains to be verified, but it is not unrealistic.

This means that the question of the likelihood of the different scenarios becomes open to empirical treatment, and the issue turns to the best methods to be used to assess how likely and, more importantly, how desirable different stakeholder groups consider each scenario to be. As a next phase, it would be valuable both to refine the method and to broaden the stakeholder groups being surveyed in order to bring in, for instance, teachers at different levels, pupils and students, parents, political groupings, and the business community. Do these groups differ fundamentally in their views on the future of schools or is there sufficient convergence that might permit strategic agreements and alliances? Ideally, the full spectrum of opinion should be tapped, and the resultant findings interpreted to take account of respondents' positions in society, especially their opportunities for proposing and imposing their vision of education. This approach would serve two purposes. It would, on the one hand, help to gauge the chances of any particular scenario becoming reality. It would, on the other, help clarify the policy debate about the timeliness, risks and opportunities involved in pursuing any particular main direction for schooling.

Broader still, such an exercise emphasises the value of a more culture-based approach to educational development. In democracies, the political support for schools – the first of the five dimensions around which the scenarios are constructed –

ultimately depends on the judgements and opinions of the public at large. Hence, forward-looking analysis in the field of education will call increasingly for a better knowledge of mentalities, attitudes, expectations, values, aspirations and plans relating to schools and education, against the context of a wide range of settings and situations, now and in possible futures.

Yet, if done thoroughly, such an exercise would amount to little short of a cultural revolution for schools. Despite the ubiquity of pluralist rhetoric, educational institutions still function to judge the mentalities of their users as incorporated cultural capital (Bourdieu, 1986). Every school has pupils who are "not cut out to be there" and who must either adapt or go under. In this respect, epistemologically, many schools place normative, even ideological, judgements ahead of knowledge, analysis and understanding. Considering that the mission of schools is to forge mentalities, it may seem surprising that the education world has always been reluctant to make any systematic effort to grasp the mentalities prevailing in society, their social and cultural rationales, their diversity and the changes that affect them. Yet, attitudes, expectations and visions – irrespective of whether they fit in with educational standards or even whether they are realistic – are very revealing of how pupils, their parents, and the public at large regard schools and education policy, and ultimately of how people will vote.

It is also worth noting by way of contrast the very high degree of attention focused by businesses and the media on the perceptions, expectations, aspirations, even imaginations, of their clients, and increasingly of their staff too, as part of their business and marketing strategies. There is a much better grasp in these sectors that confidence stems in some measure from beliefs, images and opinions. They have adapted a sophisticated range of social science concepts and methods in order to measure attitudes and to follow, even anticipate, change, as part of product development or communication strategy.

Education systems in some countries may be moving in this direction, as Söderberg suggests in Chapter 9 of this volume. In Sweden, available data have made it possible to chart trends on a number of opinion parameters over the past decade. For instance, during the 1990s, the public's confidence in schools tended to decline but to a lesser extent than it did in relation to other public institutions. Drawing on international data obtained for the INES project (OECD, 1995), Söderberg points to broad public approval for demanding educational objectives set for schools but the relative lack of confidence in their capacity to fulfill them. What is more, the degree of confidence does not necessarily relate to the actual performance of the education system compared with other countries. This points to the potential role of communication strategies to address such misperceptions.

Yet, trends in public opinion may be paradoxical. For instance, parents are generally more critical about schools in general than about those attended by

241|

their own children; those with higher levels of education, who have gained most also tend to criticise the education system more (Söderberg in Chapter 9; Hutmacher and Gros, 1994). Hence, we need a much better grasp of the complex mechanisms that shape opinions on education, across diverse settings, situations and lifestyles, as well as of the growing individual and collective stakes at issue in educational institutions. We need to develop the conceptual base and refine the methodologies, capitalising on the experiences already gained and the expertise available across different countries.

Notes

1. The scenarios evolved as part of the "Schooling for Tomorrow" programme. At the time of the St-Gall Conference, the scenario entitled "Schools as focused learning organisations" had not yet been constructed, and hence was not included in this survey. Since both conferences, "the market model" has been re-classified and a new scenario added in Chapter 3. In earlier versions of the scenarios, the "market" scenario was considered as an example of "de-schooling", while above it has been shifted under the "status quo" umbrella, and a sixth "meltdown" scenario has been added under "de-schooling". Which is more convincing depends importantly on the starting point of each country in terms of political/social culture and on the level of schooling.

2. The concepts of "likelihood" and "desirability" were not defined or discussed in any detail, so that the answers given were based on personal, rather spontaneous criteria. There were four possible answers for each criterion:
   • highly or rather likely; rather or highly unlikely;
   • highly or rather desirable; rather or highly undesirable.

3. The "don't knows", who accounted for less than 5% in every case, have been discounted.

4. Retitled as "Learner networks and the network society" in this report.

References (Part II)

ADLER, M. (1940),
   This Pre-war Generation, www.realuofc.org/libed/adler/preawar.htm

AFAE (1999),
   "Fractures sociales, fractures scolaires", XXIe colloque de l'AFAE (1999), Administration et Éducation, 1 and 3.

ASSISES NATIONALES DES ZEP (1998),
   Actes des Assises nationales des ZEP, ministère de l'Éducation nationale, de la Recherche et de la Technologie, Paris.

ATKINSON, A.B. (1975),
   The Economics of Inequality, Oxford University Press, Oxford.

BALLION, R. (1982),
   Les Consommateurs d'école, Stock, Paris.

BAUDELOT, C. and ESTABLET, R. (1971),
   L'École capitaliste en France, La Découverte, Paris.

BAUTIER, E., CHARLOT, B. and ROCHEIX, J-Y. (1992),
   École et savoir dans les banlieues et ailleurs, Armand Colin, Paris.

BECK, U. (1986),
   Risikogesellschaft. Auf dem Weg in eine andere Moderne, Suhrkamp Verlag, Frankfurt am Main.

BENSON, R. (1994),
   "Computer-mediated Communication: A Literature Review", Research Paper, Department of Sociology, University of California, Berkeley.

BENTOLILA, S. and DOLADO, J. (1994),
   "Spanish Labour Markets", Economic Policy, pp. 55-99, April.

BISON, I. and ESPING-ANDERSEN, G. (1998),
   "Unemployment and Income Packaging in Europe", unpublished paper, University of Trento, January.

BLACK, P. and MICHEL, A. (1998),
   Learning from Pupil Assessment: International Comparisons, CSE Monograph Series in Evaluation 12, UCLA, Los Angeles.

BLOSSFELD, H.P. and SHAVIT, Y. (1993),
   Persistent Inequality: Changing Educational Attainment in Thirteen Countries, Westview Press Inc, Colorado.

BORJA, J. (1988),
   Estado y ciudad, Promociones y Publicaciones Universitarias, Barcelona.

243

BOURDIEU, P. (1986),
"The Forms of Capital", in J.E. Richardson (ed.), *Handbook of Theory and Research for the Sociology of Education*, Greenwood Press, Westport, Conn.

BOURDIEU, P. and PASSERON, J-C. (1970),
La Reproduction, Éditions de Minuit, Paris.

BRUNSVICK, Y. and DANZIN, A. (1998),
Naissance d'une civilisation, UNESCO, Paris.

BURKHAUSER, R. and POUPORE, J.G. (1993),
"A Cross-national Comparison of Permanent Inequality in the United States and Germany", *Cross-national Studies on Ageing Program Project Paper*, No. 10, SUNY-Syracuse.

BURKHAUSER, R., HOLTZ-EAKIN, D. and RHODY, S. (1995),
"Labor Earnings Mobility and Inequality in the United States and Germany during the 1980s", *Cross-national Studies in Ageing Program Project paper*, No. 12, SUNY-Syracuse.

CAPELLI, P. (1993),
"New Work Systems and Skill Requirements", paper presented at the workshop on New Trends in Training Policy, ILO, Geneva, October.

CARNOY, M. (1994),
Faded Dreams, Cambridge University Press, New York.

CARNOY, M. (1999),
Sustaining Flexibility: Work, Family, and Community in the Information Age, Harvard University Press and Russell Sage, Cambridge MA and New York.

CARNOY, M. and LEVIN, H. (1985),
Schooling and Work in the Democratic State, Stanford University Press, Stanford CA.

CASTELLS, M. (1983),
The City and the Grassroots, University of California Press, Berkeley CA.

CASTELLS, M. (1993),
"The Informational Economy and the New International Division of Labor," in Carnoy et al. (eds.), *The New Global Economy in the Information Age*, Pennsylvania State University Press, University Park PA.

CENTRAL COUNCIL FOR EDUCATION (1996), *The Model for Japanese Education in the Perspective of the 21st Century*, First report by the Central Council for Education, Tokyo.

CHARLOT, B. (1999),
Le Rapport au savoir en milieu populaire, Economica, Paris.

CHARLOT, B. et al. (1994),
L'École et le territoire, Armand Colin, Paris.

COLEMAN, J. and HUSÉN, T. (1985),
Becoming Adult in a Changing Society, OECD, Paris.

CORCORAN, M. (1995),
"Rags to Rage: Poverty and Mobility in the United States", *Annual Review of Sociology*, Vol. 21.

COUNCIL OF EUROPE (1998),
European Youth Trends 1998, www.vereniging31.nl/documenten/rve_youthtrends.htm

COUSIN, O. (1993),
"L'effet établissement. Construction d'une problématique", *Revue Française de Sociologie*, Vol. XXXIV, No. 3.

COUSIN, O. (1996),
"Construction et évaluation de l'effet établissement", *Revue Française de Pédagogie*, Vol. 115.

COUSIN, O. (1998),
L'Efficacité des collèges: sociologie de l'effet établissement, PUF, Paris.

DANZIGER, S. and GOTTSCHALK, P. (1993),
Uneven Tides: Rising Inequality in America, Sage, Beverley Hills, CA.

DENKSCHRIFT DER BILDUNGSKOMMISSION NRW (1995),
Zukunft der Bildung – Schule der Zukunft, Luchterhand.

DEPARTMENT OF HEALTH AND AGED CARE (1999),
1998 Suicide Statistics, www.health.gov.au/hsdd/mentalhe/pubs/pdf/suicstat.pdf

DEPARTMENT OF HEALTH AND AGED CARE (undated),
How do Suicide Rates among Young People in Australia Compare with those in Other Countries?, www.health.gov.au/hsdd.mentalhe/nysps/back/compare.htm

DERBER, C. (1994),
"Clintradictions: Clinton, Co-operation, and the Contradictions of Capitalism", *Tikkun*, September/October.

DEROUET, J-L. and DUTERCQ, Y. (1997),
L'Établissement scolaire, autonomie locale et service public, ESF, Paris.

DOGAN, M. and KASARDA, J. (1987),
The Metropolis Era (2 volumes), Sage, London.

DOSI, G. (1988),
"Sources, Procedures and Microeconomic Effects of Innovation", *Journal of Economic Literature*, Vol. XXVI, September.

DOTTER, D. (1994),
"Rock and Roll is Here to Stay: Youth Subculture, Deviance and Social Typing in Rock's Early Years", in J. Epstein (1994).

DRYFOOS, J. (1992),
"Schools as Places for Health, Mental Health and Social Services", *Teachers College Record*, Vol. 94, No. 3.

DUBET, F. *et al.* (1989),
"Mobilisation des établissements et performances scolaires", *Revue Française de Sociologie*, Vol. XXX.

DUNCAN, G., GUSTAFSSON, B., HAUSER, R., SCHMAUSS, G., MESSINGER, H., MUFFELS, H., NOLAN, B. and RAY, J.C. (1993),
"Poverty Dynamics in Eight Countries", *Journal of Population Economics*, Vol. 6.

DURKHEIM, E. (1951),
Suicide, Free Press, New York.

DURU-BELLAT, M. and MINGAT, A. (1993),
Pour une approche analytique du fonctionnement du système éducatif, PUF, Paris.

DURU-BELLAT, M. and MINGAT, A. (1998),
"Le déroulement de la scolarité au collège : le contexte fait les différences", *Revue Française de Sociologie*, Vol. XXXIX.

DURU-BELLAT, M. and HENRIOT-VAN ZANTEN, A. (1999),
Sociologie de l'école, Armand Colin, Paris.

245|

DUTERCQ, Y. (1999),
"Vertus et limites d'un gouvernement local éducatif", *Administration et Éducation*, Vol. I.

EPSTEIN, J. (1994),
Adolescents and their Music: If it's too Loud, You're too Old, Garland Publishing, New York.

ERIKSON, R. and AABERG, R. (1991),
Welfare Trends in Scandinavian Countries, M.E. Sharpe, Armonck, NY.

ERIKSON, R. and GOLDTHORPE, J. (1992),
The Constant Flux, Clarendon Press, Oxford.

ESPING-ANDERSEN, G. (1993),
Changing Classes, Sage, London.

ESPING-ANDERSEN, G., ROHWER, G. and SORENSEN, S.L (1994),
"Institutions and Class Mobility: Scaling the Skill Barrier", *European Sociological Review* Vol. 10.

FAHNRICH, B. (1998),
Reflections on Suicide among Adolescents in Finland and Germany, www.student.oulu.fi/~bfahnric/sui cide.htm

FERRÉOL, G. et al. (1998),
Intégration, lien social et citoyenneté, Presses Universitaires du Septentrion, Lille.

FISCHER, C. (1984),
Dwelling among Friends, University of Chicago Press, Chicago.

FREDERICKS, B. (1994),
"Integrated Service Systems for Troubled Youth", *Education and Treatment of Children* Vol. 17, No. 4.

FREEMAN, R. (1999),
"The Youth Job Market at Y2K", in OECD (ed.), *Preparing Youth for the 21st Century – The Transition from Education to the Labour Market*, Paris.

GARREAU, J. (1992),
Edge City, Doubleday, New York.

GIBBONS, M. et al. (1994),
The New Production of Knowledge: The Dynamics of Science and Research in Contemporary Societies Sage Publications, London.

HABERMAS, J. (1998),
Die postnationale konstellation, Politische Essays, Suhrkamp, Frankfurt.

HAHN, C. (1998),
Becoming Political, State University of New York Press, New York.

HALSTEAD, T. (1999),
A Politics for Generation X, www.theatlantic.com/issues/99aug/9908genx.htm

HASSAN, R. (1990),
"Unlived Lives: Trends in Youth Suicide", in *Preventing Youth Suicide*, Proceedings of a Con ference held 24-26 July at the Australian Institute of Criminology, www.aic.gov.au/publications proceedings/13/hassan.pdf

HENRIOT-VAN ZANTEN, A. (1990),
L'École et l'espace local. Les enjeux des ZEP, Presses Universitaires de Lyon, Lyon.

HIRSCHMAN, A.O. (1970),
Exit, Voice and Loyalty: Responses to Decline in Firms, Organisations and States, Harvard University Press, Cambridge.

HOLMBERG, S. and WEIBULL, L. (1997),
Ett missnöjt folk, SOM-institutet, Göteborg.

HUTMACHER, W. and GROS, D. (1994),
"Attentes, priorités et attitudes à l'égard de l'école", GfS-Forschungsinstitut and Service de la recherche sociologique, Zurich and Geneva.

IN'T VELD, R., DE BRUIJN, H. and LIPS, M. (1996),
Toekomsten voor het funderend onderwijs(beleid), Ministerie van Onderwijs, Cultuur en Wetenschappen, Zoetermeer.

OHSUA, S. (1999),
L'École entre crise et refondation, La Dispute, Paris.

OUTARD, P. and THÉLOT, C. (1999),
Réussir l'école, Seuil, Paris.

KAMO, Y. (1990),
"Husbands and Wives Living in Nuclear and Stem Family Households in Japan", Sociological Perspectives, Vol. 33, No. 3.

KENNEDY, K. (1999),
"Schools for Tomorrow: Cyber Learning Organisations for the Techno Generation or Social Anchors in a Fast-changing Global Order", in OECD/CERI Working Document Schooling for Tomorrow: Future Societies, Future Schools: Trends, Methodologies and Policies, Report of a Seminar held 24-25 June.

KENNEDY, K. and MILLS, G. (1996),
"Curriculum Policy Developments in the Asia-Pacific Region: A Cross-country Analysis", paper presented at the 20th Annual Conference of the Pacific Circle Consortium, Sydney, 12-15 May.

KRUSE, H. (1993),
"Sub-cultural Identity in Alternative Music Culture", Popular Music, Vol. 12, No. 1.

LEAL, J. et al. (1993),
La desigualdad social en España, Ministerio de Asuntos Sociales, Madrid.

LE GOFF, J-P. (1999),
La Barbarie douce, La Découverte, Paris.

LEVY, F. and MURNANE, R. (1992),
"US Earnings Levels and Earnings Inequality: A Review of Recent Trends and Proposed Explanations", Journal of Economic Literature, Vol. XXX, September.

LINDBLAD, S. and PÉREZ PRIETO, H. (1998),
Elevers, föräldrars och lärares bilder av inflytande I skolan, in Skolverket (ed.), Vem tror på skolan?

MAYOR, F. and BINDÉ, J. (1999),
Un Monde nouveau, Odile Jacob, Paris.

MCCRACKEN, G. (1997),
Plénitude, Fluide, Periph, Toronto.

MICHEL, A. (1993),
"Pilotage d'un système complexe: l'Éducation nationale", Administration et Éducation, Vol. 58, No. 2.

247

MICHEL, A. (1994),
"L'éducation à la citoyenneté", *Administration et Éducation*, Vol. 61, No. 1.

MICHEL, A. (1996a),
"Les compétences de base pour le XXIe siècle", *Futuribles*, p. 210, juin.

MICHEL, A. (1996b),
"Pour une approche systémique du changement", *Administration et Éducation*, Vol. 69, No. 1.

MICHEL, A. (1999),
"L'école en quête d'équité", *Administration et Éducation*, Vol. 81, No. 1.

MINZBERG, H. (1994),
The Rise and Fall of Strategic Planning, Prentice Hall.

MOISAN, C. and SIMON, J. (1997),
Les Déterminants de la réussite scolaire en ZEP, INRP, Paris.

MORIN, E. (1990),
Introduction à la pensée complexe, ESF, Paris.

NATIONAL INSTITUTE OF MENTAL HEALTH (1999),
Suicide Facts, www.numh.nih.gov/research/suifact.htm

NEW ZEALAND HEALTH INFORMATION SERVICE (1997),
Youth Suicide Statistics for the Period 1991-1995, www.nzhis.govt.nz/publications/Youth_suicide.htm

NOLAN, B., HAUSER, R. and ZOYEM, J-P. (2000),
"The Changing Effects of Social Protection on Poverty", in D. Gallie and S. Paugam (eds.) *Welfare Regimes and the Experience of Unemployment in Europe*, Oxford University Press, Oxford.

NOMURA, N. *et al.* (1995),
"Family Characteristics and Dynamics in Japan and the United States, A Preliminary Report from the Family Environment Scale", *International Journal of Intercultural Relations*, Vol. 19, No. 1.

OECD (1985),
New Policies for the Young, Paris.

OECD (1995),
Education at a Glance – OECD Indicators, Paris.

OECD (1997a),
Employment Outlook, Paris.

OECD (1997b),
Literacy Skills and the Knowledge Society, Paris.

OECD (1997c),
Education and Equity in OECD Countries, Paris.

OECD (1998),
21st Century Technologies, Paris.

OECD (1999a),
Preparing Youth for the 21st Century – The Transition from Education to the Labour Market, Paris.

OECD (1999b),
The Future of the Global Economy, Paris.

OECD (2000a),
   Education at a Glance – OECD Indicators, Paris.
OECD (2000b),
   Knowledge Management in the Learning Society, Paris.
OECD (2000c),
   The Creative Society of the 21st Century, Paris.
OECD (2001),
   Governance in the 21st Century, Paris.
ONTARIO ROYAL COMMISSION ON LEARNING (1994),
   For the Love of Learning, Publications Ontario, Toronto, December (four volumes and summary version).
PLATO,
   The Republic, translated by R. Sterling and W. Scott (1985), W.W. Norton and Company, New York.
PRIGOGINE, I. and STENGERS, I. (1979),
   La Nouvelle alliance, Gallimard, Paris.
PUTNAM, R. (1995),
   "Bowling Alone: America's Declining Social Capital", Journal of Democracy, Vol. 6, No. 1.
RHEINGOLD, H. (1993),
   The Virtual Community, Addison-Wesley, Menlo Park, CA.
ROSANVALLON, P. (1995),
   La Nouvelle question sociale, Seuil, Paris.
ROSENBERG, N. (1982),
   Inside the Black Box, Technology and Economics, Cambridge University Press, New York.
SCHNAPPER, D. (1994),
   La Communauté des citoyens, Gallimard, Paris.
SCHUMPETER, J.A. (1947),
   Capitalism, Socialism, and Democracy, 2nd edition, Harper Row, New York.
SERRES, M. (1991),
   Le Tiers-instruit, François Bourin, Paris.
SHAVIT, Y. and BLOSSFELD, H.P. (1993),
   Persistent Inequality. Changing Educational Attainment in Thirteen Countries, Westview Press, Boulder, Col.
SKOLVERKET – National Agency for Education, Sweden (1993a),
   Val av skola (Choice of School), Report No. 40, Allmänna Förlaget, Stockholm (in Swedish only).
SKOLVERKET (1993b),
   Tankar om skolan (Thoughts on School), Dnr 92:1825 (in Swedish only).
SKOLVERKET (1995),
   Attityder till skolan (Attitudes towards School), Report No. 72, Allmänna Förlaget, Stockholm (in Swedish only, summary available in English).
SKOLVERKET (1996),
   Att välja skola – effekter av valmöjligheter i grundskolan (To Choose a School: Effects of choice in basic compulsory schooling), Report No. 109, Allmänna Förlaget, Stockholm (in Swedish only).

SKOLVERKET (1998),
Vem tror på skolan?, Report No. 144, Allmänna Förlaget, Stockholm (in Swedish only, summary available in English).

SÖDERBERG, S. and LÖFBOM, E. (1998),
"Who Believes in our Schools? A Practical Example of Policy-Orientated Evaluation", paper for the Third International Conference of the European Evaluation Society, Rome, October.

SOU (1990),
Demokrati och makt i Sverige. Maktutredningens huvudrapport (Democracy and power in Sweden. Main report of the Swedish Public Commission on the distribution of power in Sweden), Allmänna Förlaget, Stockholm, p. 44.

STERN, D. et al. (1995),
Research on School-to-Work Transition Programs in the United States, Falmer Press, London.

STEVENS, A.H. (1995),
"Climbing out of Poverty, Falling back in", NBER Working Paper, No. 5390, Cambridge, Mass.

TAYLOR, B. (1990),
"Swept under the Carpet: A Community Initiative to Youth Mental Health", Preventing Youth Suicide, Proceedings of a Conference held 24-26 July at the Australian Institute of Criminology, www.aic.gov.au/publications/proceedings/13/taylor.pdf

The Spirit of Raving (undated),
www.hyperreal.org/raves/spirit/

THORNTON, S. (1995),
Club Cultures: Music, Media and Subcultural Capital, Polity, Cambridge.

TILLER, C. (1994),
"Dream Net", Macworld, Vol. 11, No. 10, October.

TOHARIA, L. (1997),
The Labour Market in Spain, ILO, Geneva.

VALENTINE, G., SKELTON, T. and CHAMBERS, D. (1998),
Cool Places: Geographies of Youth Cultures, Routledge, London.

VAN DE HEIJDEN, K. (1996),
Scenarios: The Art of Strategic Conversation, John Wiley and Sons, New York.

WEINSTEIN, D. (1994),
"Rock: Youth and its Music", in J. Epstein (1994), pp. 3-24.

WIEVORKA, M. et al. (1997),
Une Société fragmentée: le multiculturalisme en débat, La Découverte, Paris.

WILSON, W.J. (1987),
The Truly Disadvantaged, The University of Chicago Press, Chicago.

YOUNG, M. and WILLMOTT, P. (1973),
The Symmetrical Family, Pantheon Books, New York.

ZALDIVAR, C.A. and CASTELLS, M. (1992),
España fin de siglo, Alianza Editorial, Madrid.